Completing the Circle

Taking Gestalt to Asia

Completing the Circle

Taking Gestalt to Asia

Paula Bottome

Completing the Circle

 Published in the United States of America by Clear Glass Press, San Francisco.

First Edition 1997

Bottome, Paula

ISBN: 0-9314-2524-7

For individual orders of Completing call 800-372-4238, pin=10.

To order on the World Wide Web: www.well.com/user/mp/books.html

Bookstores order from Bookpeople, Oakland, California

10 9 8 7 6 5 4 3 2

CONTENTS

ACKNOWLEDGMENTS

Many people have lent their time and energy to allow me to accomplish my journey to the west.

From the past, I thank first and foremost Fritz and Laura Perls for their wisdom, their recognition, and their friendship; Larry Bloomberg for introducing me to Gestalt and to the Perlses; the members of the San Francisco Institute for Gestalt Therapy for allowing me a place to practice and learn; Tadao Shinozaki for coming to San Francisco; Rickie Wolfe for bringing me to Japan; Yu Kawamuro for helping me stay and work there; Noriyoshi Okada for encouraging me to return; Lu Grey for returning with me, and Kenny Lo for introducing me to the social work community in Hong Kong.In the present, I am more grateful than I can ever say to my current partners in Gestalt. In Japan: Masa Mometake, Rieko Tawara, Takabumi Funazaki, Izumi Kayanuma, Shignori Maeda, Sachiko Shirai, Yasuko Okada, and Kazuhiko Umemoto. And in Hong Kong: Johanna Jen, Timothy Leung, Anita Wong, James Wong, and Candice Mok.

I could never do all the traveling I do without the help and friendship of Sharon Lee from Jeanette's Travel in San Francisco.

For the past twenty-five years I have relied on Lois Brien, Marilyn Joyce, Elaine Kepner, and Stella Resnick: friends and colleagues extraordinaire.

Susie Schmidt and Anne Blasing were editorially supportive and encouraging as I worked on the manuscript.

From my Tai Chi friend Henry Look, who first introduced me to the possibility of working in Asia, I have learned much about Asia, the Pacific Rim, and myself.

My living sons, John Allen, David Allen, and Lawrence Bottome, as well as Frank Allen who died in 1988, have been my dearest, wisest teachers and loving friends. I can never express my thanks for the deep good fortune that has allowed me to be both their mother and their companion in life's adventures. My daughters-in-law, Patti Hutton Allen and Kathleen Tays Allen, have brought female friendship and delight to the family life which enhances everything I do. My lifelong friend and brother, Edgar Bottome, has always encouraged and supported my desire to write a book. I value his respect and encouragement, as well as his example, more than I can say.

To all these people I say thank you for opening your hearts and allowing me to be myself in your presence. When you do this I feel loved, and so I thank you for loving me. You have given me the greatest of gifts and I am grateful.

I dedicate the book to all we have done together, to all we have yet to do, and to all you will do without me.

Paula Bottome
Yokohama, Japan, 1995

Chapter 1

The End of East and West: Taking Gestalt from San Francisco to Tokyo

«That excitement which is the one sign by which we can recognize remarkable things the instant they come to us.»
—Marcel Proust

Wednesday, November 20, 1991, 12:15 A.M.

Lying awake at home in San Francisco, I listen to the cable cars rattling comfortably around the block as their keepers settle them into the barn for the night. Outside my window the moon gleams in fleeting glimpses as it moves among small white puffs whose resemblance to Hokusai's neat, stylized clouds remind me once again that this is the last night before I go back to Japan. Tomorrow I will enter the world of international business travel: a maze of fluorescent lights, shining floors, and fake marble, where, in duty-free shops, highly polished salespeople push legal drugs and other icons of material success while serious immigration inspectors sit behind counters and eye an endless variety of passports and faces. This is the chute that moves travelers from one national entity to another. After my ride through the chute I will board the massive 747 that lifts and carries me over the Pacific, to the group of islands that lie along the coast of Asia just as the British Isles rest beside Europe's shore. The medieval navigators called them Cipango, and Columbus thought he had found them when he entered the Caribbean. In the United States we call them Japan, and I've been working there teaching Gestalt for five years.

Gestalt, which was called Gestalt Therapy by its founders Fritz and Laura Perls, is much more than a psychotherapy. It is an operational existentialism based on awareness, which the Perlses created by synthesizing existentialism and phenomenology with the discoveries of Freud, Reich, and the Gestalt psychologists. Gestalt is a method—the how-to of present awareness, which offers to its practitioners the excitement and freedom that come with aware living.

Awareness is invaluable regardless of the content of our current experience because awareness allows choice and we experience aware choice as freedom. In Martin Buber's words, "To be freed from the belief that there is no freedom is indeed to be free." Furthermore, people who are aware of their moment-to-moment choices are willing to take responsibility for their actions, thereby becoming responsible participants in their own lives. Lived in this way, life takes on a clarity and intensity that enhance experience and satisfy our deepest longings for integrity, meaning, and authenticity.

In the beginning . . . .
—Genesis

East is east and west is west
And never the twain shall meet.
—Rudyard Kipling

As Kipling's era vanishes into the elaborate oblivion we call history, we notice that his observation is twice inaccurate. On a globe, east and west shift with the location of the observer, so that to a person standing on the west coast of the United States, Europe, contrary to all expectations, is the Far East. From San Francisco, Japan and China are the Far West, while New York and Boston are the Middle East. Clearly, slicing the world into the Eurocentric designations of East and West is (to put it generously) archaic, or (less kindly) downright stupid; for when we speak in broad, meaningless generalizations, we generate unnecessary muddle in an already confused world. We can locate ourselves far more accurately by calling areas of the continents by their real names—western North America, eastern Asia, eastern Europe..

We notice, too, that as the century separating us from Kipling draws to a close, the ostensibly vast division between the civilizations of Asia and those of Europe and the Americas— the erstwhile east and west—is just one more cherished certainty that is shifting and changing before our amazed eyes. In the twentieth century, thanks perhaps to Einstein, we have become sensitive to relativities based on relationship, and the contradictions that once existed between our favorite polarities—east and west, good and bad, male and female, even life and death—have begun to blur as we become aware that what once appeared to be opposites are instead points of a continuous progression, or positions on a globe. And as we see continuums where before we saw dualities, we begin to understand that we can peacefully integrate differences that for centuries we imagined to be absolute. We have reached, in the words of Edward Said, "the possibility of discovering a world not constructed out of warring essences." Where before we saw only separation and conflict, suddenly we are free to embrace reconciliation.

Perhaps, as we come to accept that in our human imperfection light and shadow are forever intermingled, we will further acknowledge that no one or no culture is ever blessed—or cursed, according to one's personal outlook—with knowledge of the absolute truth. Each of us is allowed to perceive only a part of the elephant of reality; and it is in dialogue, freely entered and openly engaged, that we may enhance and refine the small amount of truth that each of us is privileged to know. The dialogue among the unique and overlapping elements of our ever so varied existences gives color and movement to the life and time we spend together, and reveals more of what is than any of us can possibly discover on our own. In our world, with its ever-shrinking time and space, jet airplanes, telephones, satellites, electronic translators, and the other technologies of connection weave an invisible net that is a nearly irresistible invitation to dialogue. Flying nonstop from Tokyo to Frankfurt or from Hong Kong to San Francisco, travelers experience directly the continuum stretching from Europe to Asia to America and on again to Europe. Separated by a meal, a snack, and two movies, we are all neighbors now.

This book is the story of my dialogue with people in Asia. It is an assertion that Kipling's polarities, both of content ("East is east and west is west") and of process ("Never the twain shall meet"), have been transformed into a new gestalt. The new gestalt recognizes relative differences capable of integration where previously there were acute divisions based on blunt certainties that often led to dogmatism and war. Our perception of continuity where previously we saw dichotomy gives new perspectives from which to understand the past and integrate it into the present. As the people in this book have come to understand, those who do not know their history are doomed to repeat it because the denied and disowned past endures within us and controls the present. Comprehending the past is absolutely essential for the creation of real and lasting change, because the new can be stable and lasting only when it includes all that has gone before.

Integrating our own history, both personal and public, will take far longer than any of us imagined when, sometime in the 1960s, we began the profound cultural transformation born of the implicit ultimatum that unless we as a species learn to live in peace we will become extinct. Becoming personally integrated opens us to learning from others; becoming culturally integrated enriches us beyond the boundaries of before. Both are liberating, and both foreshadow the integration of the human and non-human which is necessary for the continuation of life on our planet.

Longer than anyone would dare imagine, nomadic people have journeyed around and across the Pacific Rim. Guided by a genius for navigation that recalls migrating birds, they traveled in tiny boats over the vast waters of the Pacific Ocean. They explored on foot as well: innumerable families and tribes crossed and recrossed the land bridge that once connected the land of the great fiery basin which holds the largest of the Seven Seas. Everywhere that people went on their migratory explorations, they established communities and cultures. Many, like the Iroquois, the Miami, the Aztec, and the Inca, were destroyed by the

Europeans; others, like the amazingly adaptive and long-lived Inuit (Eskimo), Pueblo, and Japanese, are still here. Whoever these early explorers were—and some believe they had their origin in the Americas—they created an ancient Pacific Rim culture whose existence is recorded, not in words, but in the symbols and patterns of Native American artifacts and the remarkably similar designs of the Shang bronzes of ancient China, as well as the Neolithic pottery uncovered throughout the region.

To begin again.
—Gertrude Stein

East is West and West is East
And ever the twain have met.
(Thanks again to Rudyard Kipling)

The archaic Pacific Rim cultures, whose original unity remains in bright fragments scattered like specks of confetti from a party that ended eons ago, have largely been replaced. The Pacific Ocean has become a highway over which European culture, in its particular American hybrid, directly encounters eastern Asia without the intermediaries of the Arabs and other traders of the old Silk Road. Meandering across the deserts and mountains of the Eurasian land mass, this route—the one Marco Polo traveled—required years of dangerous travel to complete, and the exotic stories told by the travelers tended to intensify rather than diminish the historical and cultural differences between the cultures of Europe and Asia. Verified by Kipling's famous lines, these differences came in the nineteenth and early twentieth centuries to represent an archetypal polarity in the minds of both Europeans and Americans.

This confusion of perspective continues in official circles even as Americans and Asians, from both the North and South continents, experience the continuity of the Pacific Rim. We are joined in a great circle of land and culture whose fundamental unity is marked by the geological activity of the various plates and volcanoes that compose the ring of fire. It is the new destination of the ongoing westward journey of the Americans. And from the other side of the great saucer, the past century and a half have seen the people of Asia rediscovering their eastward migrations into the rising sun, the journey whose landfall is the Pacific shore of the Americas. The American railroads were built by Chinese labor. San Francisco is already a Cantonese city, and Vancouver is becoming one. The president of Peru is a Japanese-American named Fujimori. And this is just the beginning.

We are meeting. The great ocean that was once a barrier is now a thoroughfare connecting the communities on either side, the same ones that were once considered opposites, incapable of meeting. Now from each shore, people and ideas leap across the old polarity, igniting sparks of creativity and enlightenment as over and over again the old differences are joined and integration begins.

I was seven years old when the Japanese bombed Pearl Harbor. Shortly thereafter my father enlisted in the navy, and from my eighth to eleventh years my family joined the migrations of wartime: Ithaca, New York; Cambridge, Massachusetts; Bremerton, Washington; and San Diego, California. After my father went to the South Pacific from San Diego, I returned by car with my mother and brother to West Virginia, where we lived with my aunt. Fearful my father would be killed, I remember praying every night with my mother and brother for God to "bring Daddy safely home." In West Virginia I played soldier on the river bank, crawling over the coal-flecked sand on my belly and, when I was shot, falling down for an instant before leaping up shouting "new man!" and re-entering the fray. That was the closest I came to the war except for movies and their fearful impression; I can still see a doomed soldier hopelessly shooting a machine gun into the advancing Japanese soldiers at the end of "Bataan."

Going to the movies at all was a sort of war benefit for me; my mother had been strict and selective about my entertainment until she became preoccupied with more important things, like moving every few months and my father's safety. Besides movies, the war meant butter wrapped in a red ribbon for a Christmas present, crossing the border at Tijuana in search of unrationed huaraches for my rapidly growing feet, and watching my mother clean an identifiable cow's tongue while I made her angry with my comments about how "gross" it was. Most of all it meant growing up without my father. Like so many men, he never fully returned from the war, and for years I mourned and raged at his loss without realizing it.

The war ended on August 14, 1945, my eleventh birthday and the day my daddy arrived home unexpectedly. When I told my mother I saw him coming up the walk, she replied, "No, it's just the mailman." After the jubilation of his arrival, my brother and I pestered the adults to begin the party as they sat with their ears close to the radio— a common sight in West Virginia, where the reception was not all that good. Finally their excitement and the wail of distant sirens announced that the war was over, and my party, which became a great celebration, began.

While I never blamed the Japanese for any of this, when I began studying Tai Chi Chuan on December 7, 1974, the symbolism of the date was not lost on me. I always imagined it was, in Jung's words, "one of those coincidences which the unconscious arranges." My Tai Chi studies, which drew me to San Francisco's Chinatown, were the beginning of my reconciliation and integration with Asia.

This is the story of my continuing journey westward to Asia, of what I give and what I receive. I am certain that as more people make this journey, beginning from either side, we will generate in the library of the human spirit light and energy sufficient to read the texts of harmony and rapport, lost at Babel and recoverable at last by our discovery, with the help of jet airplanes and electronic media, that we are all far more alike than we are different.

Fritz and Laura Perls came to the United States as part of the Nazi brain drain, a massive intellectual and artistic immigration which included Freud and Reich as well as Arnold Schoenberg, Walter Gropius, Thomas and Henrich Mann, and many other famous and not-so-famous contributors to the human endeavor. When the Perlses fled Germany in 1934, Ernest Jones, Freud's biographer, helped them relocate in South Africa, where Fritz established a psychoanalytic institute in Johannesburg and became acquainted with Jan Smuts, the philospher-politician who first articulated the philosophy of holism. From the Boer War through the creation of the Union of South Africa to the installation of apartheid, which he wholeheartedly rejected, Smuts was a central figure in South Africa. In 1924, when the racial extremists introduced the color bar in industrial relations, he prophetically told them, "If you pass this law, you will surround South Africa with a ring of hatred."

Holism emphasizes the power and significance of the whole. A natural progression from the ideas of the Gestalt physiologists, who had demonstrated how wholes operate differently from what might be predicted from adding up the performance of their various parts, Smuts's holism focused on the value of greater wholeness and integration on every level of existence. Most significant for the Perlses in their development of the Gestalt approach was his assertion of the wholeness of the human organism and the corresponding rejection of the body/mind split, heretofore a defining characteristic of European thought. (When many humanistic therapies began to focus on "bodywork," a word I never liked because it seemed to treat people like cars, Laura Perls sniffed indignantly and pronounced, "There is no such thing as Gestalt bodywork." She's right, because in the Gestalt approach there is no body. There is only the organism in its entirety, in which everything is connected to and interacting with everything else.)

Gestalt represents a major break from the analytic tradition, which takes wholes apart into ever smaller elements for purposes of understanding and manipulation. After dismantling the whole, the analyst tries to put its component units together again in a meaningful way. Gestalt, on the other hand, asserts that meaning resides in the organization of the whole, and this organization creates both thought and action in constant and delicate interaction with the environment. Since holism refers both to the unity of the human being and to the integrity of the organism/environment field, it was an early expression of the comprehensive network of interdependent processes that are more recently subsumed under the word "ecology."

Gestalt emphasizes a further attribute of the integrated organism: its ability to regulate itself in its constant interbeing with the environment. It is the disruption of the elegant self-regulatory adjustments by fixed gestalten, or patterns of unfinished business, that the methodology of Gestalt addresses. In Martin Buber, the Jewish Existentialist with whom Laura studied at the University of Frankfurt, the Perlses found a teacher who took holism a step further. Buber emphasized relation as the essential aspect of being. In his famous book *I and Thou*, he states unequivocally that "...the real, filled present exists only insofar as actual presentness, meeting, and relation exist." Buber saw that although we live in constant interaction with the world, the decision to live in the mutuality which he calls relation is, to some degree, a choice. He writes: "You cannot make yourself understood with others concerning it [the I-Thou relationship]; you are alone with it. But it teaches you to meet others, and to stand your ground when you meet them. Through the graciousness of its comings and the solemn sadness of its goings it leads you away to the Thou in which the parallel lines of relations meet. It does not help to sustain you in life, it only helps you to glimpse eternity." He goes further and makes it clear that mutuality requires that the quality of relation defines the "I" as well as being defined by it. "For the I of the primary word I-Thou is different from the I of the primary word I-It." It is in his recognition of the relentless mutuality of the lived present that Buber influences Gestalt.

The aspect of choice in mutuality is everywhere visible. During a break in a recent group session that I conducted, Koji gave Noriko a book. As soon as the group reconvened, Noriko, a tall, graceful woman whose delicacy of bearing and demeanor could be slightly oppressive, left her place in the group and sat formally in front of Koji, respectfully holding the book in both hands. She explained to him that she had read the book in childhood and found it frightening. She didn't like it and wanted to return it to him. No one could have been more proper than Noriko as she performed the thoroughly improper act of returning the gift. Koji, who was able to recognize that in returning the book Noriko was giving her authentic self, received the book and gravely stepped into the moment of meeting that she offered. I believe that everyone in the group recognized the moment Buber describes when he writes of the "graciousness of its comings and the solemn sadness of its goings."

We can choose the I-Thou relationship, which recognizes the other as unique, aware, and with an independent agenda for living, or we can choose the I-It relationship, which views the other as an instrument to be used to further our own designs. The other so chosen can be a person; it can be the natural world of animals and trees and rivers; it can be the world of spirit. Although we cannot escape our interactions with the field in which we are embedded (try to imagine life without breath or food or infant care), we can choose the quality of relationship, and it is the choice to move into a mutual relationship with another that gives Gestalt its generosity and its effectiveness. When I speak with my whole being and define myself by mutuality, I am incapable of manipulating or using the other person. Claudio Naranjo wrote perhaps the most succinct definition of Gestalt when he entitled an essay "I and Thou, Here and Now."

After the war, the Perlses came to the United States and worked inconpicuously in New York and Cleveland teaching their particular form of existential psychotherapy, which, since there was already a school of existential psychoanalysis, they called Gestalt Therapy. Grounded in a recognition of and respect for each person's unique existence, the basic method is facilitation of present awareness as it flows through one's experienced reality; the Perlses called their fundamental technique the awareness continuum. When fixed patterns of response block the flow of awareness, they hold the person in a fantasy of the past and prohibit an aware response to the conditions of the present moment. The fixed patterns, which the Perles called unfinished business, are strong and convincing intrusions into the present of feelings connected with past events. These feelings are by definition unbearable; otherwise, they would have been experienced when they emerged, and the gestalt would have been completed and returned to the background. The reason the unfinished feelings were not expressed and integrated when they were originally evoked is that the person did not have the safety and support to experience and express their feelings fully, which would have allowed them to complete the gestalt and integrate the experience into the whole of their being.

Unless we have worked to express and integrate the pain of the past, all of us are haunted by the specter of unfinished business. In a recent group a woman named Shizuko sat with me and told me she was happy. But as she was telling me her children were doing well and her husband was kind and successful, tears rolled down her cheeks. Clearly puzzled by her own behavior, she spontaneously began to tell me of her mother's death when she was five. She said that just as her mother was dying, her younger brother pushed in front of her and took the place beside her mother. As Shizuko tried to approach the bed, her mother died, and her relatives held the five-year-old girl back, refusing to let her touch her mother for the last time. In Shizuko's words, "Time stopped then. I can't die until I meet my mother." I encouraged her to talk to her mother as if the mother were sitting on an empty pillow. When she did, she allowed herself to lie on the pillow and tell her mother how sad she was. She wept heavily for some minutes. Then she sat up and played her mother's side of the dialogue, letting her mother tell her how sad she was to leave her daughter. This is a classic example of unfinished business. The relatives, in holding the young child away from the mother's body, had interrupted her expression of grief. I think the happiness of Shizuko's present life had served as support and allowed the past scene to effortlessly emerge with us in the present, where she could express the feelings and perform the actions necessary to begin their completion.

The facilitation of here-and-now awareness will inevitably lead a person to her or his major unfinished situations, which emerge as fixed gestalts distorting present reality. The completion of the unfinished situations and the accompanying liberation of the bound energy for present awareness is a major goal of Gestalt work.

In another recent workshop, a young woman tells how she imagines that people are judging and condemning her for her stuttering. As she talks, she clasps her right hand inside her left, and when I ask her to create a dialogue between the two hands, she, speaking as the left hand, says, "I'm trying to open you up." As she speaks, she separates her hands and turns her right hand palm up. When she says, "I am open," I suggest she say it to someone. She says it to three people and then she closes both her hand and her eyes, and says, "I want to hide. I'm afraid you'll condemn me as a person who stutters." I urge her to open her eyes and say this to the person she was facing when she withdrew. She opens her eyes and repeats, "I want to hide." Then she gazes silently at the person before her for a minute or more and she says, "I know you won't judge me." This signals the completion of the old gestalt, which has now receded into the background, allowing a new figure, the person who is before her right now, to emerge. She opens both her hands and, turning her palms up, partially extends her arms. Her expression softens as she awakens from the fixed gestalt of her unfinished business and experiences the present moment of acceptance rather then the many past instances of judgment and condemnation. Her eyes fill with tears as she repeats, "I know you won't judge me." The other woman draws near and silently lays her hands on the extended palms. It's a moment of completion and contact. The woman who began says, slowly and mindfully, "As long as I live, I will always be changing."

I have been working with this woman for five years. To see her awaken to the infinite possibilities of her existence is so gratifying that I feel tears slip from my own eyes and down my cheeks. She embraces me and says "*Domo arigato gozaimashita*" ("Thank you so much"), and I imagine my gratitude is nearly as great as hers. I reply, "*Do Itashimashite*" ("You're welcome"), and experience the precious joy of knowing I have been beneficial in a person's life.

I studied Gestalt with Fritz and Laura Perls in the 1960s, when they became minor celebrities in humanistic psychology circles. I met Fritz in 1966, just before he went to Esalen in California and became well known for his powerful and beautiful Gestalt work as well as his often outrageously confrontive encounters with people. Fritz was the kind of person who, when asked if he had a match, would reply, "Yes." If you wanted a light, you had to ask again. The first time I rode in a car with him we went to a flute concert at the Los Angeles County Museum, where he entered the parking lot and whipped his Volkswagon into a space for which another driver had been patiently waiting. I was shocked, and delighted, to meet this wild, cultured man. Fritz was a wonderful combination of bad boy and sage. I always thought he resembled the Chinese poet Li Po, who had drowned himself drunkenly reaching for the moon in a lake.

Fritz was sexy, too, although a little old for my taste at the time. Nevertheless, I must have been seduced in some way, for when I left his motel to go on to Mexico with my soon-to-be-second husband, I left two pairs of underpants drying on a hanger in his bathroom. I used to tell Fritz that the best thing about him was that he was right—accurate in his understanding of the world; from the very beginning, Gestalt's practical phenomenology and operational existentialism created meaning and sense in my world. Of course the combination of sexual attraction and intellectual appreciation was a great basis for a friendship. In a significant way, Fritz was a father to me, because he taught me how the world works and how to make my way in it; and for that I am eternally grateful.

While Fritz vagabonded around the United States and later the world, Laura Perls remained in New York doing private practice and Gestalt training until shortly before she died in 1993. She was the stable, patient partner in what was undoubtedly a rocky relationship. Fritz's sexual adventures were legend, as were Laura's, and by the time Fritz died it had been many years since they had lived together. Nevertheless, there was often an easy familiarity between them; I know he called her to be with him before he died in March of 1970 because I was with her in San Francisco when she received the summons. Of course she went. Once I asked her once why she had never divorced him, and she said because he was the most interesting man she had ever met. Theirs was a lifelong friendship, not at all easy for a thirty-year-old to understand, but a relationship I have grown to appreciate increasingly as I have matured.

I have heard each of them disparage the other as "not a Gestalt therapist;" yet, as in many families where the parents don't get along, the children benefit from knowing both. This is certainly true of the Perlses' students. To have studied with only one was to have missed the complete gestalt. Laura's patient attention was a useful corrective to Fritz's exasperated dismissals of people who were having difficulty touching their pain. Fritz's keen sense of drama and timing balanced the boredom that sometimes overtook members in Laura's groups. They were a far better team than many people realized. In Germany, when my friend introduced me as "a personal friend of Fritz and Laura Perls," the newcomer looked at me incredulously and said, "I didn't know there was such a person." Of course there were many such people, but such is the power of legend that many people believed that everyone in the Gestalt family had taken sides.

In my own cultural heritage—WASP with a French accent— there is no tradition of lifelong learning with the accompanying notion of an honored teacher. When I met the Perlses, I still imagined that teachers worked in schools and schools were for children, that when one has been graduated, she or he is prepared for life. As someone who has always loved to learn—even in school where some teachers' only skill is teaching that learning is a boring waste of time—meeting the Perlses just as I was completing a Ph.D. in European history was one of life's unexpected bonuses. I had just finished my dissertation on aspects of the German emigration from the Nazis, and meeting Fritz and Laura was like stepping into the pages of the history I had been reading and writing. Here they were: the Germans who had fled the Nazis and brought their abundant culture and intelligence to the United States. Coming to know the Perles was coming to understand far more fully the history I had been studying. With their help, I was able to transform existentialism and phenomenology from abstract theories into matters of daily practice and experience. Working with them, I learned to dissolve the artificial boundaries I had created and began to experience my own wholeness.

I moved to San Francisco with my husband and four children in 1968, while Fritz was still at Esalen. After a two-year stint as a mental health educator at Marin General Hospital and numerous Gestalt workshops with Fritz and others, I abandoned history and applied for the recently created California license in Marriage, Family, and Child Counseling. Upon receiving the license, I was accepted into the San Francisco Gestalt Institute, where I taught for fifteen years and continued to study with Laura Perls, who came regularly to San Francisco.

I went to Japan to teach Gestalt for the first time in 1985 and stayed for a year and a half. I lived in Shanghai in 1988 and 1989, and since then have traveled back and forth across the Pacific more times than I can readily count. Visiting and working in both China and Japan, I have come to know some of the people and localities of Asia. On this 1991 trip, I will go from Japan to Hong Kong, where I've been working since 1989. Then, with colleagues from Hong Kong, I will travel to Taipei and facilitate a Gestalt group there for the first time.

I'll be leaving North America, a huge land mass that stretches inland for thousands of miles in every direction, for an island that by *Shinkansen*—the super-express that Americans mysteriously call the bullet train—is a three-hour journey from coast to coast. Japan is an archipelago, a small nation of great variety that, while narrow, stretches through so many degrees of latitude that a traveler from Hokkaido to Okinawa will encounter the same range and intensity of climate as one who journeys in the United States from Maine to Florida. I know that I have just begun to experience the variety of Asia, and I think of my journey as one into the unknown of my own ignorance. Tonight in San Francisco the cable is still running beneath the street outside. Its whine is the last thing I remember before I drop into my last night's sleep at home.

WEDNESDAY, NOVEMBER 20, 5:30 P.M. PST
40,000 FEET ABOVE THE PACIFIC OCEAN

Because war is menacing the Persian Gulf, the plane is nearly empty, and I stretch luxuriously across three seats by the window of the 747. Coach class, the steerage of the jet age, normally is uncomfortably packed, and however much both passengers and crew enjoy it, the present spaciousness is surely temporary. Travel, which is among life's great pleasures, is one of the first things to vanish as war systematically removes the fun from life. Since warmongers are inevitably those who don't know how to enjoy themselves, they don't mind—and, in fact seem positively relieved—when wartime comes and there are "good reasons" to force everyone to share their own bleak and paranoid existence. "C'est la guerre" is the ultimate justification for deprivation, one we are all supposed to accept without question. George Bush's exercise in machismo is no exception, and I feel lucky that his war is far away and affects me only marginally. In fact, even as a civilian with no financial interest in the military-industrial complex, I receive a war fringe benefit—being allowed to sleep my way to Japan. C'est la guerre!

The Pacific Ocean, which was once a barrier, has become a highway over which dozens of jumbo jets cruise through the confusion of night and day that high-speed travel creates. On this particular day/night the scene outside my window vanishes into an incoherent medium that must surely be air, but could just as easily be water. As we fly through the heaving, bouncing, jolting grayness which miraculously upholds the gigantic plane, I marvel at my sense of safety. I rest comfortably in the cold, oxygen-deprived stratosphere where I could not remain alive for sixty seconds without the protection and support of the sheltering machine—a tiny dot of human organization moving through the chaos of the sky. If all goes well, I will remain in this inhospitable environment for ten hours before returning to earth in a different place. In my case, if organization prevails, the new somewhere will be Narita in Chiba prefecture (in Japanese, Chiba-*ken*, a far easier word to say). Jet travel is time travel: a retreat into the timelessness of life inside a metal cylinder from which one emerges into an entirely different time and space. Einstein knew it all along.

During dinner the sky clears and the wing emerges distinct and lucid over a ring of smooth white clouds that surround the dark vacancy like the shore of a heavenly beach. I drink wine with the standard cardboard meal and remind myself to order vegetarian next time. After dinner I have a tiny bottle of amaretto, served by a flight attendant who, enjoying her leisurely labor in the nearly empty plane, shares my good mood.

We talk a while about the impact of the impending war on our respective businesses. The clouds have now merged into sloping fields of palest pink accented by puddles of dark gray outlined in purple. The eternally setting sun which lies just below the horizon will lead us all the way to Japan in a perpetual dusk.

The movie comes on, and a voice directs us to close the blinds to create a "let's-pretend" night. From their researches into psychology and physiology the airlines have learned to use liquor, darkness, and movies to coax the stubborn diurnal cycle into believing that a night has passed before they land us in Japan on the evening of the day after we left San Francisco. With the help of my extra seats, I gladly succumb to the artifice. From time to time the plane enters rough air, where it momentarily shakes and groans in protest against the forces of the sky. Remembering that the plane is as big as a skyscraper lying on its side, I am properly impressed with the powers that surround me and don't have to be reminded to keep my seat belt fastened while I sleep.

Awakened at 11:40 p.m. San Francisco time, I recognize another effort to fool the canny cycle that knows full well it's not morning and feels insulted at being awakened from deepest sleep and offered a nasty midnight snack masquerading as breakfast. Because I have slept well in the empty plane, I go along with the charade and tease myself into a semblance of waking consciousness that will enable me to navigate immigration and customs in Narita and get myself and my bag into Tokyo for a real bed on the real night of what is now tomorrow, November 21. I have lost a day, compliments of the International Date Line; it will be returned on my return to San Francisco, where I will arrive before I have left. So much for the constancy of time and the reliability of clocks!

As the plane lands, a deep red glows in the western sky. In the race with the setting sun, the sun has won and leaves us to disembark at Narita in the dark. I stumble through immigration and customs before beginning the ninety-minute train ride to Tokyo. This direct route, the Narita Express, has recently been completed and finally allows one to go directly to Tokyo by train without long delays in the eternal traffic jams that persist in the Tokyo-Yokohama urban complex.

THURSDAY, NOVEMBER 12, 7:38 P.M.
ON JAPAN RAILROAD'S NARITA EXPRESS

The new train is comfortable, with no smoking allowed in any of the cars. Between the sets of four spacious reserved seats is a small table to hold food and drink. The Japanese seem to eat and drink more or less continually as they travel —an easy habit to acquire, I muse as I munch chocolate-filled koala bear cookies, a taste I share with Japanese children.

The train is full of well-dressed people, none of whom are fat and many of whom are sleeping, both sure signs I'm in Japan. The woman across from me stares fixedly ahead and suppresses a yawn as, probably aware I am watching her, she shifts uneasily. The heavy mask of make-up on her face contrasts strangely with the translucence of her beautifully manicured hands. The train glides smoothly through the dark, which is soon sprinkled with lights from the great metropolitan sprawl of the Kanto plain. I am entering the greater Tokyo area, where twenty million people live and work in the largest and safest city in the world. At Tokyo station, I change trains and spend the last fifteen minutes of my journey traveling to Iidabashi station, a short walk from my destination: the Ryokan Seifuso, a traditional Japanese inn in a residential neighborhood in the center of Tokyo. For this commuter segment of my trip I join a crowd of men in business suits and notice that they wear a variety of styles and fabrics, quite different from the stark black and blue suits they wore when I first came to Japan just six years ago. In fact, everyone is more stylishly dressed now, including me.

I work my way through the crowd around the station and past a group of construction workers laboring under bright lights in their traditional costume of bright baggy jodhpurs and black cloth boots with a cloven toe made for clinging to precarious perches. I have often imagined that these unique garments have fad potential in the United States, but have been too timid to take them home and try them out.

Leaving the main street, I wander into the maze of narrow lanes that gives Tokyo much of its charm and all of its quiet: the tiny streets, along which even a motor scooter must proceed with care, are far too narrow and curving for speeding automobiles. Closely packed houses sit behind walls with elaborate entrance gates often accented with plants in a variety of containers. Occasionally a tree raises its bare branches above the geometry of the city street. The evening air is sweet and my bag is light. I am content as I stroll toward my room for the night.

THURSDAY, NOVEMBER 21, 10:00 P.M. IIDABASHI

I arrive at the inn just as a large party is leaving, and enter the *genkan*—the entry from which one must take a shoeless step up into the Japanese dwelling—through a jumble of shoes and people. A young woman employee I know from previous visits greets me and hurries me through the departing crowd. Straining with exhaustion as I haul my bag up the wooden stairs, I am relieved to feel my load lightened as she takes it from my hand and moves in front of me. She leads me down a familiar wooden hallway, and I follow clumsily in the backless slippers I have put on after abandoning my shoes in the *genkan*. A pathway of large, smooth stones runs down the center of the hallway like the bed of a stream and feels comfortably stimulating on the bottoms of my feet.

When the woman shows me to a room with a bath, I am pleasantly surprised at its unexpected luxury. Business must be better than I imagine, I think gratefully as I slip out of the slippers and onto the soft, sweet-smelling tatami floor, on which lies an impeccably arranged and inviting futon covered with an immensely fluffy white quilt. I repress my impulse to leap into this soft cloud until she has gone. Rousing myself before sleep comes, I take an American-style bath, which means soaking in the same water I wash in and which the Japanese, just like people in the U.S. who always shower, consider a dirty habit. I read for forty seconds before tumbling into sleep.

FRIDAY, NOVEMBER 22, 3:00 A.M.

Suddenly I am wide awake and alert on the futon, with sleep as elusive as a bat in the sunshine. Lost in time, I lie awake, listening to the conversation between a soft rain and the leaves in the small garden, and marvel at the silent center of this metropolis that extends outward at least thirty miles in every direction from this spot. Breaking all the rules of recovering from jet lag, I turn on the light and begin to read. I'm in the middle of a biography of Rebecca West, and spend the next hour alternating reading with worrying that I will not have the presence I need to work when my group begins on Saturday. Recognizing this for the futile and perfidious activity it is, especially for a professional existentialist who has come to teach Japanese people how to live in the present, I struggle to keep my attention on the printed page, and am struck by Rebecca West's observations about Saint Paul. In Tokyo's early morning I ponder the convolution of institutions that human beings have created from Jesus's simple gospel of love.

As the sky begins to brighten and birds stir in the garden, I slip from the warm futon into my first day in Japan. Even at six in the morning the neighborhood remains quiet as I walk to nearby Yasukuni Shrine, where I practice Tai Chi Chuan. It was Tai Chi that brought me to Asia in the first place, and in Yasukuni I study next to giant red and gold carp who teach the grace of languor as they drift in their pond. Inspired by their movement, I temper myself in an effort to move as softly as they do. Bright red maple leaves linger on the trees surrounding the water, and occasionally a fish leaps into the air in a wild expression of pure aliveness. I sense a slow murmuring vibration: somewhere deep within the sanctuary a Shinto priest has struck a taiko, a large drum.

I spend the rest of the day in a stupor of jet lag, and after an intense struggle to remain awake until something resembling a normal time for going to bed, fall asleep at 6:30 p.m. pondering the audacity of national leaders who make decisions affecting the lives and deaths of millions while they are in such a zombie-like state.

SATURDAY, NOVEMBER 23, 4:00 A.M.

I awaken refreshed by a dream of snow clinging to high mountains, and congratulate myself for having slept ten solid hours. The gray dawn opens slowly to reveal a pale blue sky filled with long strands of white stretching overhead like ribbons that shred and spread as I practice by the pond. I eat breakfast at Denny's: American coffee, broiled salmon, rice, and *miso* soup—a perfect Pacific Rim breakfast. As I eat, I read *The Daily Yomiuri*, one of Tokyo's three English-language daily newspapers, and feel wonderfully at home in the world.

After breakfast, I leave for the Shimane Inn in Aoyama, where the group of fifteen I'll be facilitating will begin at 10:00 a.m. I'll surely know some of the members, and I feel a rush of pleasure in anticipation of meeting them again. Relieved to be rested, I am anxious as I approach the unknown of a new group. I leave the inn early, allowing time to spare for getting lost to assure that I will find the place on time. Japanese people are particular about punctuality, and I use this knowledge as a instrument of self-torture as I ride Tokyo's efficient subway system which, although crowded, seldom needs the pushers so popular in American photojournalism. The Japanese are quite content to jam themselves on the trains without outside help, and I join them cheerfully.

After getting off the train at Shibuya station, I take a taxi. Since I don't have a map showing the location of the hotel, the driver can't find it. This is not unusual in a city where a building's address gives information about the time of its construction rather than its location, and nearly every business address is accompanied by a small map. Ignorant of my whereabouts and with anxiety approaching panic, I get out of the cab and begin to walk in what I hope is the right direction, feeling better as I move my muscles instead of my brain cells. When I recognize a familiar children's clothing store, I relax, knowing that once more I have found my way.

Walking the last few minutes of my journey, I feel the excitement, very like stage fright, of the upcoming group. I am trembling slightly in anticipation of the adventure of sitting with a group of people who have set themselves the task of focusing on awareness—an amazing activity that inevitably brings each one to the direct experience of her or his own here-and-now existence, the only possible content of awareness and the source of the power and energy that inevitably accompanies it. From our distinct experiences we will create a shared reality that is both fascinating and healing—the existential-experiential group, a voyage into the unknown and an art form one might call the theater of the absorbed. I am enlivened and flattered as I realize that these people whose backgrounds and origins differ so emphatically from mine trust me enough to invite me to be their guide for such an adventure.

As I enter the lobby of the hotel I see Hatsue, Koji, Masa, and Satako sitting at a table in the coffee shop. The cloud of jet lag dissolves, and I know I have arrived in Japan. My heart opens to my Japanese friends, who sit drinking coffee, framed by a wide window that opens into a small garden of nearly perfect Japanese mood and sensibility. They turn their faces toward me, and we welcome one another into the realm of sincerity and trust that we have created together.

"*Hisashiburi*!" ("It's been a long time!"), we say to each other. We embrace and rejoice to be together again.

Chapter 2

JAPAN:
WHERE HEART AND MIND ARE THE SAME WORD

«The stars, everything, are involved in creating greater forms of awareness, and by creating greater forms of awareness continue the fundamental task of creation.»

—Laurens van der Post

SATURDAY, NOVEMBER 23, 10:00 A.M.

Entering the room where I'll spend the next two days, I recognize several of the people seated in a circle on the soft tatami floor. When I first came to Japan, people asked me how I felt working on the floor and were invariably surprised when I told them that, in San Francisco, my colleagues and I nearly always worked on the floor. Like so much of life in California, pillows on the floor were an early, unaware encounter with the Pacific Rim.

Fifteen people from various parts of Japan have gathered in Tokyo for the weekend workshop. Linked together by an excellent rail system, the Japanese travel freely around their islands—sometimes traveling as long as three hours to attend an evening event. Since most of the people in this group have worked with me or seen me work in various settings, I can plunge into the creation of the group community without introducing Gestalt principles or theory. From now on everything I say is mediated through a translator who repeats my words in Japanese and the words of the group members in English. She is the interface through which the group works—one of the people whose help is essential to my work here. Although I understand quite a bit of Japanese and can follow much of what people are saying, I often do not understand details and nuances. Since I am shy about speaking Japanese, I don't give instructions in Japanese although I know the phrases for much of what I say. I notice that the translator becomes confused if I shift back and forth from English to Japanese, although this may be no more than a rationalization for my timidity.

I first did Gestalt with a translator in 1982 when a Japanese psychologist came to a summer program at the San Francisco Gestalt Institute. I felt an instant affinity with this man: a joy in meeting like that of a child tunneling in the sand who has broken into her friend's tunnel and touched hands. Shige wrote a report of his experience in an article, "The Four Seasons of Gestalt Therapy: I. The Fascination of Dream Work," published in the Child Guidance Consultation Center Bulletin, and the excerpts quoted below are translations from his essay. Note that while every word spoken was mediated through the translator's bilingual capability, she herself has disappeared from the transcript. The event reported here has actually been through two translations: one in the original dream work and a second with the return to English from the article in Japanese.

> *The training staff that day in 1982 was Paula and Sid, both Ph.D.s, in a group with thirteen members. They discussed how the program would proceed. The present writer volunteered, saying, 'I want to work on my dream.' As a result we divided into groups to study our separate issues. A small group joined the writer for his dream work, and Paula spontaneously agreed to be supervisor.*

Shige, the translator, and I went with two other members of the group into a small side room to explore the existential message of Shige's dream. The translator, Shioko, a Japanese woman who had been living in the United States for many years, was skillful in both languages as well as sensitive to both cultures. She and Shige and I have remained friends and recently spent a day together at her home in San Francisco. I am grateful to her for this splendid introduction to what was to become my life's work.

The assumptions underlying Gestalt dream work are almost embarrassingly simple: first, the dream is an existential message created by the dreamer; second, the dreamer is everyone and everything in the dream; third, the dream is recreated with awareness in the present; and fourth, the integrative work of the dream occurs in the dialogues the dreamer creates among the various elements of the dream.

Of his dream work, Shige writes:

> *Right before beginning the dream work Paula said, 'Please wait a moment,' and contemplated a short while to increase her mental concentration. She then faced Shige and said, 'Please tell the dream in the present tense.'*
>
> *Shige: I am meeting my friend on a road and he says, 'You went to the U.S. to study? There's big trouble in store for you.' Hearing that, I become anxious. We part and disappear in opposite directions. What does he mean? I'm anxious. Now, there is something like a thin cloud covering my surroundings. The front side is becoming covered by black clouds. Vague white clouds are forming at my back. This side feels as though some rays of light are coming in. The black clouds out in front are growing thicker and thicker; I cannot go forward. The black clouds are enveloping me. It feels as though the few white clouds are barely confronting the black clouds. Many black clouds and white clouds are going round and round about me. Ah, I cannot see my body anymore. Both clouds are spinning around me. I cannot see my body. Where did it go? But it is such a wonder that I feel no suffocation nor anxiety. I feel empty as air.*
>
> *Paula: Repeat that sentence.*
>
> *Shige: It is such a wonder. I feel no suffocation nor anxiety. I feel empty as air. Oh, the black clouds are disappearing a little and I'm beginning to be able to see my body.*
>
> *Paula: Have a dialogue between you and the black clouds.*
>
> *Shige: Black clouds, why do you go around me? You can crush me, and yet you don't. Why don't you do so?*
>
> *Paula: Be the black clouds and respond to Shige.*
>
> *Shige: The black clouds say, 'You are a sincere guy. That is why we don't crush you. Don't worry.' Now I'm being sucked into a place like a swamp. The bottom of the swamp is so deep. Ah, the surrounding is pressing me.*

Paula: Repeat that.

Shige: Ah, the surrounding is pressing me, pressing me. But it's such a wonder. I feel neither fear nor anxiety. I am truly in silence. Why?

Paula: Have a dialogue with the swamp.

Shige: Why aren't you crushing me? Why not? (As the swamp) 'Because you are a good guy. I cannot do that to you. Don't worry.' (At this moment, Shige himself feels tears well up in his eyes.) Tears well up, tears well up. Oh, they come to press me. They gradually push me in between rocks. Why do you push me? But it's surely a wonder. There is an opening, just enough to support my body. Very quiet. No anxiety.

Paula: Have a dialogue with the rocks.

Shige: Why do you oppress me? Why don't you crush me? (Shige as rocks) 'Take a look at my face; am I not smiling? I like you. You're a guy with favorable friendly impressions. You're really such a sincere guy. No need to worry.' Oh, look, the bottom of the rocks' crevice is moving upwards like an elevator! It's rising higher and higher. Ah, it's finally come out to the land's surface!"

Paula: Repeat that part.

Shige: It's rising higher and higher. Ah, finally out to the land's surface! There's a hill, trees, and a pasture. A bright feeling. Weather like a balmy Indian summer. Lots of sunshine. Warm. Silence. Wondrously stable.

Paula: Have a dialogue with the hill.

Shige: The hill. Oh hill! Teach me where to go.

Paula: Repeat that.

He repeats and the hill replies, 'Shige, I don't know.' Then Shige says, 'That's right, you wouldn't be the one to know.' (Silent for a while.) You wouldn't know.

Paula: Say that again.

Shige: You wouldn't know. Please teach me.

Paula: Be the hill.

Shige: (As the hill) 'As I told you now, I do not know. Just go wherever you want!'

Paula: Say it again in full power, in a loud voice!

Shige: Just go wherever you want! Go to where you want! Yes, I got it! (Repeats loudly, in full power.)

Paula: Say that in full power!

Shige: Go forward to your goal!

Paula: Repeat that!

Shige: Go forward to your goal! Shige, go forward to where you believe! I will go forward! Going forward stepping on ground and earth! Yes, I'll do it! The best to do is to go forward on the path that I believe, as I ground each step powerfully on the earth! After some time of silence, Shige says, 'Now I am quietly and slowly walking on the earth, walking on the earth, walking in silent stillness, into the future,' and the dream work ended. Right after the ending, tears had welled up from the writer's eyes. A sense of confidence and fulfillment was felt as well as comfortable fatigue. Shifting my view to Paula's eyes, I saw tears in her eyes. She was smiling silently, pouring her feelings into mine."

I, too, remember that moment when the work was finished and the five of us sat quietly marveling at what we had done. Since Shige discovered the meaning of his dream pretty much on his own, he had the experience Fritz Perls described when he said, "Learning is discovery." And so did I, for I was astonished at our success.

When I was offered a job in Japan in 1985, I accepted, confident I could do Gestalt with Japanese people through a translator because of my initiation in San Francisco with Shige and Shioko.

I cannot overemphasize the importance of the translator for my work in Japan. The only group in which I had difficulty getting Gestalt across to Japanese people was one in which I worked with a pro tem translator called in as a last-minute replacement for a regular translator who didn't show up. With not the foggiest notion of what I was doing, he was unsympathetic as well as ignorant; to my amazement, no one in the room seemed to understand what I was doing and saying. I entangled myself in a net of questions and doubts from which I never extracted either myself or the Gestalt approach. It was a thoroughly frustrating and disappointing experience, tempered by the fact that it happened only once. Other translators I have worked with have ranged from adequate to highly competent partners; among the latter I would like especially to thank Ayano Makiya, Hiromi Watanabe, and Yoshiko Otsuka for their brilliance and conscientious commitment to the work we have done together.

Of course, the more Japanese I learn the better partner I become in the fascinating enterprise of moving information through the interface of cultural and linguistic differences. Recently I heard a translator repeat my instructions in the command form usually used with children, and I was able to ask her to use a more polite form. Much of my part of Gestalt work is giving instructions, and the form in which I make these requests is of the essence. If I talk to people as though they are children, I am in danger of becoming another authority figure rather than an ally in our joint exploration of the present moment.

When I work in English, I hear every word, and this sensitivity to language has been a major tool in my work. The more correspondence there is between one's experience and one's words the happier and healthier a person will be. When the bond between experience and language frays, personal integrity is threatened. Loss of integrity means loss of orientation, for as the inner gyroscope of sensation and feeling becomes disconnected from the rudder of action, the person comes to rely on cues and clues from others to direct their behavior. When "What will people think?" becomes the source of orientation, the person experiences a sense of bewilderment which, when openly acknowledged, emerges in sentences like "I don't know what I want," "I don't know what I like," or "I don't know what to say."

One who lives with uncertainty is much better off expressing it directly rather than faking preferences. It is the importance to human well-being of truth—of matching words and feelings, words and thoughts, words and intentions—that makes the lies of politicians and advertisers such a baleful social influence. When powerful people model deception, the one who tells the truth often feels like a patsy—an ignoramus who doesn't know how to play the game—and it becomes nearly impossible for parents and teachers to teach truthfulness to children when apparently successful people publicly and blatantly lie. Pervasive public dishonesty is a major and unnamed cause of the much discussed moral decline in the United States—the one that is often blamed on young mothers.

Now that I work with a translator, the verbal ways of coming to know another person are far less available, and I have learned to pay more attention to the whole person, and especially to the organ Rebecca West designated as uniquely human—the hands. Awareness directed toward the hands will usually be a potent teacher. When working in Japanese, I attend to the deeper and more subtle levels of expression such as tone and pace and the many tiny movements and gestures that people makes as they (in Gertrude Stein's words) "express the whole of them." Since my Gestalt perspective is holistic, no action is irrelevant, and I see everything a person does as an expression of who they are at that moment. Naturally I have sharpened my observation skills in the process of relying on non-verbal communication. The Japanese language allows for immense vagueness, and Japanese people, like everyone else I have known, tend to become vague and confused when they are uncomfortable expressing themselves. Gestalt, however, is such a powerful method of discovery that I have been able to make effective interventions when even the translator does not know what the person is talking about.

Me (to translator): What does she means?

Translator: I don't know.

Me (to client): What are your hands saying?

And the work proceeds.

Since Japanese has several levels of politeness, a good translator will inform me of an unusual level of formality in a person's speech, of incoherence that she can hear and I can't, or of carefully crafted sentences. Often I hear Ayano soften my questions by adding, *Chigau,* (Is that right?") at the end, making it easier and less threatening for the person to differ with me and say it in their own way.

The group's members need to recognize the translator as a full person, for it belies the whole process of the Gestalt group if she is treated like a machine and her feelings, desires, and thoughts are denied recognition. I once worked with a translator who, becoming involved in the client's experience, cried so hard she couldn't talk. While she wept, I held hands with both her and the client until she returned from her own unfinished business. Like everyone else, I often don't need words to express myself. It is one of the pleasures of being a professional existentialist that my job is to accept and respond to whatever happens; I don't have to worry or fuss when something unexpected occurs. As the African saying quoted by Chinua Achebe in *Things Fall Apart* so wisely recognizes, "No one knows the way. Together we will find the way." That is an amazingly accurate description of what we do in a Gestalt group.

Since Japanese people often mistrust verbal agility, and tend to see words as superficial aspects of personality covering deeper, less articulate inner states which, in their culture, are best indicated by inference, my lack of verbal skills may, at times, actually be an advantage. Not that I don't wish my Japanese were better; I do, on many occasions both at work and at play. Nevertheless, because its basic value is awareness, Gestalt allows a purity of intention in its practitioners that frees them from any need to control, or even to understand, what the other person is doing.

This freedom to focus on awareness for its own sake allows the Gestalt practitioner to swim in various cultural waters with an appreciation of the choices that awareness allows. Choices I might not make myself, I can value because the other person makes them with awareness and with the responsibility that accompanies it.

SATURDAY, NOVEMBER 23, 10:30 A.M.

During their self-introductions at the beginning of the group, several people mention finding increased awareness and power during the workshop in July, and then a month of so later discovering that they had lost the brightness of their awareness to the routines of everyday life. This is, of course, not exactly the case, for if it were, they would be unaware of the change; nevertheless, I remember people in the United States reporting this exact experience after groups in the 1960s. It was in response to their desire to continue to practice awareness in a supportive setting that my husband, Larry Bloomberg, and I began a community development experiment in Albuquerque, New Mexico, where we were living and working at the time. People benefit from a community which supports their authenticity and the new behavior that arises from—to quote Vaclav Havel—"living in truth." New behavior, attitudes, and even so basic an experience as awareness are threatening to the status quo, which by definition does not value change.

Japanese people, even more than Americans, live embedded in established groups, especially the powerful work group, which has far more control over a person's life than in the United States. Edwin O. Reischauer, in his book *The Japanese Today: Change and Continuity*, observes: "To operate their group system successfully, the Japanese have found it advisable to avoid open confrontations. Varying positions are not sharply outlined and their differences analyzed and clarified. Instead each participant in a discussion feels his way cautiously, unfolding his own views only as he sees how others react to them. Much is suggested by indirection or vague implication. Thus any sharp conflict of views is voided before it comes into the open. The Japanese even have a word, *haragei*, "the art of the belly," for this meeting of minds, or at lease the viscera, without clear verbal interaction.

People in Japan are not necessarily more conformist than those in the United States. The Japanese are only too aware of the conflict between the desires of the private self—which they call *honne*—and *tatemae*" the behavior that satisfies the demands of the group. Since the conflict between social conformity and the demands of individuality is explicit, it is perhaps less of a burden for Japanese people than for Americans, whose individual desires often unconsciously resist the demands of the absolutistic morality fostered by organized Christianity. With its emphasis on harmony, the value-neutral Asian duality of yin and yang—whose literal meaning is "shadow and sunlight"—perhaps gives more permission for individual solutions than does the absolute Euro-American duality of good and evil. In Japanese, the word *kokoro* means both heart and mind, further modifying the dualities that have been such an essential part of European and North American culture.

Japanese morality tends to be relativistic in terms of what would be best for the group, and this allows a rational approach to personal decision making, as opposed to the resolutely moralistic social pressure Americans experience. Thus the American discussion of abortion has a hysterical tone that is altogether missing in Japan, where choice is quietly left up to the mother—who is, however, embedded in a powerful social system which through its system of birth registration explicitly values family lineage through the father.

Reischauer notes that, in Japan, "In contrast to normal Western perceptions, social conformity is not a sign of weakness, but rather the proud, tempered product of inner strength." The conflict between *honne* and *tatemae* is a human problem, not confined to any particular national group. The stereotype of Japanese conformity is, at best, a statistical observation, which is to say that it tells absolutely nothing about the behavior of any individual person at a particular time. I have met original and creative people in Japan, and slavish conformists in the United States.

The beauty of the Gestalt approach resides, I think, in its consistent reliance on awareness. Awareness and the pure joy of existence which, from time to time, it discloses are our sources of reliable information about the organism/environment field, whose events we are. To touch the authentic existence of these events is perhaps as close as we can come to realizing the immanence of the sacred in our daily lives. In Gestalt there is no other imperative, no should or shouldn't, beyond present awareness, for the Perlses accurately discerned that existentialism and moralism are differing systems for engaging the world. Of course, if one is to have precedence over the other, it must be existentialism, for everyone exists. Within an existentialist framework, morality may be described as the sum of the choices that each person makes.

Moralism differs from morality in that it aspires to make choices for everyone and thus becomes a dogma or ideology superimposed upon one's existence by outsiders. Because the Japanese do not make organized monotheism central to their vision of the world, I imagine there are many more aggressive moralists in the United States than in Japan. Perhaps this is one reason the people I work with are so open to existentialism.

Another general difference between the two cultures is the Japanese emphasis on formal hierarchy. This is reinforced by the language, which has levels of polite usage for people above and below one's own standing. The polite language, called *keigo*, that one properly speaks to a superior—literally an "above person"—is the major reason name cards are so important in Japan. A Japanese person needs to know the position of a new acquaintance in order to speak to him or her in the proper language.

Formal hierarchy, however, exists side by side with a sharing of authority in decision making which is the exact opposite of the custom in the United States, where formal hierarchy is downplayed in the name of equality and yet the authoritarian boss is very common. Aldous Huxley wrote that democracy is being able to say no to the boss, and by that definition Japan and the United States are probably on the much—discussed level playing field.

I am interested in national tendencies and, in fact, am amused when I or others conform so blatantly to the stereotypes— for example, when I refuse to learn *keigo* because it offends my sense of equality (a refusal which my son Lawrence assures me means that I will never speak good Japanese), or when after nearly every group in Japan we gather to have our picture taken—but at the same time I struggle to remember the limitations and dangers of statistical truths and stereotypes. Often I warn myself with the classic observation: All Indians walk single file; the one I saw did.

Like astronauts preparing for takeoff, people at the beginning of a workshop exhibit courage and determination as they await their venture into the unknown. The tension between uncertainly and excitement creates an ambiance that vibrates with anxiety and anticipation as we embark, and I often hear the words "*Doki-doki suru*," (My heart is pounding") as people report their experiences in the initial round of self-introductions. No one knows where we are going or what will happen as we launch ourselves into inner space.

The Japanese usually call each other by their family names with the suffix "*-san*" attached. In English this would be the equivalent to calling one another Mr. or Ms. Recently during an evening eating and drinking with a group of physicians, I was amazed to learn that after ten years as colleagues, they still address each other as *sensei* (Doctor) I discourage people who call me *Sensei*, for I am strongly identified with my name and dislike the impersonality of titles. In the groups I ask people to introduce themselves by their given names, which is often identity-reinforcing in and of itself. The translator invariably renders the name as "____*-san* while I, stuck in my American informality, cannot bring myself to add "-san" except on rare occasions, and almost never in the groups.

I imagine that formality of language and society contributes to the loneliness which Japanese people express far more often than Americans. I am unsure whether Japanese people acknowledge loneliness more often because they feel more lonely than Americans or because it is more acceptable to admit loneliness in their culture. In any case, the use of given names is a preamble to enhancing individuality and intimacy among the group members. The instant the introductions are complete, Aiko grabs a pillow—the thin, flat kind the Japanese call a *zabuton*—and throws it into the middle of the group, staking her claim to the group's time and attention. She tells us about her friend and classmate from medical school who died of cancer last month. As she talks about her friend's death she begins hitting her chest with her fist. Since I see any physical assault on the self as a retroflection—an active behavior turned toward the self rather than outward into the world where it could effect change—I put a pillow in front of her and hit it with my fist. She follows at once, hitting with first one fist and then another as she tells her friend how sad she feels.

When, after a minute or two, Aiko realizes that she is expressing anger rather than sorrow, she begins to reveal her anger in words and becomes animated and alive. When words and actions come together, like the joining of words and music, they make a song—the song of the self, aware and vital in the here and now. The aliveness which comes with being integrated is enormously self-reinforcing: it feels good to be wholly oneself, and this is one of the reasons Gestalt works. Moments of meeting and integrating the denied self are self-reinforcing because they return a person closer to natural wholeness. The encounter with one's authentic self is exhilarating. As awareness of the self becomes strong, the pleasure of being comes to outweigh the fear of disapproval and censure from others This is part of the dynamism of authenticity and freedom.

Expressing her anger at her friend for dying, Aiko gradually recognizes that in raging against her friend's death she is raging against her friend. When she begins to tell her friend what she didn't accept and what made her angry, she becomes even more alive. If not expressed directly, the great surges of grief, helplessness, anger, and fear that death calls forth may be directed into spillways of loathing and revenge. Blaming someone, even the one who has died, is a way to avoid the helpless loneliness that death evokes in those who are willing to face it directly. After Aiko expresses her anger, I ask her to change places, to move to the empty pillow and play her friend.

To many people, the empty chair is the defining technique of Gestalt practice. While I see the essence of the Gestalt approach in its existential and phenomenological emphasis on the integrity and reality of the experienced present, my respect for the empty chair as a source of learning and integration grows each time I use it. The disowned and disavowed self continues to exist within the organism, and the instruction to change seats and play the missing part inevitably evokes new experience. Often I tell people to change seats and simply sit in the new place and be aware of their experience. To their absolute amazement, the feelings of a few seconds earlier shift and something new emerges. While I do not completely understand this process, I know it is a powerful way to touch feelings and experiences that have long been hidden and denied.

Playing her friend, Aiko points out to herself (now on the empty pillow) how when Aiko refuses to accept her death she is refusing her life as well. As Aiko sits with the awareness of what she has been doing, she is able, at last, to grieve. Weeping heartfelt sobs, she expresses her loss. After crying, she is able to say, "Sayonara" and, at the same time, continue to feel close to her friend. She takes the pillow that had represented her friend and places it behind her back, a bit of non-verbal behavior that clearly demonstrates her acceptance and integration of her friend's life and death.

This acceptance and integration is a significant part of the mourning work each one must do before he or she can continue to live fully after a loved person dies. If we grieve and say good-bye to our beloved dead, we are able to keep them in our hearts long after they are gone, for while people die, love is forever if we choose to have it so. In Emily Dickenson's wonderful words:

Unable are the Loved to Die
For Love is Immortality,
Nay, it is Deity
Unable those who Love to Die
For Love transforms Vitality
Into Divinity.

I think it is pessimistic folly to say things like "All paths lead to the grave." Given the total subjectivity of human existence, each death is as unique as each life—is in fact knit to that life so tightly as to be inseparable from it. All lives have their own completions, which resemble each other very little from the outside and, of course, must be totally different as they are lived—for even death must be lived. The composer Arnold Schoenberg died saying, "Harmony; harmony," while Fritz Perls's last words were, "Don't tell me what to do." Aldous Huxley, by a prearranged signal, was given LSD for his journey. Some are carried aloft by angels; some turn their faces into contorted masks in response to the horrors they perceive while others walk through the gate fully conscious and smile. In death, as in life, existence precedes essence.

Yuriko, who had also known the dead woman, is crying vigorously by the time the group members finish sharing their response to Aiko's work. I invite Yuriko to work, something I rarely do. Her issue is guilt for what she sees as her abandonment of the dying woman because she had been frightened by her visible deterioration and suffering. Aiko couldn't forgive her friend for dying, and Yuriko can't forgive herself for not giving more support to a dying friend. Both had lessons to learn from this death. I ask Yuriko to be the dead woman and talk about her life. As her friend, Yuriko says she had done the things she wanted to do and was ready to die.

I really don't know how Yuriko came to be more accepting of herself; she cried, and maybe in touching her sorrow she touched her compassion as well. Compassion is a seamless garment, and in wrapping it around others I warm myself; for whenever I meet pain, I touch the suffering we all share.

In this work, I avoided Yuriko's anger, and this might have been a mistake. I often make mistakes when I work, and in the spirit of practicing what I preach I accept myself as a person who in doing new things—and Gestalt work is always new—often does them wrong. Since I think guilt is retroflected anger, turned against the self rather than the other, I hear "angry" when a person say "guilty," and often I direct their attention toward this possibility. It's hard to be mad at dead people, and yet anger is, I think, a universal response to death, both to being left alone and to being reminded that someday we, too, will die.

We all die, and if we live long enough we all meet the deaths of others. In responding to these encounters, each person makes momentous choices which define significant aspects of their existence. Nothing is more intrinsic to our being than the ability to recognize and respond to issues of life and death. Our choices as to how we will participate in these defining events of human existence comprise a significant part of our responsibility for aware self-creation.

In their responses to these two pieces of work, the group members share the sense of commonalty that comes with facing death together. Teaching groups members how to respond to one another's work is an important part of the workshop. So much of how we relate to one another in everyday life is comprised of judgments and advice, neither of which is helpful. Most people do not know how to be with another person's feelings while remaining attentive to their own. We are obsessed with the need to "do something," when we will far more helpful if we simply "stand there."

I encourage group members to share how they have felt during the work as well as any similarities they may have experienced in their own lives. Many people are so locked into the negative responses they have received from certain people in their past that they are genuinely surprised when other people respond to them with compassion and understanding. The sharing of feelings allows people to feel connected in a community which supports and allows experiment and change. Since this group's members are experienced, they share their responses in a simple, direct way. At the completion of the group response to Yuriko's work, as we break for lunch, we have become a community.

The intensity of group work can be heightened by keeping the group together for periods as long as twenty-four hours. Although I have done this in the past, I have since become more sensitive to people's need for time to withdraw and integrate. In order for profound emotional experiences to have maximum impact, there needs to be an ebb and flow between deepest intimacy and everyday human interaction, between contact and withdrawal. Perhaps as each one becomes familiar with their own rhythm of contact, they will realize that what enlivens experience is not dramatic intensity, but the quality of awareness and attention with which one illuminates present existence. This is what Zen Buddhism teaches as well, for it is in being fully present with everyday experience that the Zen student transforms the ordinary into the luminous. By attending fully to the mundane, we transcend it, and by reveling in the ordinary we enter the realm of the mystical which is a function of our willingness consciously to participate in the sweet stillness lying at the core of the life we share. The group breaks for lunch, and together we wander down the busy street to an Italian restaurant where we share a basket of garlic bread as we await our pasta. I eat a wonderful linguine with cream sauce.

SATURDAY, NOVEMBER 23, 1:30 P.M.

After lunch several people explore their difficulties in knowing and accepting themselves. One member speaks about her discomfort with free time. As a person who loves free time, I am baffled by this problem until she reveals that she creates her fear of free time by saying, "If I am not doing what I've been told to do, who am I?" Her discomfort with freedom is masking a deep sense of non-being—a fearful unwillingness to choose for herself that her caretakers created, most likely by terrorizing her for her childhood choices.

Hers is a profound existential dilemma which she and I can only begin to address in the group. I know that contact with another person amplifies contact with one's self. Because of this, people who are protecting themselves from unacknowledged suffering cannot make satisfactory intimate relationships because the contact of intimacy thrusts them into the pain they seek to avoid. Lacking sufficient support to experience the ancient suffering, they retreat—either by blaming the other person for their suffering or by withdrawing from the relationship with a feeling of helplessness and despair. In her essay "Comments on the New Directions" (1976), Laura Perls gives an excellent definition of support:

> *Support is everything that facilitates the ongoing assimilation and integration for a person, a relationship, or a society: primary physiology (Like breathing and digestion), upright posture and coordination, sensitivity and mobility, language, habits and customs, social manners and relationships, and everything else that we have learned and experience during our life time. In short, everything that we usually take for granted and rely on, even and particularly our hang-ups and resistances, the fixed ideas, ideals, and behavior patters which have become second nature precisely because they were supportive at the time of their formation.*

Partners in couple relationships often experience the discomfort of anxiety caused by unsupported contact. The emotional and physical intimacy of coupling takes one deep into his or her own experience; and should there be ancient misery waiting there, the intimacy will appear to be creating the pain that emerges. The unaware couple will blame each other for their suffering rather than seek deeper causes, a mistake that often leads one or the other of the partners to end the relationship. Our entire program of emotional education, both conscious and unconscious, allows us to blame others for our suffering. Most English speakers remember the childhood sentence, "Look what you made me do!" and many would be embarrassed to use it as adults. However, although most people become less blatant with maturity, they continue to blame, for it is nearly impossible to take responsibility for a situation one does not experience creating. Until I can meet my childhood pain—or, at the very least, recognize that I am avoiding it—I will blame others for my emotional misery. I will continue to do so until I meet someone who will listen to my suffering.

Since symptomizing—which the Perlses called a dummy behavior, an avoidance of the meeting which comprises true living—is socially acceptable, many people will listen to the most tedious elaboration of symptoms for which the possessor disclaims all responsibility and yet withdraw from direct statements of grief, anger, fear, or loneliness.

The isolation and loneliness that either symptomizing or make-believe well-being create are more than just personally unfortunate: they are a community disaster, a pattern that leads to such tragedies as Susan Smith's 1994 murder of her two young children in Union, South Carolina. Imagine the utter despair of a young woman who trusts no one to listen to her desperation. If there had been such a one, the terrible act would not have been carried out, for such a perverse plan could never survive the exposure of being discussed with another human being. It's the kind of plan that can only seem practical so long as it is unspoken, which is another way of saying that it's an insane idea. To speak it is to know its madness. Most people could not dare to imagine Smith's loneliness, for if they did, they would touch their own despair.

We could, if we wished, create communities that value talking about oneself to others, communities with the explicit social expectation that members of the community will listen and lend support to those who suffer. How we prevent ourselves from doing this is one of the most interesting topics of our time. At the present stage of our emotional community development, it is far easier to hate and blame the victim—and, make no mistake about it, people who commit unthinkable murders are victims, too—than to consider how we might learn to open our hearts and act in ways that would avoid such tragedy.

Contact with others demands contact with the self. The basis of aware self-acceptance is support, both self-support and support from others. Support from others is fundamental, for the ability to give and receive support is essential to human wholeness. There is, however, a difference between support and dependency. The dependent person projects his or her confidence and imagines he/she needs the other person to survive. Dependency demands control—domination and manipulation—rather than meeting. To the extent that I require support from another, my need precludes respect for their unique personality and destiny and prevents my joining them in the mutuality of the I-Thou relationship.

As people come to trust one another in the sheltered group environment, they can experiment with contact and the mutuality of I-Thou because they know they will receive support for their suffering.

To this woman now sitting before me, I suggest she move in front of each person and make simple self-affirming statements, such as "I'm here" or "I'm okay." Such a modest task. Yet she fills it with meaning as she sees her here-and-now existence mirrored in the eyes of others, an experience she had been denied in infancy and childhood and has since denied herself. Because she has long been unaware of her innate value as a living being, the recognition and acceptance she receives from others is a rare affirmation and touches her deeply.

Another person, a man this time, wants to explore his discomfort after speaking before a group. When I asks him to return in fantasy to this experience and attend to what the discomfort is saying, he discovers that he is saying to himself, "You should have done better." This is an "Aha!" insight for him and an example of how awareness in and of itself has the power to alter experience. As Werner Heisenberg reminded us years ago, the observed phenomenon differs from the one that is unobserved, and aware behavior is an observed phenomenon which differs intrinsically from that which is unaware.

When I ask this man how he feels about his work, he says he is satisfied and the voice that says, "You should have done better" is silent for now.

After a short break, a young woman works on a recurring flying fantasy in which each time she is about to leave the ground she stops herself. She says that whenever she experiences this failure she feels devastated as it seems to portend her inability to achieve what she wants. Again, I encourage her to stand up and, in fantasy, return to the place of difficulty so that she might become aware of what she is doing. It is a marvel of human creativity that imagined events have an impact similar to events lived, and it is this uncanny imaginative power that allows Gestalt work its peculiar authority. In its existential and experiential purity, Gestalt encourages people to become holistically aware—with their muscles and viscera, as well as with words—of what they are doing to create the present. The facilitated intensification of awareness is a potent source of information and learning. No one has to trust or believe what I say, because they can learn from their own experienced truth. It is such information that I am encouraging this young woman to access when I ask her to act out the fantasy. When she does, she learns that at the moment of takeoff, she closes her chest and locks her shoulders. I tell her to go through it again and this time intentionally perform the behaviors that stop her from flying. Doing this, she is amazed to discover that she is flying. Her discovery is an example of the workings of paradoxical intent, the process whereby a person can gain control of an undesired behavior by doing it with awareness. Because people often lie to themselves, they feel extremely frustrated by their inability to do what they think they want to do. Of course, what one thinks one wants to do and what one truly desires are often quite different, and paradoxical intent allows us to explore and learn from this difference.

The clusters of behavior which we call procrastination give a good example of how this might work. Procrastination is signaled by such sentences as "I wanted to finish the paper, but...." What comes after the 'but' can be any number of reasons: "...I didn't have time," "...didn't know how," "...didn't understand," etc.; these allow an endless round of self-deception which, while it might leave the player feeling righteous, will surely leave her or him feeling frustrated and impotent. Using paradoxical intent, one says, "I don't want to finish the paper," and deliberately avoids finishing it by going to the movies, hanging out with friends, or any other desired activity.

Deliberate performance of the disowned behavior allows me to experience the other side of my ambivalence—the part that desires the thing I deny. When I do consciously what I am already doing, I bring the force of will and awareness to the activity which has seemed in some mysterious way to be doing me. Further, by acting with awareness and deliberation, I become able to accept responsibility for the behavior I have chosen. With or without awareness, I am responsible for everything I do. Regardless of how undesirable I may think a bit of behavior is, I am the one who is doing it, and it is only by first acknowledging my power and responsibility that I can do something different. No matter how profoundly I have been victimized in the past, I am the one who does what I do now. I am the one who can change what I do now.

From the very beginning choice and responsibility have been among the defining elements of existentialism, and working with Gestalt—which is operational existentialism, the "how-to" of existentialism—I emphasize over and over again the progression of awareness, choice, and responsibility—the triad on which human freedom rests. Paradoxical intent allows people to experience the choices they make and to understand their responsibility better, perhaps, than they had before.

As I discuss this with the group, I bring my fists together on top of each other to stress the inner connection and wholeness that responsibility for one's choice allows. The establishment of an authentic inner connection with one's self is the essential first step to reinstating the process of natural growth and evolution.

Just as, in Lincoln's words, "a house divided against itself cannot stand," a divided person cannot grow. A divided person suffers an internal war between the one who, acting on behalf of a role, seeks to kill vital parts of the self and the hurt and angry self trying to maintain its integrity. Learning that a role or set of roles is more valuable than one's authentic self is always a painful lesson, for as Rickie Marcuse (the widow of philosopher Herbert Marcuse) taught me, in order to teach someone something that is not true, it is necessary to hurt them. Reality reinforces truth, and the teacher of lies has to inflict pain to counter the natural reinforcements that comes with acting in harmony with what is. The notion that any role is more important than the unique authentic self is a lie. So long as a person is hostage to this deceit, they may change roles, but will be unable to connect with the deep impulse and growing power of the life force that, although often encapsulated in pain and anger, remains at the core of each of us. Disconnected from its source in the authentic self, human power becomes perverse, destructive, and demonic, lending itself to compulsive behavior as a way to occupy its wasted and blasted energy and to avoid the terror of its loss. From hand washing through sex, food, and drugs, and on to the will to domination over others, compulsive behavior is the endless striving of a being who perceives itself as doomed to suffering in isolation.

Without connection to the self, a person will never find ease or pleasure, love or compassion. Such a person wanders homeless over the Earth, an angry wraith seeking revenge on all, even on the Earth itself. He or she cannot, in William Blake's words, "to the stilled Earth say: I flow, to the rustling water speak: I am." This internal exile from one's authenticity is the greatest loss a human being can experience.

People suffering severance from themselves have been taught much that is not true and have suffered gravely in the process. It is inevitable that when they first touch their authentic selves they experience pain: the pain of the punishment meted out to assure the replacement of what is, or was, with the version of reality the one who punishes wished to teach. In the early Gestalt groups I did in New Mexico, we used to say, with the seriousness that abides in true wit, "I cry, therefore, I am;" and for many people, this is all too true.

Rigidity, compulsivity, and unaware roles are solutions to the problem of how to live with the pain and humiliation that comes when the childhood caretaker rejects the emerging self as it seeks to expand into the world; they are the solution to the problem of childhood survival amidst the unbearable suffering occasioned by the rejection of who and how one is. Avoidance of feeling, which as the source of alienation prevents one from knowing either one's self or the life in which she is embedded, is not the problem, but an outgrown solution to childhood distress. It is the core of the existential dilemma.

In a more recent group an attractive woman with the sculptured facial structure I associate with Native Americans comes forward and sits silently in front of me kneading a towel-like handkerchief. She seems to be aware of this behavior, and when I asks her what her hands are saying, she says, "You don't need to be afraid." When I inquire if she is afraid, she says she is and continues, "I don't know what I want. I don't know who I am. I don't know what's real." Beside me, Ayano, who is translating, strains to follow the pale words which barely ruffle the silence. Apparently exhausted, the woman lapses into a breathless stillness that reminds me of a young animal frozen in the bush as the predator stalks nearby. Inserting myself into her stillness, I reply, "We'll have to find something real for you to start from," and as I say this I feel myself calling on the strength of my own being in hopes that in meeting me, she might touch the reality of her own existence. When I draw her attention to her failure to breathe, she inhales and says, "When I do or say something I always feel like I'm faking." Her dark, round eyes peer gravely from a palpable atmosphere of misery, and I see her as one who had lost contact with the ground of her being, truly a lost soul drifting through life in a miasma of sorrowful unreality. I surprise myself with the tender patience I am able to summon as we sit together and create a here-and-now reality that she can begin to trust. Perhaps, in meeting the patience of her endurance, I was able to touch my own.

"Are you aware you aren't breathing?" I ask. She nods slightly and breathes a little deeper. I encourage her to do it again. She presses a towel hard against her face as, nourished with oxygen, the tide of tears rises before she succeeds in forcing it back. I say, "Are you aware you're breathing?" Again she answers with a nearly imperceptible nod. I say, "If I were to ask you what you doing right now, you could reply, 'I'm breathing.'" When her eyes glow with a moment of recognition, I say, "Let's do it," and ask the question: "What are you doing right now?" She replies, "I'm breathing." "And this is real, this part of your existence," I respond. A look of what I imagine is relief flashes through her features, vanishing more quickly than lightning crossing the night sky. I tell her that I see her and that she is real. Again, she nods her tiny agreement. Then I ask her if she sees me, and when she nods again, I assure her that I am real. She is taking the baby steps of awareness, and although she walks ever so tentatively, she walks. All through our dialogue, she struggles with her tears, and when I direct her attention toward them she becomes aware that she is stopping them. I assure her that both wanting to cry and stopping her crying are part of her existence. She fills out in front of me, gaining dimension as she allows herself to taste the misery and the companionship of this her present existence. She tells me that at home she was always considered *jama* (troublesome). I assure her that she's not troublesome to me now and ask whether I am troubling her. When she says, "No," I ask Ayano if she's troubled by either of us. As the three of us agree that we're not troubled by one another, I begin to feel light.

Then she says that sometimes she knows her feeling and sometimes she doesn't and wonders if that is okay. I suggest we check with the group and ask how many have had the same experience. Everyone, including me, raises a hand, and I encourage her to look at this expression of her similarity with other people. When I ask her if we can stop, she nods a solid agreement. As I move forward to shake her hand, she falls into my arms and begins to cry. She has touched the misery that, for her, is the beginning of self-awareness. As I hold her, I rejoice silently. I never imagined she would cry, and was satisfied when she had begun to know that she existed. She begins a long path of re-creation—truly a phoenix rising from the ashes of her destruction. I am awed in the presence of her tenacity as she struggles to be present with the pain of her present moment. As she returns to her seat, I am aware of both the graciousness of her coming and the solemn sadness of her leaving, just as Buber described.

Hamlet had it right: "To be or not to be?" is the question, and each one answers it for themselves. The answer involves more than the decision not to kill one's self, although, as Camus has indicated, this is an essential component of our existential responsibility. After a certain age, we are all alive because we choose to be. Once I choose to live, however, the next step is to become aware of how I live, to recognize the choices I make in my living, to take responsibility for these choices, and to be willing to see the world I create with my choices. I am not a carrot (although once I said I was in Japanese, in which the words *ninjin*—carrot—and *ningen*—human being—are distressingly similar); simple existence is not life. Awareness, choice, and responsibility are the elements from which we create our human essence, and those who deny them are the living dead who drag their unfeeling corpses through the world creating pain and misery everywhere they go.

SUNDAY, NOVEMBER 24, 10:00 A.M.

Settled in time and space at last, I join the group members in a mutuality of trust that allows those who under ordinary conditions would never express their own truth to put themselves forward. Mieko is a tiny, frightened human being. As she sits in front of me, I am momentary overwhelmed by the extent of the work I imagine she has before her; and yet, in her courage to come forward, I see the spark of being. This is not a defeated person. My task is to cherish her tiny spark in a way that will sustain and foster her sense of her own life.

I rarely feel this way. Usually my trust in people's ability to take care of themselves makes me willing to let come what may. In my first work with Mieko, however, I deliberately set out to facilitate an awareness of her own deepest sense of being, to provide an experience that will support and nourish her fragile self-esteem. Until a person is ready to reinforce and support him or herself—and she isn't—I want to lend a hand. At the same time I want to be authentic and true to myself.

While being phony doesn't work, being kind does, and Mieko's plight touches me. As she shares her experience, her delicate hands float up from her legs and I can see power in her solar plexus when she straightens her back. A glow comes into her eyes and her face relaxes into a repose that I find adorable. From this inner connection she speaks in the teeny, tiny voice of a child, long intimidated and frightened into silence. The ember of her existence glows softly in the silent room. I work to be a mild wind nurturing her flame. Mieko's work is focused on her childhood and her difficulty in talking to her mother. In the present, she presents a bundle of repressed energy, fearful and holding back. Her inner world is filled with messages that say "Don't speak," "Don't move," "Never tell." As she articulates these secret demands to the group, she relaxes and begins to express the painful feelings that this suppression created for the little girl she once was.

The role of the obedient child is an especially compelling one for girls; in Japan, as in the rest of the world, parents and other adults are more likely to indulge the energy and buoyancy of boys. Girls' desires and realities are usually challenged and squashed as the caretakers mold them into the narrow roles male-dominated societies require for women. For these roles to work satisfactorily, women and girls have to appear to be satisfied, even happy, with their situation. Mieko had been taught never to talk back. It seems that in Japan, as in America, many parents invariably hear children's words not as talking, but as "talking back"—a good example of the often unconscious truthfulness of idiomatic expression.

I remember my own confusion as a child when I was told not to talk back. How could I talk if I didn't talk back? Of course the implied answer, to me and to Mieko, was, "Don't talk." Since it's often pleasurable to be the obedient child, this role offers a good example of how it is not particular behaviors that creates alienation so much as the state of the inner connection to the self. If one is obliging and cooperative from compulsion rather than choice, there is an inner dynamic of incongruity and separation. The same behavior can be chosen and life-enhancing or compulsive and life-depleting. Since people are excellent actors, it is not easy for an observer to know which dynamic is in place. Over the long run, however, compulsive role playing creates depression because the self, removed from its natural sources of energy, becomes exhausted and filled with rage whose further repression demands the expenditure of even more energy from an already depleted organism. Depression, in fact, results from the violence of repression—socially condoned, especially among women, because it is turned against the self.

The power of the parents to establish rules that the child will obey—even though such obedience will inevitably create an inner split between the good child obedient to the parental demand and the dark, alienated self crouched angrily within—was demonstrated recently and inadvertently by George Bush. Shortly after being elected to the Presidency of the United States, arguably the most powerful position in the world because of the nuclear button to which it allows access, he, with some fanfare, announced to the world that henceforth he would no longer eat broccoli. Apparently, neither the role of Congressman or vice-president or head of the CIA had allowed him sufficient status to stand up to the parental mandate, "Eat your broccoli, George." Now that he was President, however, little George could free himself at last from the disgusting labor of choking down the vegetable he despised. This is a stunning example of the power of parents to shape the immature organism, creating a false self that eats its broccoli even though it hates the taste. The inevitable partner of the "good child" who eats his broccoli is a denied, repressed self that hides his choking, gagging hatred of the despised vegetable and of those who have forced him to eat it—in Bush's case, perhaps this is the persona whose vote twice broke a tie in Congress to assure the United States's continued manufacture of chemical and biological weapons. Bush's behavior is especially telling because taste, with its connection to nutrition and survival, is obviously a personal and idiosyncratic aspect of human individuality; there is no right taste to savor or correct way to appreciate one's food. And yet even this most profoundly personal preference can be overridden to the extent that one person had to become President of the USA before he could "just say no" to broccoli.

Clearly Mieko was able to find others who would support her growth, for when I saw her recently, her bright face and substantial demeanor were remarkable. She gleamed with satisfaction as she told me that she was now in graduate school.

When the group resumes after a short break, Chika says she wants to work. She comes forward and sits in front of me, saying that she doesn't know what she wants to work on. Usually when someone says this, I tell them to begin a few sentences with "Now I'm aware...." When a person begins to report their here and now awareness, something significant inevitably emerges. I often tell people in workshops that there are three ways to begin Gestalt work—reporting one's here-and-now awareness, reporting a problem in everyday life, and telling a dream. Telling the dream or memory in the present tense moves from the blandness of "talking about" into the lively immediacy of the aware present; further, I encourage people to talk to (rather than about) the person who preoccupies them, to act out the dream rather than report it, and to tell their stories in the present tense.

Since Gestalt is inevitably existential and experiential, each of these beginnings must be facilitated in such a way as to make explicit the implicit truth that whatever the person is experiencing is happening right now. Each of these beginnings, if skillfully facilitated, will allow a person to become aware of the major unfinished situation that he or she has the support to experience in the present.

As soon as I suggest she report her here-and-now experience, Chika settles into a deep passivity from which she stares at me as though her will has been surgically extracted. The weight of her dependency lies in the room like a blob of stellar matter, and I sit quietly, wondering what to do next. Apparently rousing herself in the face of my inactivity, she begins a story of immense confusion and obfuscation. Even with my meager Japanese I can hear the Japanese equivalents of words like "my father's mother's brother," "my mother's brother's wife," and "my older brother's daughter," which spin themselves into a clatter of confusion that leave the interpreter breathless and the group confounded.

Fortunately I am able to focus on the process of her confusion rather than the content of her narrative, and when, after a few minutes, she says, "I don't understand," I'm relieved. That sounds true, and I ask her to frame some sentences stating what she doesn't understand.

At once, she begins, "I don't understand what I like; I don't understand what I dislike; I don't understand who I am." The clarity of her expression is refreshing after the terrible sink of her confusion, and the group seems to emit a collective sigh of relief as she finds her moment of truth. I acknowledge both her truth and her suffering, and ask her to tell someone in the group what it is she doesn't understand. After she does this, I ask her what she feels. She replies, "Regret," and says she has a pain in her chest. I direct her to focus her awareness on this pain and give it a voice; then she says it has shifted to the back of her neck. As she says this, her hands come together in a strangling motion. I hand her a pillow, which she twists briefly before exploding into violent flailing and hitting. She has touched her rage.

Although the ability to split from one's essential self might seem a human tragedy, it is a survival mechanism which allows people, children and adults alike, to endure the unendurable. Whenever people are helpless, wherever honest expression might endanger survival, denial and fragmentation are protective responses. It is safer to decide that one isn't really angry after all than to confront the rage of a person five or six times one's size or the ferocity of a guard holding an automatic rifle. One might be wiser to return and close the door nicely rather than face rejection as a feminine being just as one is coming to know what femininity is.

The man who hits his sobbing son and shouts, "No son of mine is going to be a crybaby!" quickly teaches the boy not to cry regardless of how miserable he is feeling. These are entirely rational choices made by people who are doing their best to stay alive and maintain their integrity in desperate and unalterable situations. The tragedy occurs when the split remains after the aggression that occasioned it has vanished, after the situation has changed. Then, without full expression of the repressed anger and pain, the torment continues, now internalized and perpetuated as self-destructive behavior by the injured person themselves. The desire to avoid suffering caused by internalized aggression drives some people to deny their aggression and project it onto others.

Many people rationalize their rage, saying something like, "I'm not angry. You are. And since I need to protect myself from your aggression, it's all right to hit you first or deprive you in such a way as to make you helpless." Such projection underlies racism, sexism, and other irrational fears and hatreds in which one's own feelings are imaginatively placed on someone who is defined as not me, or not us: the other who becomes the stand-in for the denied self. So long as I refuse to experience my own suffering and the feelings of misery and rage that accompany it, I will reenact my personal drama by harming myself and/or seeking to inflict a similar suffering on others. I will believe that they and/or I deserve to be punished for the terrible qualities which, under the relentless persuasion of those who are more powerful, I have convinced myself I possess. This will be my way of avoiding the pain that I am afraid to feel.

Compulsive hating allows only temporary relief from self-hatred, for, as Alice Miller said, "Nobody achieves freedom by blaming people who never harmed them." The suffering people inflict on others in their attempt to avoid inner pain has no limits because the release from stress and pain that hurting others allows must, like drug use which accomplishes the same purpose, be endlessly renewed. Since hating people who never harmed us cannot complete the unfinished business, the figure of past suffering will continue to emerge into awareness. Persons who have chosen projection as their comfort will have to soothe themselves with new, and escalating, expressions of hate and anger. Surely the Holocaust makes it horrendously obvious that this process does not work. This must be one reason some people want to deny that it ever happened—because to recognize the Holocaust is to accept that projection is not only cruel, but useless. Far from the final solution, it is no solution at all.

If scapegoating others were removed as an acceptable source of comfort for internal suffering, many people would collapse into the unbearable misery from which scapegoating had been a sanctuary. (An example was the noticeable upsurge of calls to mental health clinics in South Africa after apartheid ended.) Others, desperate to avoid their painful feelings, do literal battle to protect their right to hate regardless of the misery which their psychological accommodation creates for others. To complete the gestalt of past suffering, one needs to direct the unexpressed feelings toward the appropriate person or a well-formed fantasy of that person. One does not have to seek out one's aged parent and scream her or his childhood resentment in their ears in order to complete the unfinished business. One does, however, have to express the feeling directly to his or her fantasy of the parent whose ignorance, fear, or preoccupation created the injury. The parents' motives are irrelevant because the effect on the child is the same regardless of the parents' rationalizations—even though, as in the case of illness or economic deprivation, parental behavior may be understandable from an adult point of view. For the child caught in the grip of a violent or neglectful parent, reasons are unimportant.

Each person is free to find a secure environment in which it is possible to enhance the compulsive reenactment of the unfinished situation with the powerful, and heretofore denied, emotions which the events evoke. In such a place, they may also express the desires they were afraid to express at the time: "Stop it;" "I don't like that;" "I want to run away." When the person adds heretofore unexpressed emotion and desire to the reenactment, she or he may gradually integrate the past experience and release the energy bound in repression for fresh responses to the ever-new present situation. As we complete the unfinished business of the past, we become free at last to enter the newly accessible present which perpetually invites our aware participation.

I have often wondered at the way present events trigger the repetitive response of unfinished business. After years of thinking about this problem, I have decided that unfinished business shares with the hologram the characteristic that the whole is present in even the tiniest part. This means that, for the sensitized person, whenever a portion of the unfinished situation is present—in a harsh tone of voice, an authoritarian attitude, or even a gender or age similarity, the entire unfinished situation emerges. I was once in a group where within five minutes a perfect stranger was screaming at me and calling me a bitch. Another stranger once expressed the desire to cut my carotid artery and watch my blood spill on the floor. While these are clearly extreme examples, they make the point. When some bit of my behavior called up the hologram of their unfinished business, they quit the present and began responding to me as though I were someone hateful from their past. Their unfinished business was like a trap waiting to snap shut on any moment of the present containing a bit of the unresolved past. They expressed their rage as though I were the one who had hurt and humiliated them. For such people, time collapses like a fan, and the present becomes identical with the unfinished past.

Everyone is born with the capacity to experience their here-and-now emotions. Anyone who has lived with children knows this is so, for children express their feelings. They don't stop until the caretakers teach them that feelings are dangerous to themselves or threatening to those around them. Sometimes these two sources of repression overlap, as when the parent's discomfort results in violent actions toward the child. And sometimes the relation is more subtle, as when, for example, the parent teaches that the child is responsible for the parent's happiness and must never show or do anything upsetting to such a parent's invariably delicate equilibrium.

Many children learn to hold back their feelings when they become aware that the expression of their emotions, especially pain and anger, appears to create distress in the caretaker. In *Villette*, Charlotte Bronte captures this process perfectly. When six-year-old Polly asks to accompany her father on a journey, he says, "It's only great strong people who should travel. But don't look sad, my little girl, it breaks my heart. Papa will soon come back to his Polly."

> *"Indeed, indeed" [she says], "I am not sad, scarcely at all."*
> *"Polly would be sorry to give papa pain; would she not?"*
> *"Sorrier than sorry."*
> *"Then Polly must be cheerful; not cry at parting, not fret afterwards. She must look forward to meeting again and try to happy meanwhile. Can she do this?"*
> *"She will try."*

Papa teaches Polly to quash her feelings in order to protect him from his discomfort at leaving. The best thing about learned behavior is that it can be unlearned. The blocking of emotional responses can be unlearned, but first one must become aware of what one is doing and how he or she is doing it. Gestalt, with its emphasis on the precise tracking of awareness, is particularly effective for unlearning because it encourages people to become aware of exactly what they are doing. As one becomes practiced in present awareness of actual behavior, she or he will realize they may choose to do something else. On several occasions I heard Fritz Perls say, "The present situation is the only thing we should allow to control us." With this pithy remark Fritz, with his genius for the obvious, expressed the goal of the Gestalt approach: to be aware of and responsive to ourselves and the events around us in our present time and place. Taking the obvious one step further, Fritz emphasized the ability to respond: response-ability, responsibility.

When a woman changing clothes in a department store dressing room caught and sued the security guards who were spying on her, a California jury awarded her more than one million dollars in damages. "This wasn't about money," the 36-year-old victim told the newspaper. "It was about making them take ownership for what they did." Ownership for our actions—another (and, in our intensely possessive era, perhaps more appropriate) way to say "take responsibility" for what we do.

Gestalt work facilitates the expression of feelings in a safe and supportive environment by taking advantage of the power and creativity of the human imagination to evoke the presence of the previously hurtful person in the here and now. By speaking and expressing emotion directly to the here-and-now fantasy of the abusing person, one begins to complete the unfinished gestalt and gains freedom to go on with one's life responding to present people and situations rather the painful past.

Invariably, in all cultures where I have worked, suffering and anger are the denied feelings that encapsulate the authentic self and separate people from the wisdom of its guidance in daily life. Working in Japan I often heard the word *kuyashii*, which carries the nuance of combined anger and sorrow that accompanies denial of the self. Chika uses it before she goes through her cycle of pain and anger. First she pounds and twists the pillow and then she sobs over it. When her anger emerges again, she repeatedly screams, "*Bakkayaro*" ("Stupid!"), before she collapses sobbing in Yuriko's arms. Her expression resonates deeply with others in the group, and at least three people, including a young man, sob aloud during her work. Their grief may signify that they have touched the shell of their own suffering, which perhaps has been softened by their participation in Chika's expression.

I notice that each sobbing person has a comforter who holds them, which confirms my experience that people in groups are superb at taking care of one other. The path to freedom and security is an inner path of feeling and acknowledging suffering. Each person experiences the emotions that were too painful or life-threatening to feel at the time of injury and directs them toward the person or people who originally evoked them, even if the mature adult recognizes that to hate and fear these ancient enemies is totally irrational. It is another paradox that one can become rational only after she or he has allowed the irrational feelings of childhood to emerge into full expression. To avoid re-traumatization, this is best done in a sheltered environment where there is sufficient support for integration. Laura Perls said that any experience that has been fully integrated becomes support, and I think this is obvious. It is the disintegrated (and therefore disintegrating) experiences that take us away from our natural support and wholeness.

Blaming one's parents for one's suffering is hardly more irrational than blaming Jews, single mothers, or a snake and an apple. Further, directing one's rage toward the one who actually caused the suffering will allow completion, while directing it toward innocent scapegoats will not. Ultimately focused expressions of anger and blame are steps on the path to wholeness, for regardless of how cruelly others have treated us, each of us—whether we like or not, whether we are aware or not—is responsible for our own actions. Who but ourselves is pushing the buttons and pulling the levers? Even when I pretend to be Oz, the great and powerful, I am still I.

As I gain courage to face forbidden feelings and desires, I begin to meet myself in my wholeness. The more nearly whole I am, the more vividly I participate with all that surrounds me. This sense of connection, the experienced certainty of being embedded in a living nexus of feeling and sensation, allows me to find the place Karl Jaspers describes where "what seemed abyss becomes the space of freedom: the seeming nothing becomes the space from which true being speaks to us." As I become whole I awaken into a universe suffused with spirit, one in which everything is holy. Those who avoid their wholeness transform the unexpressed self into Jasper's abyss. They choose, as Perls observed, to actualize a self-image rather than a self, and the self-constructed and highly symbolic self-image will never lead us to the place where true being speaks to us. People who evade and avoid their own existence cannot approach wholeness until they are safe enough to feel and express the whole of them—hurt and anger, rage and sorrow, joy and orgasm, the whole mishegoss of human emotion.

Sunday, November 24, 1:00 p.m.

During lunch I spend time alone in my room making notes on the morning session. Reviewing the work, I remember my very first group, when I saw the people there as hurt children masquerading as adults. The crude disguises behind which most people live are only credible to those who agree to be deceived or who have scant energy available for observation and awareness because they, too, are hiding. Maintaining an act and avoiding the obvious requires enormous energy creating a personal economy of scarcity which makes people appear dull and stupid. Through eons of existence and evolution, the human species has evolved such a host of intelligence-affirming survival skills that it is impossible for people to be as stupid as they often appear. It was one of Fritz and Laura Perls's great insights that many people are "playing stupid." Rather than an innate inadequacy, stupidity is often the aftermath of learned denial, an avoidance of reality that invariably results in a depletion of energy for awareness and activity. It is this deliberate, forceful avoidance of what is happening in front of one's eyes—those organs superbly adapted to observing the present situation, that makes people act stupid and feel depressed. It is the confluence of millions of people playing stupid that creates the horrible dramas of our lifetime—nuclear, chemical, and biological weapons; racism and genocide; starvation amidst abundant food supplies; and unemployment in the face of massive healing, teaching, and environmental clean-up tasks in which everyone could effectively participate at half the cost of the wasteful manufacture of armaments.

Intimacy, too, is a great threat to the delicate equilibrium of denial and pretense that in many people passes for personality. To feel connected to another person, I must first be connected to myself, which, for many people, means to feel pain that, by definition, is too great to tolerate. This explains why many people are lonely. It is only under very special circumstances—such as those created in certain groups or by people who are fortunate enough to be able to love—that injured people can risk the pain required to contact the self and, therefore, another person. In avoiding contact with our own pain, we avoid contact with other people, with animals, and with the Earth itself; it is this absence of intimate contact that creates the hysterical feeding frenzy that passes for economic life and the minuet of avoidance that passes for social contact in the postmodern world. As Eric Hoffer once wrote, "You can never get enough of something you never wanted in the first place," and no one alive ever wanted money in the first place.

During the afternoon session Sunday, Sachiko works on a dream in which she wanders in a *kuroi mori*—the black forest, a profound symbol in many cultures. Dante begins his journey with the sentence, "Midway through my life I found myself on a path through a dark wood."

The Japanese do not "have a dream;" they "see a dream." Nor do they "have time;" instead they say "there is" time. It is literally impossible to ask if the store "has" apples or oranges or T-shirts. All you can ask is, "Are there apples?" Pondering this difference has sensitized me to the possessiveness of we English speakers who "have" time, and dreams, and relationships. In fact, we even say "I have gone," and, thus, speak as though we possess the ephemerality of our own past. No other people "have" as much as English speakers, and this "has" to affect our experiencing the world in subtle ways that are quite impossible for us to see from our position within our language.

A theme of this workshop has been entering the illusion of inner emptiness to make an internal connection with the self. As she dreams her dream in the present, Sachiko wanders in her black forest and becomes aware of the sweet pungency of the forest. The smell is her affirmation, and, from it, she gains courage and encouragement to continue on through the darkness.

Listening as she explores her fantasy, I remember that the Japanese have been involved with Buddhism for over a thousand years and that the inner connection that I am reinforcing is not very different form what Sakyamuni, the historical Buddha, meant when he talked about the Buddha within. Jesus, too, insisted that the kingdom of heaven is within. Buddhism, according to my friend Stella Resnick, is a religion based on psychology and offers both maps of the inner world and, in meditation, a way to navigate with those maps that is not necessarily mediated through a priesthood. Of course, organized religion everywhere has the same vested interest in coming between the believer and her/his divinity in order to raise money and gain influence. Since Buddhism offers more than stories, no matter how beautiful, and obedience, no matter how satisfying, perhaps it allows people in Japan a little more psychic freedom to wander in the black forest and smell its sweetness.

In meditation Buddhism offers a technique for touching one's ultimate reality which, especially in the school of Soto Zen, is similar to Gestalt in its emphasis on present awareness. When I met Fritz Perls he had just returned from Japan, where he sat zazen for a few months at Daitokuji, one of the largest Zen temples in Kyoto. Gossip has it that he was too rebellious to be a successful Zen student. I can identify, for I, too, lived in a temple, and although I enjoyed the practice and the food, I was ready to leave for a less structured environment after two months. Traditional Japanese Zen is not a good practice for those who don't wish to be ordered around by others. Fritz, with characteristic understatement, summarized his Zen experience thus: "The value of the empty mind cannot be overestimated." I will summarize mine with this short statement I saw displayed in a Kyoto temple: When conditions allow, we meet When conditions fail, we don't. These conditions softly glow.

I respect the tranquillity of Buddhist iconography, just as I love the pictures of Mary and Joseph and the baby Jesus. Together they represent peace and love—the perfect text for me, a person who still values the 1960s and what we both did and tried to do then. Although my dreams for a just and peaceful world didn't come true, they were the inspiration for shared work and the fun and celebration that comes when the working day is through. My goals haven't changed since then. I have. I have become more patient, a word I once thought was code for "copping out," and understand that the task of creating a peaceful and just world is far larger and its accomplishment far more gradual than my under thirty-year-old self could possibly have imagined.

The next person works on an experience when she was ten years old and her mother had a heart attack in the toilet. The only person at home was the ten-year-old girl, who heard her mother's call and came to her in the toilet where her mother lay smeared with feces. She cleaned her mother as best she could and yet, through the years, had never felt that she had done enough. I suggest she talk to her ten-year-old self, and as she does this she is able to accept that what she did was the best she could do at the time, that it was good enough. Her acceptance allows her to comfort the frightened and grieving child who lived through the traumatic experience of nursing her ailing mother without sufficient support for her own pain and fear. Her sympathetic acceptance of the young girl's trial is moving and beautiful.

Next Asako wants to work. She had cried during Chika's work. For years Asako was always angry. Now sometimes she weeps, and her eyes, once cold and hard, glow brightly while the same honesty that made her anger intimidating now shines through softer and more compassionately as she comes to feel and to integrate her childhood misery, hidden for years under the prickly crust of her rage. She is happier and kinder now that she has touched more fully the pain and grief of her own life. She has enhanced her understanding of what it is to be a human being by acknowledging her anguish as part of a mosaic of pain that she shares with many others.

One of the functions of groups like this one is that in sharing their pain people come to understand that, rather than isolating them, their suffering binds them into the community of tribulation they share with all living creatures. In this regard, Sakyamuni is right: suffering is the legacy of all who live, as natural as rain which, as the Bible reminds us, falls on the just and unjust alike.

I am convinced from my work that contact with the inner self, the authentic self, allows compassion, for as each one experiences the quandaries and suffering of their existence, they understand the pain and dilemmas of others. The similarity between myself and others infuses the most profound meaning to the golden rule: love thy neighbor as thy self. Those who have no love and compassion for themselves cannot possibly love others. If I cannot love this one whose life and suffering I know so well, how can I possibly love the other whose pain is relatively distant and abstract? It is only because I value my self—not my self-image or role, not my place in society, but my living, aching, raging, laughing, crying, soon-to-die self—that I am capable of feeling compassion and understanding for the myriad of selves that surround me.

I ask Asako to choose someone to talk with, and she chooses Nori. Asako's and Nori's reaching and touching is awkward, even comical, as they brush elbows and nearly bump heads. Sometimes, the group laughs. Still, genuine meeting is so precious that even the most rudimentary attempt brings delight. The true living of meeting is well worth the discomforts, first, of contacting one's own pain and, then, of embarrassment which invariably comes with doing something new.

Sightseeing in a temple during our early days in Japan, my son Lawrence and I were resting when a young woman came up a flight of stairs nearby. When her friend asked her how it was, we were pleased to understand when she replied, "*Kirei*," the Japanese word for beautiful. Lawrence and I bolted down the stairs to see the beautiful thing and discovered the toilet before we remembered that *kirei* also means clean. Of course, we were embarrassed and amused by our mistake; nevertheless, the event stamped on my mind for all time that among the Japanese, clean is beautiful, and beautiful, clean. Even the Zen emphasis on emptiness, which is a kind of cleanliness, has been illuminated by this silly mistake.

A life devoted to avoiding embarrassment is stale in its compulsive repetition of the familiar. People who cannot support the mild discomfort of embarrassment and awkwardness will be afraid to experiment with new people and places, not to mention unfamiliar cultures. In our early months in Japan, Lawrence and I found ourselves in a seemingly endless pageant of strange social situations. Am I really supposed to eat these tiny fish? Heads and all? What do I do with these long legs at this low table? In the shrine, do I kneel now? And how do I stand up on numb legs? What if I fall? When am I supposed to drink from this tiny cup? And what I am to do on this ancient Noh stage while my friend chants beside me? In a fit of eighteen-year-old frustration, he accused me, "I see what you're doing. You just wait and then you do what they do." And he was right. Years ago my mother advised me, "Do what your hostess does," and although she had in mind more conventional settings like dining tables with lines of silverware extending to the horizon on either side of one's plate, she got me through my introduction to Japanese society. I wouldn't have missed the awkwardness and embarrassment of those days for anything, and sometimes, now that I am knowledgeable and secure, I miss it, for it was my "merit badge" for daring in cultural exploration.

According to Laura Perls, "Embarrassment is the boundary state par excellence." When we are embarrassed we are at the threshold between the known and the unknown, and to the degree that we allow ourselves to feel embarrassed, we may extend our contact into new realms of the expanding universe we inhabit. If we deny our embarrassment or withdraw from the situation because of it, we limit ourselves. If we accept our embarrassment, then we can begin to make contact with the different, the other. Laura continues, "As you go with the experience [of embarrassment] your boundary expands. If, on the other hand, you try to avoid acknowledging your embarrassment and present a well-structured front, you'll stay within your self-set boundaries, resulting in a feeling of safety and security. But at what a price." The price will be boredom and numbness which are necessary in order to avoid the excitement and insecurity of contacting the unknown and experiencing embarrassment. Once again, here in my group in Tokyo, it is enhanced support, and ultimately enhanced self-support, that allows people to experience embarrassment and, thus, to extend their contact into the new and unexpected.

The contrast between the behavior of people in small groups and those in social settings or on television is often so great that they seem to be members of different species. And yet the images—the public presentations of talking heads with their perfect coiffures and measured speech without a trace of spontaneity or exuberance—become the models from whom many people, especially children, learn. And what they learn is that life is an act, a ritual of perfection—which is another lie, for perfection is a mental construct that never exists here and now. By contrast the people I meet in Gestalt groups are lively and interesting from the very instant they touch their inner being; a person whose own inner connection to existence shines through is authentic, creative, unpredictable, and wonderful.

It is one of the tragedies of teaching people they need to be cool and in control that such people will be unwilling to experience the unknown and will, therefore, spend their lives limiting themselves to circumstances where accepted behaviors are well known and carefully prepared. As the Beatles reminded Jude, "It's only a fool who plays it cool by making the world a little colder."

It is difficult to imagine a culture whose role demands are more disparate from the American than the Japanese, and yet, because human beings are so much more alike than we are different, the basic process remains the same. In childhood the authentic self is devalued and denied by adults intent on bringing the child into membership in society rather than nurturing her or his uniqueness. In place of the authentic self, a role or series of roles is taught and valued, elevated and encouraged, praised and reinforced while the child's deepest being is, at best, abandoned and ignored and, at worst, attacked and violated. Gradually buried beneath the roles, this authentic being suffers and is outraged that its unique and precious attributes are denied while the puppetlike actor is valued. It is an excruciating nightmare of reversal, one that never ceases even for an instant. Waking and sleeping, the suffering of the denied self is always present, a rejected and ignored bass line to all other rhythms imposed upon it. The instant that a person allows themselves space, focus, and support in the present, the denied self leaps forward and demands attention.

Depending to a great extent upon the desperation of the mother, the social roles will be enforced more or less insistently; the most desperate and unsupported women will inevitably be the strictest enforcers. These are the intimidated women who do as they are told because, cut off from their own life force, they can imagine no other role for themselves than serving the expectations of others, even if it means sacrificing the respect and love of their children. The more secure and supported the mother, the more allowing she will be of the child's authentic expression. This is one of the reasons the women's movement is so important: there is no way that a woman who is denied value by her society can impart value to her child. Perhaps those who insist on second-class citizenship for women are more conniving that we realize, for suppressed life in women means stupid puppets in the next generation, and there are definitely those among us who imagine they benefit from the absence of enlightened people living fulfilling, self-determined lives.

In Japan, early childhood training is done in a loving and accepting environment with many full-time mothers at home with their children. Since there is practically no baby-sitting, the Japanese mother spends more time with the young ones than most American mothers do, and small children are indulged to a degree that would be seen as "spoiling" by most American parents. The Japanese school system, however, is relentless in its exercise of control over children, and *chanto*, which means "properly," is a Japanese word I hear often. Because Japanese education is controlled by the central government rather than local school boards, parents in Japan have less influence in the education of their children than involved American parents have. Nevertheless, the Japanese child has at least as good a chance as the American to know when a role is a role, and child rearing in Japan does not necessarily demand the destruction of the connection with the inner self. In fact, the concepts of *honne*—the inner desires (easy to remember because it is similar to "honest")—and *tatemae*—the behavior required by the group—make this difference explicit, and perhaps easier to keep in mind than in the United States. In the U.S. a morality based on absolutes of good and evil may make the situational adjustments of *tatemae* more difficult to accept and create more guilt about choosing to play a role in order to accommodate other people. Roles may be perceived as dishonest by people raised with not bearing false witness as an absolute value. Nevertheless, the process of alienation from the self seems much the same in both cultures where some parents—and no one knows how many, for domestic violence is the deep and dirty secret of all societies—enforce alienation with violence.

With half an hour remaining in the group, I ask them what they want to do. Hiro, the young man who had sobbed so passionately during Chika's work, tells of his experience with *ijime* during his fourth year in grade school. *Ijime* a Japanese word usually translated as "bullying," is more systematic and better organized than the usual schoolyard bullying in the United States. It is a powerful form of social control aligned to the Japanese proverb which states that the nail that sticks up must be pounded flat. When Hiro says that everyone stopped speaking to him, I gasp and remember an incident in the third or fourth grade when the teacher asked me to play with one of the girls who was having trouble with the other children. I don't think this would happen in a case of *ijime*, where the outcast child is often abandoned by the teacher, too. The bullied child may be blamed while the tormentors are ignored. Even parents are helpless since they have little influence at school, and keeping the child home from school doesn't seem to be an option in a country where the school is part of the national government and study part of the nation ethic. As an American it is hard for me to imagine the helplessness of both parents and children as they face *ijime*, and I am aghast when I read in the newspaper of a child who has committed suicide rather than continue to face the bullies at school. Local control of schools is a major difference between the United States and Japan, and while it may lead to unusual variations on the interpretation of knowledge—for example, the teaching of creationism —it is, nevertheless, a significant guarantor of democracy, especially in a country as large and varied as the United States.

Sitting on the cushion, Hiro collapses his spine and smashes his solar plexus. His hollow chest is still. I suggest that he speak to his fourth-grade self. Although this is his first work, I imagine that, since he had seen people speaking to the empty pillow all day, it would be a familiar task for him. He says, "I know it was hard for you," and collapses further. He is too weak and demoralized to comfort the hurt child, and when I ask him to become the eight-year-old boy, his helplessness becomes more obvious. I say to him, "Hiro, I'm not going to take you into this experience because we don't have time. Instead I'm going to work with you on your posture."

I ask him to be aware of how he is sitting and then slowly to straighten his back. It is magic, of course: the face on the head at the end of a straight spine is a new face, as everyone in the group can see. I then ask him to return to his original posture. He does, and says, "I'm usually like this."

I agree and tell him to straighten again, stressing awareness in each position. As he looks around the group from the upright position, I can see that he is aware. He understands that he can, by changing his posture, change his experience. I don't know what he will do with this awareness, or if he can work with it in his daily life; nevertheless, he experienced something new, and nothing can change that. Denial cannot erase what has happened, for denial itself is an affirmation of the thing denied. (If it hadn't happened, I wouldn't have to deny it.) Hiro has had an aware experience of how he disconnects himself, and now it is indelibly part of his existence.

Often I am amazed at how simple the changes that make a difference are. It was a mark of Fritz Perls's genius that he saw the obvious and recognized its significance. The change that connects a person more firmly to the self—to their existence, their soul, however you wish to name that inner "space of freedom"—is self-reinforcing. This is the most wonderful aspect of Gestalt work. By facilitating a person's authenticity, their connection with themselves and their existential source, I am encouraging them to travel a path that is natural and self-rewarding.

I feel good when I am authentic. Even when you don't approve of me or even when I don't get what I want, there is joy in "living in truth," in being true to who I am at this moment. Every time I do it, I can do it more easily the next time. I told the group members this at the end of the session. Although I am increasingly aware that lectures, even a few sentences from me, kill the group energy by putting them in the passive student role, I told them as a way of summarizing what we had done together. More and more I am coming to trust that the people I work with will discover what they need to know from the great surge of experience that seventeen people devoted to awareness create when they sit together in a room for thirteen hours. We had ten minutes to complete the group. Everyone said a sentence or two. (I told them that if anyone talked too long I would cut them off, because space is so precious in Tokyo that when your time is up in a borrowed space like the one we are using you are expected to leave at once. I notice that much of what I do in the group is in the nature of a benevolent traffic cop.) We had enough time; everyone spoke and the circle was unbroken.

"*Manzoku deshita*." I was satisfied.

MONDAY, NOVEMBER 25

It's a dazzling autumn day filled with the sounds of jackhammers, the rapacious city birds whose powerful beaks open concrete all over the world. Why can't they make city streets with zippers since, like the flies in men's pants, they are clearly places that must be opened and closed again and again? Tokyo, for many years no more than the provincial capital of the Tokogawa family, was never laid out in the regular, square blocks that Imperial Kyoto copied from the 7th-century capital of Tang China—Changan, present-day Xian—and which we now accept as the rational way to organize a city. Like Boston, Tokyo evolved as a small urban nexus expanding into the countryside along the paths between the fields. There are quiet neighborhoods in Tokyo, places like the Ryokan Seifuso, protected from the chaos of the metropolis by miles and miles of narrow streets whose size and shape prohibit the noise that comes with speeding vehicles. Now, however, I'm in a friend's apartment facing Yasukuni Dori, a frantic ribbon of activity that runs through the busy neighborhoods of Shinjuku and Ichigaya toward Kudanshita and the Imperial Palace grounds that lie behind their beautifully crafted stone moat like an island paradise in the middle of the urban Pandemonium.

Free from commitments and jet lag, I am happy in the middle of the turmoil. Free to do as I please, I pack my bag to go swimming at a nearby sports club which welcomes visitors for the outrageous price of 1700 yen—about fifteen dollars and, today, worth every cent of it.

I'm reading *H. G. Wells in Love*, and am struck by his remark, "I conceived a great disapproval of incest." That's in his favor, I reflect, as I contemplate the women's group I will work with tomorrow. Incest is one of those words whose meaning and implications are unthinkable: an experience that lies near women's lives like a hungry carnivore crouching in the grass. Will it spring and reveal itself, or will it remain hidden in the deep cover of repression? Each time women gather to speak our truth the beast lurks, for as the American TV star Roseanne so wisely said, when asked, no one can with complete certainty say it never happened to them. Safeguarded by the camouflage of repression, we may say, "I don't know," or, if we have already met the terror, we respond, "Yes it did." Some imagine that they don't want to know, and yet I observe that with knowing comes safety. Our secrets want to tell themselves, and the more successful we are in creating a satisfying life for ourselves, the more inevitable it is that we will meet the truth of our past. When it emerges into a life grown strong with love and support, one may be confident that she or he can complete and integrate the past into the present: expressing the denied feelings, freeing the bound energy, and liberating the secret self into here-and-now awareness. Nevertheless, I feel a stab of dread contemplating tomorrow's group.

I return to the present and walk to the sports club where I swim my laps in a pool that is, in every sense of the word, *kirei*"

Tuesday, November 26, 7:00 p.m.

As I join this group—ten women, mostly in their twenties—I recognize several I have worked with before. The organizer of the group, a woman of about thirty whom I have known for several years, told me that everyone had experience with Gestalt or a similar approach, and I, in my fantasy, translated this to mean that they were eager to work. Now I'm surprised at how distant they are—no flash of recognition or expression of pleasure such as I had exchanged with members of the previous group. Instead they greet me with guarded postures and lowered eyes staring into inner preoccupations. During the initial round of introductions they are so articulate about what they want from the group that my preconception is reinforced. Even as they show me that they are closed and withdrawn, I perpetuate my illusion that they are prepared to do Gestalt work and worry if there will be enough time. During the long and awkward silence after the introductions I gradually drop my fantasies and began to face them as they are at this moment. As I write this I ponder the significance of time shared—time to come to know and to trust, time to imagine I know better than I do, time to create unrealistic fantasies and expectations. It is always a challenge and a discipline to remain in the present. I remind myself that Gestalt is the lifelong practice of being in the present, again and again returning from my mental wanderings to the now, the ever-new home of aware existence. As I do this, I am aware of my own disappointment, both personal and professional. The members of this group are not living up to my expectations, and I will have to work harder than I imagined in order to create an environment of trust among us.

They want to explore the issues relevant to young women living in industrialized nations—work, love, marriage, single parenthood. One woman offers to work on a dream. I had worked with her last spring and remember her deep distress at that time. Now her face is so open and responsive that she could have been someone else, and I strain to remember that I have met her before.

In her dream, she sees a road running through rice fields with mountains in the distance. She says it is similar to the scenery around the inn where she is working. I have her close her eyes and walk along the road. She says she is seven and sees the heads and hands of children in the tall rice straw. I ask her to open her eyes and tell the person beside her what she has seen. When she does this, she adds that the children are alive. When I ask her to talk to her seven-year-old self, her face becomes puffy with unshed tears. I don't remember what she says next. When she switches seats and becomes the seven-year old girl, she jerks her head. When I ask, "What just happened?" she replies, "Maybe I don't have to be afraid." When I ask her to say that to me, she looks at me for a long time, so long I hear the silence ring in my cars and imagine I see fear in her eyes. When she speaks at last (did I question her? I don't remember), she says, "I feel like I'm not here." Then she becomes aware of the women sitting in a circle behind her, and I ask her to turn and look at them. She seems to settle into herself again as she looks at them and seems relieved. I, too, am relieved as I ask her if it is all right to stop here. She says, "Yes," and thanks me with a small bow. I say, "Thank you. Thank you for sharing your world with me."

All of this went on with a translator, and, as I write, I am aware of how little I understand this woman and her world, not to mention her impact on the group, which had become quite frozen by the time we were finished. No response, no further requests to work. At this moment, I experience what I have come to call my "water strider syndrome." A tiny creature with large padded feet moving over the surface of the pond, I step ever so gently on the water's delicate skin to avoid plunging through, knowing that my recent steps have been heavier than I realized. As I make a conscious effort to lighten the pressure, I muse wryly that perhaps I'm simply the fool who rushes in. At this moment, I am one who knows that I don't know, and, in my not knowing, I sit still, watching and breathing as I hold myself in a present that I do not understand.

After a long quiet interval during which I observe people stopping themselves before they begin to speak, I suggest we go around the group and each one express how she interrupts her self-expression. This is a typical Gestalt intervention, focusing on what is happening now and making it more explicit. If we pay attention to what we're doing, we can learn from absolutely any experience. The women willingly tell of their many ways of stopping themselves: "Waiting until I'm ready." "Breaking a pattern of usually going first." "I'm afraid of what's going to happen." "I'm unclear about what to say." The group becomes lively during this round, and I awaken from my stupor of expectation into a recognition of what is happening in front of my eyes. I am, at last, becoming aware of these people's uneasiness and their hesitation about working.

When this round is finished, I suggest we go around again and, this time, report our here-and-now awareness. Taiko says she wants to talk, and when I give her an opportunity, she says, "after everyone else has finished." Then Fuyu, who had worked with me in a previous group, asks if she might ask a question. I say, "Sure," and she says that she has read in a book that Gestalt is not good for psychotic people (the translator originally says "psychosomatic," and it takes a few seconds to clarify the confusion). What do I think?

I reply that I don't put people into categories like that. Since I work to the best of my ability (the limits of which I have just experienced in a discomfiting blaze of clarity) to meet people as they are, I consider classifications based on the medical model even less useful than those of culture and ethnicity. The medical labels are just refined stereotypes, none of which are very useful in meeting individual human beings as they create the best resolution they can to the specific predicaments of their particular here-and-now existences.

I go on, probably too long, encouraging them to trust themselves and their responses to people rather than labels or ideologies. I add a few sentences about saying "No" and what an important response this is, and emphasize my own willingness to take "no" for an answer. When I ask her how she feels hearing my response, she smiles and says she expected such an answer. She is a tall, delicate young woman who moves with the exaggerated flexibility of a young sapling that has been fertilized heavily and grown too fast. Her trust is slow in coming; but maybe, because I trust her, she will come to trust me. When the woman who had worked asks her why she asked the question, her reply is casual, an "I just wanted to check" sort of answer.

Misako, who sits as though she expects to be hit, says she can never express herself as well as the others, and weeps as she speaks these words. When I remind her that she is expressing herself eloquently this very instant, she smiles a shy smile. Eiko remembers her childhood yearning to be normal and feels large hands pushing on her shoulders.

Each of these young women shares a kindred pain from feeling unobserved and unvalued in an unheeding world, and yet each one expresses herself with a lovely precision, standing forth as distinct as a heron standing white again the shinning green of the rice fields in June. Their beautiful clarity emphasizes what the world misses when it does not pay them the attention they crave. I remember Marian Evans remark that young women carry through the generations humanity's best chance for love and nuturance. Marian Evans, who had to become George Eliot in order to get herself heard, would surely have sympathized with the dilemmas of these young Japanese women.

Yuko is soft and thoughtful. Natsuko resembles the little girl who, although she likes to play with the boys, retains a delicate femininity.

Taiko, who wanted to talk after the others were finished, speaks in a voice that is as soft and distinct as the stroke of a feather. She begins to tell of her relationship with her boyfriend, of her uncertainty whether sex should lead to marriage, and of her doubt about marriage as a choice she wants for herself. Yuko has said earlier that if marriage means what her parents did, she wants no part of it. When I say that the areas of sex and marriage seemed to among the hardest for us as women to trust ourselves, it seems the group signals a silent agreement. We all know that each woman has to make her choices in the face of fierce social pressure to conform to established patterns of marriage and monogamy which may or may not bring satisfaction to a particular woman. As Taiko shares her sexual dilemma, we huddle beneath the mythic cloak of romance and marriage, the dark garment of conventional wisdom that insists that it is women who desire and benefit from marriage. We gasp for air as we struggle to find the air holes in the thick cloth of social expectation which threatens to smoother us all. I often wonder why, if women's state of dependence is so natural and satisfying, men find it necessary to expend their energy creating coercive institutions to keep us in our place.

I tell them of own my decision to marry at seventeen as a way to solve the problem of being sexual in a world of limited birth control information, no abortion, and great maternal pressure. Someone asks me if I had quit school. When I reply, "Of course," time collapses and together we face the reality of women in patriarchy who carry the burdens of life and death as though they are ours alone.

When we sit together in a room and share our life experiences, the truth of our power, our awesome responsibility, and our lack of male support is too obvious to deny. It is only by bonding together that we can hope to survive either as individuals or as a species. I remember Alice Miller's observation that "the human soul is virtually indestructible and its ability to rise from the ashes remains as long as the body draws breath." It is this phoenix spirit within each person that draws me to this work and holds me here, a perplexed participant in the mysteries of human courage and suffering far beyond my ability to imagine or understand. The phoenix in these gentle young women draws me to them across all the artificial boundaries of age, nationality, and the strange category that some call "race" (Does that mean that some win and others lose?). Silently I salute the next generation of women, my daughters, who take up the burdens of tenderness, love, and mercy in a wretchedly violent world.

WEDNESDAY, NOVEMBER 27, 7:30 A.M.

I have finished my Tai Chi on the beach and am sitting in the sand at Miura Kaigan, about two hours by train from Tokyo. Behind me stand five metal frames, each one about twenty-five feet long and covered with rows of plump white daikon radishes drying in the salty air. An image of harvest in Japan. I have found a rusty lounge chair and am sitting on the nearly deserted beach with the daikon behind me while in front of me the wide gray ocean moistens the beach with tiny waves. Down the beach a brown dog is walking her mistress briskly along the shore. I'm waiting for the famous McDonald's with the ocean view to open.

I am fortunate to have friends like Masa, Satchi, and Eri, their eight-year-old daughter, whose guest I am for these few days between workshops. Masa also handles the administrative part of my work—a demanding job that includes publicity, arrangements for space, my accommodations, enrolling people for the groups, and money. All these things he and his staff do smoothly; and, at times, Masa translates as well. He and Satchi lived for six years in Fresno, California, and both speak English. They know American culture and, like me, straddle the Pacific Rim in their affections and interests.

Tomorrow we will celebrate Thanksgiving. I have brought my favorite stuffing mix and cranberry sauce from the U.S., and today Satchi and I will shop for turkey. When she asked the local bakery about pumpkin pie, they told her that they only make it for Halloween, a cute example of how cultural elements are transformed as they journey across the wide western ocean between the Americas and Asia. (From here, it's the eastern ocean, as the sun struggling to rise from the clouds on the horizon is quick to remind me. I have crossed to the other side.)

For me this shore is among the places where east and west meet, although like most significant locations this propinquity is an inner spot, one I take with me wherever I go. The clouds, thickening like cooking oatmeal, have brought a cold wind that accents one side of my face and body like a shadow in a photograph. I will walk again rather than shiver here until McDonald's opens at eight.

McDonald's in Japan is a phenomenon. The restaurants are everywhere. After my first year here, I used to say half-facetiously that the most surprising thing about living in Japan was that I ate breakfast at McDonald's every day. McDonald's pancakes—in Japanese, *hotto kekki*—tasted good to me, much better than they did in the United States, although I don't know if this was because they're different or simply a function of my search for familiarity in a foreign land. Now that I'm more acculturated, my favorite breakfast is broiled salmon, miso soup, crispy dried seaweed, pickles, and rice, with coffee, a combination I find at Denny's. Since there's no Denny's here, I settle for McDonald's although Denny's coffee is much better, and the Japan blend (*blendo*) sold in Tokyo's thousands of small coffee shops is best of all.

Sitting in McDonald's overlooking the long luxurious curve of the beach below, I eat a fish sandwich (no hot cakes at Miura's famous McDonald's) and read Virginia Woolf's *Moments of Being*. In it she writes that while she likes to read memoirs, she sees a serious weakness in that "they say 'This is what happened;' but they do not say what the person was like to whom it happened." At her suggestion I will illuminate the one to whom this Gestalt adventure on the Pacific Rim is happening.

I was born in Moundsville, West Virginia, in 1934, the worst year of the Great Depression, which makes me a member of what has from time to time been called the "Silent Generation." It was a time when many people were not being born because the poverty of depressions always strikes most severely at the young who are just beginning to work and to reproduce. Since by the 1930s birth control was having an impact among the middle class, many young people were able to postpone beginning their families. At the time, my father was trying to start a law practice in his hometown, and my mother, who had a teaching certificate from West Virginia University, could not work because, in those days, married women, whose knowledge of sexual intercourse was seen as potentially corrupting to their young wards, were not allowed to teach school. I think Rebecca West had the last word on this subject when she wrote, "There is so little difference between the extent to which any large number of people indulge in sexual intercourse, when they indulge in it without inhibitions and when they indulge with inhibitions, that it cannot often be a determining factor in history." Apparently, the West Virginia school officials of the time disagreed, and, despite my mother's sexual experience being both legal and sanctified, they prohibited her from practicing the profession for which she had spent four years in college preparing. She told me once that their rent was ten dollars a month and they were ten months behind when my grandfather, a well-known glass designer for the Fostoria company in Moundsville, bailed them out to keep them from being evicted.

I slipped through the baby boycott because, although my parents were poor, my mother, whose first child had died the year before, was desperate to have a baby. I was born into a baby deficiency and have continued to live as a member of a small generation which has been eclipsed by the great mob of the postwar baby boomers. While their culture has greatly affected my life, I see now that my generation, with the cooperation of Russians of the same age group under the leadership of Mikhail Gorbachav, has silently (as is our way) ended the Cold War and, thus, made our imprint on history. In this way we have returned to the baby boomers the favor of the 1960s, when their sheer numbers opened up the society by overwhelming the institutions of socialization. Further, the desire of the young men to stay alive created a peace movement among a group who later (at the time of the Gulf War) proved to be rather less peaceful than they had been when their own lives were at stake.

Shortly after my birth, my father had a chance to leave his nonexistent practice in Moundsville to join his law school roommate in Logan, a small town in the coal fields of southern West Virginia. His roommate had recently inherited a great deal of property and had more work than he could do alone. I have the impression that after this move my parents had a rather rapid rise in income and attendant improvement in standard of living. My first memory is of standing on a moist shady sidewalk between two houses with a redheaded woman who I knew was not my mother and who I later learned had been hired to take care of me while my mother resumed her social life, always a source of great pleasure to her. In this first memory, my awareness materialized abruptly, as though I had been beamed down from the spaceship Enterprise. Suddenly I'm here and I know I'm here; there's a sweet, damp smell and coolness caresses my cheek while Mary's white skin and red hair hover above me. At about this same time my brother was born, and I remember the sound of his constant crying as he and my mother struggled over what milk he should drink. He, of course, won, and she stopped nursing him. Apparently she had breastfed me for nine months, according to the fashion of the time, and was determined to do the same with him, but Ed's desire was different and, in the end, she acquiesced as she nearly always did if her children put up a loud enough fight. Although she had studied psychology in college, she was an anxious parent and transmitted a great deal of her anxiety to both of us.

[The Mcdonald's sound system is playing a Muzak version of "Like a Virgin."]

Both my parents were successful in their respective realms. My mother, whose parents lived simply on a farm among the smooth, rolling hills of northern West Virginia, had gone to high school in this same small town of Logan where her widowed sister lived with her three sons, the oldest of whom was one month older than my mother. "Just like a bunch of hillbillies," a friend once said; and it was, I believe, a source of embarrassment to the family and of acute discomfort to both my mother and her sister, my aunt, whom I once heard express her resentment at my grandmother's competition in baby-making. In any case, my mother and her three nephews were raised together, spending their summers in the country and their winters in school in Logan. She had many friends in this tiny town beside the Guyandotte River, a tributary of the Ohio, which it joins in Huntington, West Virginia, on the border of West Virginia, Ohio, and Kentucky. I remember the cooks and housekeepers of those years before the war much better than I do her, except for the time when I got the red measles. Then she sent the housekeeper to her sister's with my brother while she went to bed with me and nursed me through the misery and delirium of what was then called the "bad" measles.

My widowed aunt, who was old enough to be my grandmother, worked as secretary to the Logan County Chamber of Commerce in the lobby of the Aracoma Hotel. Her office was set off by a bright brass railing, very good for swinging on when nobody was paying attention—which was fairly often in those days when children, to our immense relief, were often neither seen nor heard. My aunt, whom we called Mimi, was a highly respected widow whose husband had died serving in the U.S. Army in Europe during the influenza epidemic of 1918. She served as unpaid treasurer for every conceivable community organization—Girl Scouts, March of Dimes, Community Chest, Red Cross—and was rewarded in her vigorous seventies by having the new Girl Scout Camp named Camp Mamie Flynn in her honor. Since she had raised three boys, she enjoyed having a little girl in the family, and it was relatively late in life that I discovered that I was supposed to be inferior to boys, always imagining that it was quite the reverse and that "girls were better than boys."

One day when I was about four, my mother went out and, perhaps because it was the housekeeper's day off, left me in the not very vigilant care of the seven-year-old boy next door. Escaping the backyard, I embarked on my first expedition, a walk along the railroad tracks that carried the mile-long chains of freight cars filled with coal from the mines nearby. I remember the harsh smell of the creosote in the railroad ties and the large gravel they rested on as I walked along the seemingly endless railway. I met a bigger girl skillfully walking on the metal rail, which roused my envy because I couldn't do that. She called me "little girl" and told me a train was coming. Looking far down the metal rails, I could see a puff of smoke moving toward me—silently because it was still far away. Suddenly my daddy seized me from behind and swung me into his arms while, behind us my mother ranted hysterically about the perils of the railroad tracks. He held me, and the three of us stood close to the tracks as the train rushed and rattled past us, making its own tempest and shaking the earth under our feet. I experienced its awesome power and, with no difficulty, understood that it could hurt me. Those dark, steaming, howling creatures were, along with wolves and witches, the monsters of my childhood, potential killers who are benevolent so long as they are treated with respect and kept at a distance. Years later, when I was in high school, my mother was still mad at Jimmy McCormick who had ignored his baby-sitting chore and allowed my first adventure—a walk on the railroad track.

I was an active, rambunctious child, sturdy and big for my age, and she indulged me in allowing me to wear heavy coveralls and making very little fuss about dirt. I supposedly had flat feet and wore heavy, corrective, boot-like shoes that were good for all kind of explorations in the woods that surrounded our next house. I loved the privacy and endless variety of things to do and see on the damp spongy floor of the Appalachian wilderness. My brother, two and a half years younger, joined me in these adventures, both in Logan and at my grandparents' house in the county, creating a bond that, apart from the years of adolescent madness, has been always been intense and powerful to the point of feeling, at times, telepathic.

I am still very much the same person I was then, and when I recall events from that time, I identify with the awareness and guiding perceptions of that child. I am her and she is me. I think that my parents loved me; they were, however, preoccupied with their own lives and so supplied me with adult companions and caretakers and then floated in and out of my life like Proust's parents in *Remembrance of Things Past*, with their beautiful clothes, smells, laughter, and caresses. I had my brother and the out-of-doors with its endless beauty and diversity, and I had books. The caretakers (who were never called maids) were instructed to read to me whenever I wanted. This had a great and beneficial effect on my life, which has been a long love affair with, among other things, the printed word in all its wonderful manifestations. Aunt Mimi, too, promoted this interest, and I remember going with her into the children's room of the Logan County Public Library and standing, trembling with excitement and delight as the walls of books saturated me with their sweet, dusky smell. I have known forever that, in Virginia Woolf's words, "The whole world is a work of art, that we are all part of a work of art."

My second husband, Larry Bloomberg, once remarked that my mother's return to the small town where she had grown up was the great tragedy of her life. Perhaps he was right, for my mother was an intelligent woman who had a degree in psychology and had worked for the head of the department at West Virginia University as an undergraduate student assistant in the days when there were few graduate students. Returning to Logan, she immersed herself once again in a dense and powerful small-town society whose power was mightily reinforced by her older sister's relentless respectability and pressure to conform. I remember my desperate impatience with what I saw as her undiscriminating preoccupation with "What will people think?" While Mimi's presence meant much to me, my mother might have developed more fully and been happier in an environment where she was less vulnerable to the power and pressure of village gossip. My father, on the other hand, was an independent man with a mild reputation for eccentricity gained in part by working in his yard in the late 1940s, long before it was the thing to do, wearing kelly-green shorts which he bought at my brother's summer camp.

I left Logan at sixteen and became a statistic in the mass migration of the young from West Virginia in particular and, more generally, in the world's urbanization in the late twentieth century. As a lawyer's daughter in a small town where I was so well known that when I said, "Shit" in the drugstore, my mother heard about it before I got home, I have basked in the anonymity of city life ever since discovering that private life is possible.

While these events happened long ago, they have a great deal to do with the person who is living the events I am describing; they compose the basic structure laid down like the foundation of a building on which the later patterns and designs are constructed. As many others have reported, the older I become the more identity I feel with this rough-and-tumble little girl with bookish tendencies whom my Great Uncle Bryan (my country grandfather's brother) used to call a "a little cinnamon bear." She has been a good friend, and her down-home good sense, hewn and sharpened by a small-town school life, has been a helpful guide through the maze-like intricacies of the crass, class confusions of adult living.

Back at McDonald's on the beach, someone is playing a video game, and the song it plays when he wins is "Old Black Joe." I am confounded by the human potential, so broad and deep that no culture can embrace it. Now, thanks to jet airplanes and electronic networks, we no longer have to force ourselves into a single cultural mold as Cinderella's sisters forced their feet into the glass slipper, snipping a toe here, chopping a bit of heel there until we achieve some kind of bloody fit. In an open world, there are shoes and slippers for every foot. I can participate in and enjoy it all—the ferocious variety of the U.S., the dense psychic stew of the Japanese, the exuberant appetite of the Cantonese. And this is just a sample of what is available. These amazing choices are the gift of our age, which has brought me to the end of exclusion and to a place where freedom takes on new dimensions because I have worlds of culture from which to choose as I discover for myself the truth of the Chinese saying that "the country which is nowhere is the real home."

One of the three sacred objects possessed by the Japanese royal family is a bronze mirror. Such mirrors came originally from China and are among the oldest archaeological artifacts discovered in Japan. One often sees them in museums, and they are lovely: one side molded with elaborate bas-relief dragons or twining plants, and the other flat and shiny as a still pond. Deep within the wooded sanctuary of the great Shinto shrine at Ise stands a building designed to resemble an ancient rice storehouse. Barely visible in its enclosure among the sky-stealing cyptomeria which consecrate the setting, the shrine sits beside an empty spot on which, for 1,300 years, workmen have constructed its exact replica. Every twenty years, in an elaborate ceremony, gods, blessings, and artifacts are transferred to the new building from the old, which is then torn down to make room for the next duplicate. Were one allowed to enter this sacred structure, she would find enshrined there the sacred bronze mirror. Should she choose to study its finely polished surface, the bronze artifact—one of the most holy objects in all Japan, lodged in perhaps its most sacred sanctuary—would reflect back to her own face.

The cultures of the world are treasures, like the species, that we must guard and cherish so that, in their uniqueness, they remain to give freedom its finest form, which includes both the ability to choose and the variety that makes choice meaningful. For myself, I want the care and consideration that has preserved the ancient serenity of Japan's Nara for over a millennium, the dark sweetness of the black forests of Europe and North America, and the exuberant joy of wild flowers in the Appalachian spring.

THURSDAY, NOVEMBER 28, THANKSGIVING DAY, 7:00 A.M.

Standing by the train station, I watch buses come and go depositing students in dark uniforms on their way to school as usual. The Japanese traditional holidays which mark the rhythms of planting and harvest within an agricultural society are celebrated with Shinto rituals. Shinto, which is an animistic nature religion, a living anachronism in twentieth-century industrial society, was discredited by the American leaders of the postwar occupation, who saw only the perversion of Shinto that the Japanese militarists created to reinforce their own ultra-modern religion of nationalism. In the separation of church and state which the Americans enforced, the traditional holidays lost their official standing, leading the Japanese to create a number of new ones with names like Sports Day and Respect for the Elderly Day. This has been done, in part, as a response to world criticism that they work too hard, a criticism with which many Japanese agree wholeheartedly. The Euro-American holidays— Christmas, Halloween, Easter, etc.—are used for commercial promotions, but since people still work, they are not holidays in any genuine sense. The Japanese mercantile genius requires that a lot of chocolate change hands on February 14, when women are supposed to give it as gifts to men, especially their superiors at work. As an additional fillip, March 14—called White Day—is another occasion for chocolate to circulate. This time men return the favor, giving white chocolate to women (the color difference instituted to make sure that all the receivers of dark chocolate don't scramble their packages and give away the chocolate they originally received).

This shuffling of gifts is something of a tradition in Japan, where vast numbers of gifts exchange hands every year—winter gift season, summer gift season, and *omiyage* (mementos) from every journey. Since it's impossible to give consistently thoughtful presents under the constant and compelling pressure to give something, many gifts are re-wrapped and re-routed and others are never opened before being sent on to someone else. I imagine streams of gifts flowing through out Japan rather like the Sacramento River in the Delta with its endless sloughs and tributaries circulating lazily in all directions.

The continuous exchange of gifts has to be a factor in Japan's economic success, because the constant flow of giving and receiving keeps things—including money, the queen of things— circulating, a fundamental requirement for a healthy economy. I find it a pleasant tradition and, like many Japanese and non-Japanese alike, enjoy the small delight of opening a present. I represent a small outlet for the flow as I often dispatch gifts across the ocean to the U.S. There, teaching my family and friends about *omiyage*, I inform them that they have now replaced Nara as the far eastern terminus of the Silk Road. Since I have love and affection for many Japanese people and numerous aspects of their remarkably aesthetic and robust culture, I enjoy being a conduit of their culture around and across the Pacific Rim.

Both the gradual integration of cultures and the intense articulation of cultural differences by, for example, Slovenes, Croats, Quebecois, Basques, Lithuanians, Estonians, Moldavians, Tibetans, Mongolians, etc., can be a source of wealth for everyone so long as people have enough confidence to be curious and friendly when they encounter the excitement that comes with unfamiliarity. We have to generate sufficient wisdom and self-respect within ourselves to value variety, tasting and trying the dishes at the great feast of diversity that the modern world allows. Respect for diversity and love of one's own land, tradition, and language are not antithetical; in fact, they are natural partners. It is insecurity and doubt of one's own merit and the value of one's belief system that creates the fearful exclusivity and hatred of difference that often passes for loyalty and is, in truth, only the hysteria of frightened people trying to establish a certainty they do not feel.

Satchi and Masa's condominium, called a "mansion" in Japan, is an ample living space quite different from the stereotype of the Japanese apartment as rabbit hutch. The toilet paper holder in the bathroom plays "It's a Small World After All" in reedy, electronic tones each time I unroll the paper. As I hear it on this Thanksgiving in Japan I feel like crying. My being here affirms that it is a small world, and so instead of crying I say a small prayer for peace.

Satchi and I go to her health club in a huge, modern shopping complex three stops away by train; she does the aerobic step class and I swim in a large, clean pool, not at all crowded on a weekday morning. Afterwards we shop for a turkey and find, instead, a frozen turkey breast which we buy along with some dark meat chicken pieces and chicken giblets for the gravy. We also buy potatoes and green beans, celery and onions, and crab meat for salad. At the last minute I throw in some nice Japanese mushrooms for the dressing. We buy an apple pie from the man who has pumpkin pie only for Halloween. As we arrive home, Rieko calls from Shinagawa station on the edge of Tokyo and says she is on her way. As I set the giblets to boil to make stock for the gravy which will be a hybrid, half chicken and half turkey, the weather has turned cold and rainy, and we could easily be in Boston; Logan, West Virginia; or anywhere in the midwestern United States.

Thawing the turkey breast in her microwave, Satchi discovers that it is rolled, so we flatten it and cover it with the Pepperidge Farm stuffing brought from San Francisco. Then we top it with the dark chicken meat, skin side up, and tie it all together in a bundle which just fits into her tiny oven. It cooks beautifully, a large, golden lump of poultry meat. The drippings are rich and brown, perfect for combining with the stock and chopped giblets to make traditional gravy. Surrounded by parsley, the woman-made bird is beautiful. We mash potatoes and steam the green beans. Satchi makes a lovely crab salad for a first course, a touch of California, and Rieko brings herb-flavored cheese and wine. At 6:30 four adults and Eri, age 8, sit down to a real Thanksgiving dinner. The food is authentic and delicious; we are delighted. Even Eri, who had never before seen such food, eats a large plateful. We eat and eat until *Onaka ga ippai*, which is the Japanese version of the traditional Thanksgiving chorus, "I'm stuffed." (First the turkey and then the people.)

While we were preparing dinner, two men brought in Masa and Satchi's new 27-inch television set, which they installed while we cooked. Rieko had brought the final proofs of the book we have been working on for several years. She and I corrected the proofs, she reading the Japanese and I the English, until the gravy called and I gave up being an intellectual to return to the kitchen. There are no words for the joy I feel knowing that I can do both—that I have "done it all."

The secret to doing it all is, I believe, being willing to settle for imperfection. I have understood intuitively that, as Gertrude Stein notes in her essay on Picasso, when a person is doing something new, she is so involved in doing it at all that she doesn't have time or energy to make it beautiful. As women evolve into the public world while refusing to abandon our roles as nurturing parent, lover, and friend, we are, even more than Picasso, creating something new under the sun. What is notable is not that we do it imperfectly, but that we are doing it at all. Men can, if they want, learn to do it, too. Of course, doing it at all requires new forms of social bonding among women, among women and men, among men, and among everyone and children.

In the process of integrating women into the public world, we are creating relationships and social structures so original and new that they are offensive and often terrifying to those who, numbed and frozen by their past suffering, are easily frightened by whatever appears unfamiliar and unpredictable. These people will inevitably experience vertigo with the slightest taste of the experience of being on the bridge and discovering, with the Zen teacher, "O marvel! It is not the river which flows, it is the bridge which moves over the torrent." For them, the throbbing cadences of the new and the excitement of the unprecedented bring fear and often terror, for the small security they have been able to create in life is predicated on their petrified grip on the illusion of control. Such people often hide their fear behind a barricade of aggressively asserted, supposedly divinely ordained truth, all the while insisting that the way life has been is how it will always be. They have chosen a harsh and angry fate as they struggle against the inevitably of change and are more to be pitied than feared.

It is in allowing the new while at the same time acknowledging the fear and suffering of these frightened souls that we may be able to do yet another new thing—create change without reaction: something we failed utterly to do during the 1960s. This is perhaps the great challenge of our time, one worthy of our most imperfect efforts. I comfort myself with the reminder from a Tibetan Lama, Sogyal Rimpoche, who says, "The effect of our actions depends entirely upon the intention or motivation behind them, and not upon their scale." As I remember my past brazenness, the desire to shock and outrage which I have transformed with maturity, I know that I have to some degree purified my intentions. Perhaps my present actions will have a more benevolent effect than those of the past. Now, as then, confident that each one has a part to play in creating the world we share while no one can do more than her or his best, I stand on the bridge and love both the bridge and the torrent.

Satchi, Rieko, Masa, Eri, and I created Thanksgiving in Japan, and it was both new and beautiful because we have all had practice crossing the expanse of the Pacific and blending the cultural elements we have found on its bountiful shores. This year, my greatest Thanksgivings are, first, for the health of those I love, and, second, for the opportunity to participate in the creation of the emerging world. There are times when my observations indicate ecological disaster coming more quickly than many imagine; nevertheless, to work together to create a reality of peace and love, variety, adventure, and fun is perhaps, in itself, the accomplishment: the achievement that is too new to be beautiful. Since in the here-and-now work of the world there are no ends, only means, even if we all vanish tomorrow, surely someone—maybe a sulfur-metabolizing someone from the vents on the ocean floor—will do it again. The universe is very large and essentially mysterious despite all our sexy metaphors of big bangs and black holes.

FRIDAY, NOVEMBER 29, 6:00 A.M.

"I am buried in the sand, my true and complete shape masked by the flowing forms that cover me. I expose only a teasing suggestion of my design, just enough to indicate that something is here, something of which I am a part although from what I show you will never know me in my wholeness. Even after Paula digs me up, she won't know what I am. I have a short column attached to a disk and have no other purpose, now, than to lie here half- buried. I am hard and durable and will be here a very long time."

Sitting on the beach on the bright, clear day after Thanksgiving, I contemplate the object described above. Describing it in the first person, as I have done, is a Gestalt exercise whose truth seems to lie in Gertrude Stein's observation that "everyone is always repeating the whole of them." No matter what I do or how ardently I pretend to be different, I am always being me, always telling my story. Because most of us are so practiced at both concealing ourselves and colluding with others as they pretend to be what they are not, sometimes, in order to discover the self beneath the pretense, we have to approach our identity obliquely.

Among the oblique ways to touch the authentic self is the Gestalt approach with its emphasis on awareness in the here and now. Each time I focus my awareness in an unaccustomed direction, I learn something unexpected about myself and the environment; I experience the flash of recognition, the "Aha!" so valued and sought after that even science acknowledges it. I remember that the first time I worked with Fritz Perls, he videotaped the session and later showed it to my husband, Larry. As we watched the tape and I was feeling sympathetic toward the woman, myself, in the picture, thinking that she looked pretty good, I heard Fritz tell Larry, "I'm calling this one 'Low Self-Esteem.'" Aha!

By performing the tiny Gestalt exercise above and identifying with the bit of buried plastic, I assert my vast and essentially unknowable nature and express myself in hopes that someone will listen and learn something of my view of the elephant we are exploring together. "No one knows the way. Together we will find the way." At the very least, we will achieve Socrates's goal: "Either we shall find what we are seeking or at least we shall free ourselves from the persuasion that we know what we do not know."

The clear air is gentle today; yesterday's storms were the turbulent edge of a warm front passing through, and today's weather in Miura Kaigan resembles San Francisco with its bright blue sky and piles of white clouds scattered over a landscape washed clean by rain. Even the surf breaking in slow white rows which trace the sweeping arc of the bay is milky bright. In the distance a wind surfer who has stolen a Friday for himself shines like a mirror moving out to sea.

Someone once remarked to me that Japanese people are too compliant to do Gestalt. This is another bit of stereotyping that my experience contradicts every time I work. While I have found Japanese people to be cooperative in the sense of making the suggested experiment—which is much of what Gestalt is about: do it and see what happens rather than remain stuck with one's fantasy of an outcome—I have not found them to be compliant. Often Japanese people will do the suggested act or repeat the words I have spoken, and just as often they will say, "No, it doesn't fit."

Recently I suggested that a young man say, "I don't want to express my feelings." I was using paradoxical intent to make explicit his implicit unwillingness to express himself. He repeated the statement as I suggested, and afterwards stopped and said, "No, it's not quite like that." I responded, "Well, say what's true for you." After some seconds, he replied in a small voice, "You have to listen very carefully to hear me," and then wept quietly. When he stopped crying, he said, "I stopped it," and I replied, "Now you're aware, and that makes all the difference." I have had dozens of similar experiences, and readily dismiss the stereotype of Japanese compliance as useless in coming to know Japanese people.

I recently read a Native American activist's statement that there is no such thing as a good stereotype, and I agree. Stereotypes are for those who don't mind consistently having the world, in my mother's words, "make a liar out of them."

SATURDAY, NOVEMBER 30, 12:00 P.M.

I'm on the train to Hachioji, where the next group will take place in a seminar house run by a group of colleges. The train trip will cost about ten dollars and take me inland from Miura and to the west of Tokyo for about an hour. There is a steady suburban sprawl all along this route, and I am amazed once again how similar the parts of Japan that are not Tokyo look—clean, well-built, crowded, and compact. Occasionally I see the stubble of a small rice field or the curved plastic buildings in which part-time farmers reap a tax break on their land by growing tomatoes, cucumbers, and other vegetables in what a friend once called a cucumber factory.

With its repetition of rice fields, small vegetable gardens, and clusters of plastic Quonset huts separating villages of neat, compact houses, the Japanese countryside, the *inaka*, leads a casual observed to see its scenes much as Ronald Reagan saw the redwood trees. This surface similarity, however, is no more than a soothing slipcover of familiarity, for just as one begins to accept the superficial message of sameness, the fine gradations of land and uniqueness of a place and people leap into one's senses like the deep boom of the temple bell sounding through the clatter of the cicadas in summertime. "Here, I am special," they say; "pay attention and learn from me."

Near the train tracks, the dry stems of lotus plants rise randomly from a small dark plot where a child in a yellow jacket sits digging in the mud with a stick. The train slips past without disturbing his project. As I approach Hachioji I see an occasional clump of trees and wooded hillsides in the distance.

I'm reading *Flaubert's Parrot* by Julian Barnes; like many other books I read, it comes from the British Council Library, a precious resource that has saved me hundreds of dollars, for English-language books are even more expensive here than in the U.S., sometimes selling for as much as three times the dollar price marked on the cover. Barnes quotes Flaubert: "To be stupid, and selfish, and to have good health are the three requirements of happiness—though if stupidity is lacking, the others are useless." Although Flaubert's cynicism goes against the grain of my optimism, I appreciate his good-natured acceptance as he meets the stupidity of the world without trying to understand or change it.

I agree with Fritz and Laura Perls, who said that people are not stupid, but deny their intelligence because they have been taught as children that to be bright and perceptive is hazardous to their health. It is far safer for most children to play stupid than to share their wisdom with adults who usually don't want to hear anything that might upset their rigid and unremarkable version of reality.

Thus children learn to play stupid, and stupidity is a habit that once acquired is hard to kick. Consider the Bottome revision of "The Emperor's New Clothes," in which as soon as the child observes that the emperor has no clothes, a nearby adult smacks her across the mouth and tells her to shut up and admire the emperor's lovely new garments. This is surely a more likely outcome to such audacious childhood behavior as pointing out to the adults that what they have agreed to see is a lie.

Most people encourage their children to be stupid, and it is here that Flaubert is right. If one does not play stupid, she or he will never be comfortable in a social system based on lies. Those who have some inkling of what's going on don't seem particularly happy. Is the opposite true? Are those who play stupid happy? I don't think so. I think that happiness comes, when it does, to those who are willing to see through the systematic lies into the fundamental reality underlying the human constructions which, like powerful nets, can capture and confine, but can never completely destroy our natural human relatedness to truth—to what is.

For me, it is the natural world—the sky, seasons, light and shadow among the trees and flowers, animals, human love and kindness, birth, and death—which affirms the truth that lies beneath the social constructions. Sexism is a lie, racism is a lie, bureaucracy an absurdity, economics a rationalization, and history a story told to reinforce the present ideology. Everyone is encouraged to become dull, which is a great help in tolerating the incoherence which multiple falsehoods create. We have been very successful in creating this perversion of stupidity—for it truly is perverse to spend millions of dollars turning bright, loving, sensitive children into ignorant, frightened, conforming adults.

I'm not ready to accept Flaubert's design for happiness, at least not until we give women a chance to participate as equals in all aspects of living and dying, to add our vision and our energy to every assignment of life's labor. This solution is one that was far beyond Flaubert's genius and imagination; nevertheless, women's contribution—their potential for freshness and originality in making the communal decisions that govern life and death—offers our best chance for survival. I remember a headline I recently saw in a Japanese newspaper: Grandmothers must rule, Swedish sociologist says. Per Gahrton, the founder of Sweden's Green Party, in his book "Let Grandmothers Rule the 2000s," says: "I don't really expect men voluntarily to abdicate their positions of power. But we could pass laws that women must hold at least half of the real power in society."

Why not? So what if it's a quota; what we have now is a quota: the allotment nobody dares to name because we are supposed to see it as "natural," just the way things are. In reality, it's just another lie that we have been punished into believing. When I see on television the various groups of people who make decisions that affect us all and notice that they are nearly all men, I wonder at our willingness to allow such incongruity to continue. It's not a question of "If it's not broken, don't fix it," because it's broken. For the most part the groups of well- dressed elderly men grind out gruesome decisions such as the massive allocation of resources for the purchase of murder machines of every size and description—land mines to splinter the legs of farmers in the fields, automatic guns for killing twenty people a second, missiles in every size from hand-held stingers that can destroy a plane to the MIRVs that carry ten nuclear warheads—rather than investing in perquisites for life: inexpensive education, safe water, clean air, undefiled soil, public health, adequate housing. It is stupidly indulgent to allow men a continued monopoly on decisions which affect us all when they have demonstrated such foolish incompetence. Let's share it fifty-fifty and see what happens. As I say so often in the groups, "It's an experiment." Might as well. Things could hardly get any worse.

I arrive at Hachioji nearly an hour and a half early, which is my way of handing the anxiety that comes with going new places or, as in this case, going to a familiar place from a new point of departure. I have time to eat lunch and read *The Daily Yomiuri*. Sitting outside a hamburger stand, I hear "The First Noel" in English—"No-e-l, No-e-l." In Japan, too, it is the time when "born is the King of I-is-ra-el." Behind the carol, a drum machine pumps out a rock rhythm. I wonder if the juxtaposition is deliberate or simply the inadvertent confusion of street sounds.

Returning to the station, I meet the people who are sponsoring the workshop, and we leave together in a taxi. At the seminar house I meet briefly with Yugiro, the translator who has lived three and a half years in the United States where, he tells me, he studied transpersonal and other forms of humanistic psychology including P.O.P. (P.O.P.? Process Oriented Psychotherapy. I contain my smile. The implicit made explicit, and why not? Pop art, pop music, pop psychology—all blend into pop culture, the United States's gift to an insatiable world.)

3:00 P.M. SATURDAY, SAME DAY

Resting in my room, I have time for a catnap. I've been up since 5:30, so it's easy to slip away for a few minutes of unconsciousness. When it's time for the group to start, I wait in my room for the participants to arrive. Since most people in Japan work on Saturday, often all day, they may have difficulty getting away for something that begins on Saturday afternoon.

The authority of the workplace in Japan is difficult for me to comprehend, although I can see that the power of the six-day, or even five and a half-day workweek in confining identity to work and, therefore, to hierarchical control is an important element of Japanese society. In order for individuality to emerge, people need free time for coming to know how they feel and what they want to do. Nevertheless, people in Japan value their leisure activities, and "*Shumi wa nan desu ka*?" ("What are your leisure activities?") is a common question, even in job interviews. Interests outside of work can range from chanting Noh choruses and ink drawing to sports of all kinds. Everyone is expected to have one or two to which they dedicate themselves with some seriousness and commitment. Perhaps the very seriousness with which people view their hobbies is another way of avoiding free time.

When I enter the group room, the members have just completed a half-hour of relaxation and awareness exercises developed by the founder of their institute, a well-known Japanese playwright. We gather in a circle of twenty-seven people: 21 group members, 4 staffers, the translator, and me. The room where we work is large and airy; one side opens into the treetops. It's warm, and each person is sitting on a folded blanket rather than a pillow. The orange blankets with their large red flowers and red borders stand out like tiny islands against the beige carpet.

I begin the session with self-introductions and ask people to mention anything special they want from the workshop. The group members are young and speak with the buoyancy of youth, laughing readily in the rare moments when someone is funny or awkward.

Their common desire is to remain in touch with themselves as they interact with other people. Since young children in Japan are treated permissively and practically never left alone, they develop a degree of dependence that is unusual in American culture. "Out of this situation," Reischauer says, "emerges a child and then an adult who is accustomed to bask in the affection of others. This attitude is defined as *amae*, the noun form of the verb *amaeru*, which is cognate with the word for 'sweet,' and means 'to look to others for affection.'"

This helps explain why confluence, the merging and confusion of self and other, is a major Japanese issue. Confluence, while often resembling intimacy, is really a defense against intimacy, for by pretending that the other is the same, I deny our differences and cling exclusively to our similarities which blur us together in a psychic mush that disallows the true meeting that is living. A person who creates confluence instead of contact is always alone, for they live beside a fantasy rather than a real, live person.

The people who study at this institute are remarkably articulate, and I could have begun work with each one from their introductory statements. I like to hear from everyone, however, before I focus on one person, and so we complete the round of the group before I ask if anyone wants to work.

The more I think about it, the more certain I am that "work" is the word that most accurately describes what people do in Gestalt workshops. It's work to be attentive to that which is usually denied; it's work to touch feelings of pain and fear and to track them as they emerge and develop in the present; it's work to allow a long-repressed memory to come forth and, then, to enter into that scene and do something different than one did in the original event. It's hard, demanding work requiring discipline and commitment as well as the greatest courage, for the unfinished business is by definition unbearable.

What continues from the past into the present are the unexpressed feelings evoked by the past events. People must speak the language of their organism: the words and phrases that express the emotion they were afraid to articulate in the past. Without more strength and support than were available before, one will not express the emotions the past experience evoked. It is the work of all of us in a group to provide the safety and support that allows people to meet the emotions of their unfinished business and express them.

Everyone knows that the most terrifying demons are the ones that live inside; those who work in my groups face these appalling creatures and, through the process of awareness, transform their demons into allies. Since any experience, no matter how hideous, becomes support once it is integrated, the experiences that lurk inside defining the present with the terror of the past are by definition unintegrated and often forgotten. Until the emotions that accompanied these events are expressed, the experience cannot be integrated and transformed into support. Unfinished situations are very expensive energetically, for not only does the fixed gestalt bind the unexpressed energy, but the energy required by the effort to keep the entire process out of awareness is also lost to the here and now.

When I ask, "Who wants to work?" I hear a loud silence. Then I take the next step and ask them to be aware how they are holding back. A slender young man with lovely skin shaping finely drawn features replies that he is afraid of failing. I reply, "You can't fail to be aware, because there's no such thing as a wrong awareness. All awareness is valuable because it's part of the present moment." When I ask him what he is feeling, only his face and hands answer. He says he doesn't have words and asks would I help him. He is kneading his hands as he says this, so I ask him what they are saying. He replies that his right hand is scared.

When I suggest he be the right hand and say, "I'm scared," he goes blank, and I know I've moved too fast.

I withdraw at once and ask him when he first felt this fear. He replies, "In kindergarten." Haltingly and with little visible emotion, he talks about how afraid he was of upsetting his mother. When I suggest he say this to his mother, he freezes again, although this time he begins visibly to tremble. Slowly, he curls over, pawing and clutching the floor like a very young child. From time to time I see him shudder, and, occasionally, he says, "*Haha*" ("Mother").

Wilhelm Reich discovered that the story of our past is encoded in our bodies. When people feel safe enough to open the window of awareness these patterns release involuntarily, and people often literally shake themselves free from the compulsions of their history.

After what seems a long time—maybe five minutes—I take the young man's hand and ask him what he wants. He puts his head in my lap and weeps dry, miserable sobs. He continues his work with very little intervention from me; I truly do not know his story and feel cautious about interrupting what seems to be a tenuous and delicate, yet deep, contact with suffering caused by years of self-denial which I imagine was created by confluence with his mother.

I can see the little boy who, as is often the fate of children, had been taught that his actions could seriously injure his beloved mother. In order to take care of her he hid and disguised his own feelings. Maria Montessori said, "The essence of the child is love," and the loving little person, despite her or his essential helplessness, wants desperately to make his caretakers happy and agonizes endlessly when he imagines he has failed in this quite impossible task.

[On the night of March 10, 1945, in the firebombing of Tokyo, perhaps 150,000 people were killed. A woman tells this story: "A sea of flames surrounded us. At the pool in the corner of the park, I had to jump in and pulled Koichi into it. Koichi was too small to understand why we were in the pool. 'I'm sorry, Mommy,' he cried. 'I'll be a good boy. I'm sorry. I'm sorry.'"]

When the young man finishes his work and returns to his seat, I look around and see the group members swaddled like babies in their bright blankets: in my eyes they have become a circle of suffering children. Several people tell him how they touched their own childhood pain as, in their role of participant observers, they shared his misery. Many met their own deprived and denied childhood selves during the work. I am moved by the generosity of the group members as they share their childhood pain and wisdom.

It's almost time to stop, and I tell them to close their eyes and go inside to feel the child they were, and are, and to discover what the child wants and needs. Then I tell them to open their eyes and feel their adult selves right here, right now, and to be aware they can help themselves get what they want. I remind them that each one is both child and adult, and that these aspects can be friends who help each other through life. I also tell them that both selves deserve love and respect.

That is the end of the first session. I don't go to dinner and instead go to my room where I take a bath and have tea and cookies before diving into the great dark sensuality of sleep.

NOVEMBER 30, SATURDAY, 7:00 P.M.

Kazuaki's work begins with his awareness of a pattern he has observed while fighting with his wife. He says that although he loves her, he also hates her, and when he is tired and out of sorts, he begins a fight. Then he tells me that he feels an aching void in his chest. I intervene here, telling him to focus on the emptiness and express what it is saying. At once his face begins to swell with sorrow, and when I ask him what his sadness is saying, he replies, "Pay attention to me when I'm sad." I suggest he say it to his wife. He finds this difficult, and I acknowledge his quandary by observing that perhaps starting a fight is a more comfortable way to get his wife's attention than expressing his sadness. He agrees.

Then I suggest he express his sorrow. As he sits on the pillow in front of me, he appears young and small, totally oblivious of the group. I am impressed at the constancy of the hurt child who lives inside most, maybe all, of us—a child in adult incognito who sets aside its mask and ventures forward to express its misery and despair only in moments of safety and support.

For those who question the value of allowing this ancient suffering to emerge, I submit that the brilliance and wonder of life emanates from the child within. It is the eyes of the child that see the world as a shining adventure waiting to be explored, and it is the child who awakens in the morning trembling with excitement in anticipation of the day to come. When unfinished business builds a wall of pain between the adult and this joyful, energetic source of existence, when the hurt and angry young self is abandoned in darkness and neglect, adult life becomes a repetition of tiresome routines—patterns whose unaware purpose is the avoidance of unfinished business. An experience that is incompletely experienced is frozen into a pattern, a gestalt that repeats itself over and over again trying to find the completion and relief that expression allows.

The persistence of the childhood trauma springs from the person's inability to express their feelings. A young man tells of making a mistake in front of his third-grade class; another, of watching his friend throw his tricycle into the river. Both have been stuck with the burden of these rather insignificant events because during all the intervening years they never felt safe enough to tell someone of their loss and their pain. After they tell the group their stories and express the grief of their immature selves, they feel refreshed and relieved.

Since emotions are the language of the organism, we must express the emotions that events evoke before the experience can be concluded. Most people have experienced the frustrating repetition of self-defeating behaviors whose source seems utterly beyond their control. This is the blight of unfinished business: the organism's struggle to complete the gestalt that is not whole. In the effort to avoid suffering the repressed pain, to avoid even knowing that I am in pain, I separate myself from the inner vulnerability and, in the name of being mature, pretend I don't care. Charlotte Bronte reports this experience in *Villette* when, in her inner dialogue, Lucy Snowe asks, "'But if I feel, may I never express?' 'Never!' declared Reason." And it is this unbending voice of senseless reason which many imagine to be maturity. Those who lose contact with the childlike part of themselves will never feel pleasure, never have fun, and never experience the true living that comes with meeting.

I ask Kazuaki to tell his inexpressive self of his sorrow, and when he does, he weeps. Once they have touched their inner pain, I tend to encourage Japanese people to remain in the child's role, which, often delicate and ephemeral in its initial appearances, vanishes utterly if they switch back into the more putative, judgmental role, which Perls called the "top dog." When I began working in Japan, I would, in order to facilitate a dialogue, encourage the person to change cushions and move from the child's voice back to the parental "top dog." When I did this, the child, or Perls's "bottom dog," would disappear, and we had to recreate the situation that would invite the hurt child to emerge again.

I came to realize that while in Japan the top dog is loud and self-assured, the bottom dog is shy and hesitant—unlike the boisterous, provocative child that often emerges in Americans. Japanese people seem constantly to worry about what the other person thinks and tend to bind themselves with *enryo* ("reserve" or "constraint"). On occasion I say, *Enryo shinaide kudasai* ("Please don't constrain yourself"), which is usually greeted with a smile.

Once, when I suggested that a Japanese person in the child's role say, "You can't make me!" (definitely one of my own childhood mottoes), I was amazed at the long complex sentence the translator had to create to communicate this (to me) rather simple idea.

Alice Miller, the iconoclastic Swiss psychoanalyst and author of *Thou Shalt Not Be Aware*, recommends that the therapist become the advocate and ally of the child, and I do this. Nevertheless, over the long run, it is important to encourage a dialogue which includes both voices because—as Pat Baumgardner, a Gestalt colleague and friend from the United States, pointed out many years ago—a harsh top dog which doesn't have ample opportunity to express itself verbally will express unconsciously in accidents of varying degrees of seriousness and can become a threat to the person's safety.

After telling me that she especially wanted to work next time, a group member once called and apologized for not showing up because she had punctured her hand with scissors. "It was just an accident," she explained. While some people recognize intuitively that when they hurt themselves they are making a statement, others do not even consider the possibility of their own responsibility for hurting themselves. I had a client in the United States who came into therapy because, in her words, "I have been working around machinery all my life and recently I have had a series of small accidents. I want to know what's up with me."

I encourage people to take responsibility for their unaware behavior. When this is just too difficult—as it often is with severe medical problems—I propose they do it as a healing fiction. For while there is a limit to personal responsibility, we don't know where this boundary is. To work with a symptom as if one is creating it will increase awareness and can sometimes heal.

Like all Gestalt work, the healing fiction of taking responsibility for behavior that is traditionally seen as beyond our control is an experiment. Because people often confuse responsibility with blame, this kind of work often has to be proceeded by work on the process of blaming.

Blame, which can be quite agreeable when directed toward others in a shedding of self-responsibility, is uncomfortable when turned toward the self in the mistaken notion that this is what it is to take responsibility. If one is raised by people who, instead of taking responsibility for their feelings and actions, blame the helpless child for their distress, it is highly unlikely that the child will learn to be responsible for his or her own actions.

Blaming, which is a learned behavior, can be unlearned. Once a person unlearns the need to blame—the "look what you made me do" syndrome which some, but far from all, of us outgrow—he or she will matter-of-factly accept responsibility for what they do. It is obvious that I do what I do, that I am responsible for what I do. No matter how abused and misused I was, regardless of what was done to me in childhood that taught me to act in unproductive and self-destructive ways, I am the one who is drinking the whiskey, alienating my friends, slicing my finger, or performing any other act. I am doing it now, and I am the only one who can stop. You can kill me before you can make me doing something I refuse to do.

This is obvious. It is the subtle inner boundary of activity on the cellular level where the limits of responsibility are still unknown and essentially unexplored. A Gestalt experiment with the healing fiction is one way to learn more about this boundary, and allows a person to practice taking responsibility without blaming themselves for their own suffering. The goal in Gestalt is the expression of all voices in an ongoing dialogue which creates an integration of organismic energy into a configuration of personal vitality. This process allows each person to become aware of their interest and power, and mindfully to express themselves in both actions and words.

Japanese authoritarianism, a prototypical top dog, draws its considerable power from Confucianism, which, with its emphasis on obedience, rationalizes the humiliation of the young who are seen as servants of the old. Confucianism encourages people to consume the present generation in the service of the elders: to live as though, by Euro-American criteria, time moves backward. Among Asian Confucian societies the concept we designate "filial piety" embraces a far more comprehensive and compelling philosophy than the benign phrase suggests. While Confucianism has its greatest authority in China, Korea, and Singapore, its influence endures in Japan, where the word *oya koko*, which we render "filial piety," means, literally, to serve the parents.

When I was living in China in 1988 we visited a house that had been completed just before the Revolution of 1911. This house had elaborately carved panels depicting scenes from a classical volume of filial piety, including one in which an adult son dressed in baby clothes and played with toys so that his parents could continue to believe that they were young. Another showed a young man who had cut off his arm to make a nice broth for his ailing mother. These are most certainly extreme examples; nevertheless, I think they give a taste of the expected sacrifices which the glib phrase "filial piety" does not express. The philosophical system supporting this phrase makes claims on young people that the rather pleasant-sounding English phrase does not convey and that, without direct experience, those not raised in a Confucian society will fail to understand.

As Kazuaki tells his "top dog," or authoritarian side, to pay attention to him, he begins to form a fist. I suggest he tell how impatient he is, and this sentence connects with him; crying, he says it over and over:

"I'm impatient with you." Next he says that the person on the pillow has become his father, and I suggest he say, "You took care of your needs and not of mine." This, too, clicks—I can see it in his face—and he says it with feeling as he hits his knees. Immediately I direct the retroflected anger outward from his body toward the pillow, which now imaginatively represents his father. He strikes it again and again, breathing heavily and releasing his anger. When he is finished, I suggest he tell his father that he made a mistake by stopping the child's expression and putting his own needs first. He says this emphatically several times.

When a person repeats a phrase I offer and infuses it with energy, I know the phrase fits their experience. I frame the phrase from my observations of their process and my fantasy of what they are trying to express. It is a hypothesis that I present for them to test. This technique is useful only if I am willing to make my suggestion lightly and to withdraw it at the slightest gesture of dismissal. When people say, "It's not like that," I suggest they make a statement that fits, which they invariably do.

Since I am teaching people to trust themselves, I have to follow them scrupulously as they do the hard work of inner exploration. Each one knows their own experience far better than I do, and I think it is better to err on the side of leniency than arrogantly to insist that I know them better than they know themselves. To do so would undercut the entire process of self-discovery and democracy that the groups promote.

In the late 1960s, when I began my travels on the Gestalt path, there was a prevailing ethic of toughness. When I supported rather than confronted, colleagues called me a Red Cross nurse, which at the time was a derogatory label, although it doesn't sound so bad now. I wish I could have accepted it with more pride in those days. From experience I know that the balance of support and frustration must be maintained before a person will dare step into their abyss. I could more easily bully a geranium into bloom than intimidate a human being into aware existence.

With the flamboyant masculine bias that was then taken for truth, practitioners dismissed the suffering of many women with the label "hysterical," as though people who were hysterical were not in genuine pain.

In Freud's day, there were even serious suggestions that men could not be hysterical—a proposition that in view of the present world situation might evoke hysterical laughter in one who is sufficiently spontaneous to respond naturally to absurdity. In no profession is a historical perspective more necessary than psychology, for no aspect of study and observation is more vulnerable to the conventional wisdom than the one that dares to define what is truly human: the study of the psyche, a Greek word that means soul or spirit.

Freud retracted his conclusions about his patients' childhood traumas and seductions because he was afraid. Given the scorn with which his milder observations and conclusions were greeted, it is hard to cast the first stone at the Viennese doctor, for who is to say what she or he would have done in similar circumstances. What I can learn from him is to avoid dogmatic assertions about other peoples' souls because I may be mistaken. Let's save our certainty for remarks about ourselves and remember, with Gertrude Stein, that regardless of how objective I imagine myself to me, I am always repeating the whole of me.

When I ask Kazuaki if he wants to stop after expressing his anger, he says, "No, I want to give my father a chance to answer." I am pleased because this is a sure sign that he has achieved some degree of completion in expressing his hurt and angry feelings and is ready to move to the other side of the dialogue. It's a dynamic process, this dialogue of unfinished business, for by the time we have reached adulthood, we have internalized both the victim and the aggressor. Both sides must be expressed before integration can occur.

Kazuaki moves to the other pillow and, without the pressure of unexpressed hurt and anger, can now be a father who admits his mistake and apologizes to the little boy whose feelings he had appropriated. After saying this, Kazuaki feels complete and wants to stop.

After the group responds to Kazuaki's work, Yasuke comes forward. He says he want to reveal his secret self who wants to dominate women. He speaks of two kinds of women—the free woman and the submissive woman. The group laughs when I suggest he play the same two categories of men. The most touching and telling moment occurs when he tells the free woman he is afraid of her, afraid he will not be able to keep up with her. His basic process is dependence, trying to get me to give him answers.

After he plays the roles of free and submissive man and free and submissive woman, I ask him to stand in the middle of the square made by the four roles. As he stands there contemplating the four identities he has acted out, he becomes aware that all four parts are himself. He takes a while to look at each one and then he says, "Life is more complicated than I thought. What should I do?" I reply, "Answer your question." He says, "I have to think about it more."

His last remark is, "I want to ask you one more question."

"Go ahead," I reply. "I won't promise I'll answer."

"I have to answer it myself," he responds.

The connection between dependence and domination so obvious in this work heightens my interest in the process whereby men are hollowed out by their socialization. The "hollow men" that T. S. Eliot observed nearly a century ago continue to clamor and strive for some activity that will soothe their emptiness and make them feel whole again. Unfortunately the masculine ethic promotes domination as the solution of this dilemma. In their desperation to fill their emptiness, many men become so senselessly cruel and stupid that, often, I forget the anguish that underlies the hollow man's swagger. When, as in Yasuke's work, a man admits the fear that underlies his need to dominate, I feel privileged to greet the real person—the real live boy that Pinocchio yearned to become—who lives inside thick plaster cast of the masculine role. I look forward to the day when boys have more varied visions of manhood than those promoted by state, church, and Hollywood.

Kota, who had organized this group, is touched by Yasuke's work and remarks that we have to invent relationships between men and women because, even though we want something different, we can't discard the old roles all at once. His balance and sincerity remind me how formidable a task it is to create new patterns to shape and ease the life tasks that every generation must accomplish in order to survive. The keepers of the status quo guard closely the structures of acceptable expressions of intimacy and condemn those, like single parents or homosexuals, who dare to find happiness outside the walls. I respect the valor of those who design new forms for intimate relationships, for I appreciate their dignity and courage in daring to know their most heart-felt desires and in acting responsibly to fulfill them.

Working with these two young men and hearing the other group members' experiences of playing the obedient child and losing themselves in other people's desires and expectations, I have a strong and agonizing sense of the betrayal of the human spirit that occurs when those whom the child trusts refuse to honor and cherish the growing being in their care. As children, we know we are helpless and dependent. Since we must rely on the adults around us for survival, we learn to fulfill their expectations, even if this means that we crush our most natural impulses of speech and movement. To the extent that the adults around us do not value us for ourselves and try to make us over into the creatures they imagine we should be, we suffer. We are hurt and angered by this process, and yet to express these feelings might possibly (depending on the severity of the adults) endanger our lives, or at the very least the sense of safety and well-being that we need in order to mature. In a process learned from parents, teachers, peers, and finally the person her or himself, the destruction of the self is transmitted and finally internalized until an outside agency is no longer needed to enforce obedience. The control and repression which people who are harshly socialized have internalized and imposed on themselves is an ongoing process of self-murder.

I am exhausted when we stop at 9:40 p.m. During the night I dream of my high school friends: Selby sings behind a closed door while Sue and I discuss the importance of looking a garment over carefully before buying. In the dream I tell her that she should shop in China because she would find the flaws in the goods and buy only the well-made ones, which would be super bargains.

SUNDAY, DECEMBER 1, 7:00

I awaken in grayness and lie in bed waiting for the light to bring its gift of color before I dress and go outside. Walking along a narrow paved road with a steep hillside rising and falling on either side, I see a break in the vegetation and gleefully scramble up the hill and into the brush. People have built so densely on Japan's land that it is always a treat to find some dirt to slip and slide in. As I approach the ridge my shoes are heavy with mud, and I pull myself upward by clinging to the low variegated bamboo. From a clearing at the top I view the valley below.

Smoke rises from blue tiled roofs in a small village crowded between the *tanbo*—rice fields, in which stand squat tepees of tan rice straw. Beside a concrete encased stream a fringe of bamboo billows softly like ostrich feathers on a woman's hat, the yin to the yang of the neighboring pines which march up the mountain in stiff military rank. The pines are all the same size; someone planted them for harvest, just as when spring comes they will plant the rice. The tall and plummy bamboo in the valley is distinctly different from the waist-high variety I have just climbed through. The many varieties of bamboo are the distinguishing feature of the Asian countryside and a continual reminder that I am not in West Virginia. The clearing, however, is the right-of-way of an overhead power line which could be in West Virginia or any other industrialized land.

Across the valley, another series of towers drapes its wires like a clothesline over the dark pine forest. Hiking in Japan, I have rarely been out of sight of these signs of human activity. Pure wildness is not easy to find here, and when one stumbles upon it—as I once did in the form of a wild monkey on the remote and holy island Kinkazan—it's a gift. A large portion of Japan's main island is covered with mountains, and even there, on the fierce alpine peaks of Honshu's mountain spine, windmills, cabins, and markers remind one that many, many people have been there before.

Disregarding any possible danger from the power line, I do my Tai Chi in its space.

SUNDAY, DECEMBER 1, 9:30 A.M.

When I join the group, they have finished their exercises and are sprawled around the room on their blankets. Since the only split between body and mind is the one we make with words, their exercises are excellent preparation for Gestalt.

Ready to work, group members come forward one after another to engage the great adventure of knowing themselves. Encouraged by ancient voices and urged onward by deep inner aspirations, they seek the passage to self-awareness.

First comes Kaneko, who, while begging for her mother's acceptance, experiences directly her own rejection of her present self, a practice she had learned from her mother's early disapproval. Her little girl voice gains power as she experiences her self-rejection and comes to realize that she is the one who in every moment makes the choice to accept or reject herself. As she becomes aware of precisely how she rejects herself, she will become free to replace the now useless pattern with sensitive responses to the present situation—which, of course, includes herself.

To disavow the self is to deny the here and now in which the self exists. It is this truth that underlies the words of the Japanese actor Zeami, the creator of the Noh drama, who said long ago, "We can only take what is happening in the present and call it good."

People who have been taught to judge find it extremely difficult to grasp this simple and obvious truth: the present is all we have, and each one is part of it. Rejecting ourselves, we reject the truth, for, as Lenny Bruce so accurately observed, "Truth is what is." When children are judged rather than cherished, they receive the mistaken notion that they are born to judge, that they must spend their lives bundling existence into judgments that create a buffer of good and bad through which they must mediate their experience. I remember once explaining this to a friend while driving through San Francisco's Marina, when an oncoming car crossed into my lane. Swerving to miss it, I incorporated the event into my conversation, and said, "I can use my energy thinking about what a lousy driver this guy is, or I can get out of his way." My friend got it, not least of all because he saw that my response save us both from possible injury. We both understood that whether the other guy was good or bad was pretty much irrelevant to the far more important task of safely avoiding him.

I witnessed another amusing example of the distraction that judgment creates when my son Frank and his girlfriend were working in the kitchen and one of them knocked over a milk carton. They argued over whose fault it was as milk poured over the counter and onto the floor. I got up from my chair, walked over, and set the carton upright while they debated blame. Responding to the situation is more relevant, more useful, and far more fun than judging.

Next Hirotaka tells of the violent *ijime* he experienced in middle school. He is willing to embrace his anger and pain at his classmates' conduct, and, as soon as I remind him that now he is safe from their retribution, he explodes with rage. He expresses himself with powerful, integrated sounds and movements in a true explosion of anger, such as Perls mentioned when he discussed the four explosive emotions: anger, grief, joy, and orgasm. Perls said these explosions are paths to the true self, paths revealed as the organism speaks its language of emotion with awareness and support in the present. With these elements in place, Hirotaka is able to express emotions which at the time of the bullying were too dangerous to impart. He has been waiting for the completion that comes with expression ever since, and as soon as he felt safe enough he expressed fully what, heretofore, had been inexpressible.

I am becoming more and more convinced that the ability of human beings to repress their response, and even to forget the incident, fosters survival. There are in most lives situations when, especially for the small and vulnerable child, self-expression is dangerous and could result in death. In their natural wisdom, children know this and inhibit the dangerous response, holding it until they find a safe place and sympathetic listener.

In the group, Hirotaka has found what he needed to express and complete the rage and misery of his *ijime*. When he finishes his explosion, he thanks Kota, who acted as his teacher, for preparing him for this work. With tears in his eyes and in his voice, Kota replies that Japanese society, just like the Chinese at Tienanmen and the Thais in the recent Bangkok riots, kill their young by prohibiting self-expression. Members of the group nod in agreement. Hirotaka, by directly acknowledging his gratitude, demonstrated his understanding and integration of what he had done. Awareness and support developed in his studies with Kota made his present contact with his past suffering possible. His expression of the suppressed emotions of hurt and anger allowed him to emerge from the cocoon of pain he had created to prevent even more serious injury at the time of his *ijime*. The completion of the past trauma frees him into present awareness and the gratitude which William Blake says "is heaven itself."

Sakae says that her problem is money. When I ask her to put money on the pillow and talk to it, many people laugh. As she tells money how important it is in her life, she makes a movement with her hands that catches my eye, and I direct her awareness to her hands. Focusing on how she is moving her hands, she looks surprised and says, "I'm counting money." She pauses before saying, "I'm always counting money and I don't enjoy it. I don't enjoy working for money." This is an "Aha!" for her. She stops, satisfied and ready to integrate.

Fumiko, the girlfriend of Yasuke, who wants to dominate women, works next. With her work we get to see the female side of Yasuke's work. Her dilemma is between taking the risk of frightening him by choosing to be open or remaining closed and inauthentic, which she rationalizes as taking care of him. As soon as she clearly delineates her choices, she sees that destroying herself in the name of taking care of him will not create the life she seeks for either of them. She stops with this awareness, a commitment to herself and a willingness to face the risks that accompany new choices.

The last work of the morning is by another person injured by cruel peers. During this work, I understand clearly that abandonment by adults always underlies the long-term effects of peer-induced suffering. When there are sympathetic adults to whom the child can turn for, if not protection, at least sympathy and understanding, the power of the peer group and the damage of their cruelty are greatly diminished.

We have worked for two and a half hours straight, without a break, and the right side of my neck is sore and stiff. I had begun tightening my neck the moment I walked into the group, and I ignored myself all morning. Being a far from perfect practitioner of what I preach, I am critical of myself for not being more sensitive to my own feelings. I am convinced that people will "do as I do" rather than as I say, and when

I don't take care of myself, I am teaching them to do the same; however, since I am teaching self-acceptance as well, I have to practice the virtue of living lightly with my own imperfections. The world will never be made kinder by people who are not kind to themselves.

SUNDAY, DECEMBER 1, 1992 1:30 P.M.

Joining the group after their relaxation exercises, I see some lying about with their eyes closed, others standing apart swinging their arms or stretching, while still others stand on the balcony and bark sharp, guttural sounds into the treetops. As soon as I enter the room, they form themselves into a circle, clearly eager to work.

Shizuyo is the first to come forward. She begins to speak of her many roles—wife, mother, teacher. She says she is thinking of quitting her teaching job, and then, hesitating a moment, she sinks into herself and utters what I think is one of the saddest sentences in any language: "I don't know what I want."

When the natural process of knowing one's preference in the present is interrupted by those who imagine they know better, the young person becomes lost. By denying the experience of felt preference, a person sacrifices the orientation of desire and floats adrift in a sea of possibilities where any choice is as good as any other. In such a void of true being, one will seek direction from others in order to know how to proceed, and will seek reward and verification from these same others because she or he has forgotten the satisfaction that comes from pleasing oneself. I always think of the folk wisdom of the old pop song which goes, "You can't please everyone, so you might as well please yourself." It's only from authenticity and truth, no matter how painful this truth may be, that the living organism can experience the natural vitality at its center and respond creatively to its environment.

In order to help her to fully experience her state of not knowing, I tell Shizuyo to say it again: "I don't know what I want." I sense that, for her, not knowing is truth and that it will be from this point of ignorance that she can gather her energies to begin again the process of natural growth that was interrupted when she lost her ability to acknowledge her desire.

Repeating the sentence, she touches her chest and begins to rub it lightly. I ask her what she experiences there. "Something is stuck," she replies. I encourage her to continued massaging her chest, which she does in silence for a few minutes before I ask her what the stuck place is saying. She replies, "Don't cry. It's better not to cry." Still rubbing her chest, she continues, "Other people don't cry. '*Gaman*' (Endure). You're supposed to *gaman* the way the others do."

"*Gaman*," a verb meaning "to endure suffering," is a highly prized virtue in Japan, especially for women. "*Gambaru*" is another and related verb which, translated freely, means, "Do your best; never give up." They are the active and passive versions of the virtue of eternal striving, and are used by Japanese people both to themselves and to each other. "*Gambatte kudasai*" is what a Japanese person would say instead of "Good luck," or "Break a leg."

As Shizuyo orders herself to *gaman*, she begins to cry thin, hard sobs that seem to force themselves through the unwilling musculature of her throat and face. She continues to massage her chest with increasing force until she does it with a frantic determination as first one hand and then another move back and forth just above her breasts. The content of this work is *gaman*, and she is satisfied with the release which she gives herself when she cries. I don't resist the impulse to explain and tell her that crying is a natural (fortunately, natural is a value in Japan) way to release feelings of sorrow and grief and nothing to be ashamed of.

Next Kanae, an adorable young woman, soft and pink as an infant, comes forward to talk about an old boyfriend who pushed her away saying he didn't want to see or talk to her anymore. She admits that she had always been tense with him and is far more comfortable with her present boyfriend. Still, watching the previous work, she noticed the return of her old feelings. She talks to him briefly, telling him that she is *genk*" (fine), and then she bursts into fierce tears. I ask if these feelings reminded her of some other time in her life. After considering for a moment, she replies, "Yes," and tells me that her mother had not liked her very well and had never given her much love.

I suggest that she speak to her mother, and she expresses a bit of sorrow and loss, as gradually she begins to cry the heavy sobs of childhood neglect. When I ask her what she wants, she replies that she wants to be hugged, and when I ask her if I might hug her, she says, "Yes." Kneeling on the floor, we hug; she holds me tightly and sobs until gradually she releases me and puts her head between my breasts where, breathing softly, she rests.

She is the beautiful child of someone who did not take time or give energy to cherish her. I hope that when my sons need someone to make up my deficiencies, they, too, may find someone to hold them as they cry, for, as Carl Sandburg said, "There is only one child and its name is all children." Everyone from time to time, needs the warmth of loving arms. Wouldn't it be a good world if we had armies with such arms? And what a lot of money we could save for important things like homes and healing.

Before I can straighten my back and catch my breath, another woman sits in front of me and begins telling about her mother who died just as she, the daughter, was giving her a drink of water. She had not been close to her mother, and continues to harbor guilty imaginings that she killed her. She dissolves in a convulsion of tears as she tells this story. Sitting with her and her sobs, I feel helpless, and console myself with the knowledge that I don't have to do anything because she is healing herself.

The ability of human beings to heal themselves is obvious to anyone who has cut her finger or recovered from a cold. Healers are, first, the sick or injured person themselves, and, second, those who create and allow circumstances that permit the natural healing process to occur perhaps a tad faster or more effectively and who, above all, do no harm. By expressing their deepest sorrow, each one heals her or himself, and while I grieve that people suffer, I feel a certain relief sitting with them as they express their pain.

The daughter's last word to me is, "*Nakunarimashita*" ("She died"). We never touch on the issue of her guilt. It remains her secret. She works herself and continues to cry long after she flees the group room into the trees outside. I feel drenched in anguish during the short break that follows. In the kitchen behind the group room, I watch as one woman massages the shoulders of another who begins to sob loudly, and the woman who had been massaging holds her while she cries. I walk past them and step outside onto a porch overlooking a narrow ravine where a small stream flows. Totally hidden under the lush vegetation, I hear water moving through the tiny valley. I comfort myself recalling that, like the stream, human tears invisibly spread their nurturing power and fertilize all they touch.

After the break, there is only an hour remaining in the group. A young man who has been playing a clownish role in the group comes forward and expresses his concern that he is wasting his life doing work that he doesn't want to do. He comes across as thoroughly confused, and I choose his posture as perhaps the best path to awareness for him in the short time remaining. As he speaks, he alternately crosses his arms and braces his hands on his knees. I have him change cushions each time he changes his posture, in essence creating a dialogue between the two positions. He crosses his arms often, and each time he does it, I interrupt him and tell him to change seats.

Gradually, he becomes aware of what he is doing and what the different postures are saying. The role expressed by the arms crossed over the chest is very self-assured and certain, saying, of course, "*Gambatte, gambatte*." The more open posture speaks in a soft, tentative voice and, since it is less of a parrot, is more interesting and responsive. He becomes the tiniest bit aware of these aspects of himself, and clearly aware that the crossed- arms posture is more familiar and comfortable than the other. I ask him to sit in the middle with a hand on each cushion while I say a few words about how awareness allows choice which is another word for freedom. When I say that choice means freedom, his eyes give off a bright spark that tells me he got it.

He got it! And I saw him get it! I end the work here.

After another sentence about the importance of endings and finishing in order to complete the Gestalt, we spend the last minutes of the group in an unstructured round. On the whole, the Japanese people I work with are uninterested in theory and want to use their time with me and the group focusing on themselves and each other in an existential, experiential way.

In this last round, a woman says that she feels blamed and dreads returning to work because "I will be blamed there." There has been much written about the Japanese tendency to blame others, especially in connection with the World War II. Blaming, however, like most human activities, is spread pretty evenly among human beings, as we observe when we hear American businessmen blaming the Japanese for their own failure to enhance American productivity and creativity. The tendency to blame others rises from internalized blame and guilt which the child has accepted because his or her boundaries were too weak to resist the accusations proffered by adults, no matter how bizarre and irrational they were.

I remember a scene from the movie "I Love You, Alice B. Toklas," in which one of the characters appears dressed for a wedding in traditional Native American attire. On seeing him so arrayed, his brother exclaims, "What are you trying to do? Kill your mother?" How many people restrain themselves because they believe their behavior will kill their mothers? Internalized blame creates inner pressures which those who lack awareness often discharge by blaming others. This is, however, a quick fix and, like a drug, has to be repeated over and over again in ever-increasing doses. It is rare that anyone speaks out against the evil of blaming children for their immaturity, which is where the terrible cycle begins. The failure to protect the immature from the frustrations and blaming judgments of their suffering elders is at the basis of the whole blame game, which serves no one because it only deepens the trench of the mass grave that is the status quo.

Blaming is the polar opposite of taking responsibility for the choices I make. When I blame, I am implying that somehow you control my behavior, and this is never true. The rebellious child knows that "You can't make me." Anorexia is the statement of an oppressed person claiming their most fundamental right: the hunger strike, the right to starve themselves.

Because the child is small and does not have the power of exit, however, it is relatively easy to coerce a child with an offer they can't refuse. As children from relatively non-violent homes become adults, they realize their power to come and go, to think, feel, and act on their own volition. Such a one understands that although another person can kill them, no one can force them to perform without their cooperation, and this leads to awareness of responsibility and to the ability to respond.

Responsibility is the acknowledgment that I am the one who makes the choices and takes the actions that create my life. It is, perhaps, the major goal of Gestalt work to foster aware choice for which a person willingly takes responsibility.

In the final round, a woman who hadn't worked makes an interesting comment. She says, "I didn't work because I kept saying my issue wasn't important enough, and then today, I realized that my saying my issue wasn't important was my issue." This is a stunning insight, and, in the only remark I make during this round, I tell her so. In becoming aware that she makes herself and her concerns unimportant, she has touched the child who denies herself expression in order to take care of the parents.

Often during the Gestalt dialogue I hear Japanese people say to their parents, "*Kawaisoo*" ("I pity you"). And indeed parents who rely on children for protection and support are pitiful. Nevertheless, the pity of the all-forgiving child-saint hinders access to the more profound and less socially acceptable self who, hurt and betrayed by the parents' incompetence, needs to express an immature and—to the adult mind—perhaps irrational rage and pain in order to grow up. Adults do not love with the all-forgiving love of childhood. When they do, this love is labeled masochistic because adults, who have the right to exit, do not have to suffer whatever people in their vicinity do to them.

The group ends with most people feeling satisfied. I am too tired and stiff to feel good about what we have done. I think I've done good work when I can enhance my energy rather than deplete it, and I have worked too hard in this group to feel satisfied.

After the group, I return to Tokyo's muffled urbanity, where my friend Rieko shows me a video of a clinical psychologist friend and colleague performing traditional Japanese dance. Watching the video, with its unfamiliar forms and music, I wonder that one person can be both the clinical psychologist and the Japanese dancer, and remember Yeats's famous line, "How can I tell the dancer from the dance?" The answer is, of course, "I can't. The dancer is the dance."

The dance of modern Japan is a profound challenge to the practical citizen of a multi-national country like the United States who sees history beginning with the colonizing of the wilderness two hundred and fifty years ago. At that time in Japan, after more than a thousand years of high and brilliant culture, the Tokugawa family sealed the islands from foreign influence and cultivated a historical particularity that is perhaps unique in the world. Reischauer notes that Japan's "natural geographic isolation, magnified later by human design, forced the Japanese to live more separately from the rest of the word than any other comparably large and advanced group of people. This combination...enabled them more than most other peoples to develop on their own and in their own way."

During the Tokugawa period (which lasted roughly from 1600 to the 1860s) the Japanese developed in Edo, the site of modern Tokyo, a city of skilled workers, talented entrepreneurs, and popular culture, such as *ukiyoe* and Kabuki, which became the foundation of the modern Japanese economy. As Reischauer notes, the Japanese miracle is not its successful economy, which evolved naturally given the traditions of hard work and excellence; the Japanese miracle is democracy, which in the generation after the second world war flourished in the unpromising medium of decaying bureaucratic feudalism.

While the Japanese may logically be designated as a tribe, they can, in no sense of the word, be seen as primitive and undeveloped. The very fact that they have been able to continue their own cultural development in the face of massive Euro-American intrusion is a powerful testimony to the ability of their culture to both speak and listen to the deepest needs and strivings of human life.

It is, I think, the very intactness of Japanese culture that makes Japan and the Japanese difficult for many Americans to understand. Japan is the only major culture that was not demoralized by European and American colonialism before it began to play its role on the world stage—

the unique venue created by the vast communication and transportation networks of the twentieth century. As such, Japan suggests, as (say) the Eskimos or Peruvian Indians do not, a viable and possible alternative to the mainstream of Euro-American civilization.

Japanese civilization cannot and must not be dismissed, which means that it must be met; and for many people an encounter with what is different is a threat to their own shaky—and, therefore, violently espoused—values and convictions. Insecure people see a meeting among equals as a threat rather than an opportunity. My encounter with Japanese people and culture has brought to my life the joy and challenge of the true living, which is meeting. I am grateful to my Japanese friends, colleagues, and students who have welcomed me into their hearts and lives, where together we create the exciting adventure of love and learning that comes with meeting.

TUESDAY, DECEMBER 3, 7:00 P.M.

Just as with Heraclitus's famous river, I can never step into the same group twice; and tonight the women's group, although composed of the same women who came last week, is a significantly different gathering. We are all far more relaxed than before, and seem to have breached some kind of barrier, perhaps no more than the wall of ignorant expectations.

Fuyu, a shy, graceful young woman, speaks with great deliberation, telling, for the first time ever, of the misery she feels in the presence of people. She expresses concern that she is acting spoiled (*wagamama*), and when I suggest she become the spoiled child, she refuses, choosing, instead, to talk to the child, which she does softly and sweetly. With the clear intention to protect, she says, "Hide! Hide! Make yourself small and be quiet. That is the way to be safe." After she says this, she recalls her loud and intrusive mother, in whose presence she was restless and fearful. She chooses to stop her work when I suggest she talk to her mother. Since her basic challenge is setting boundaries with others, which will often mean refusing their requests, I am gratified when she says "No" to me. Several times during her work, she smiles a shy smile which reminds me that, while we have worked together once a week for eight weeks this past spring, this is the first time I have seen her smile.

Eiko begins her work by saying that she is afraid of falling. When I encourage her to imagine falling, she does, and in the fantasy becomes aware that she would rather continue falling than touch bottom. I urge her to find a bottom, which I imagine might be her ground. She refuses, however, saying she doesn't want to touch the bottom. After this refusal, she says her chest is empty, and when I ask her what she feels, she replies, "Sad." She begins to cry, saying, "I don't feel that what's inside me is valuable."

I ask, "When you see other people's sorrow, do you think it's valuable?" Still crying, she replies, "Yes, I think it's valuable." She looks at the ceiling and continues to cry. I suggest she look at someone in the group and tell them of her sadness. She selects a woman and tells her, "I don't have any confidence and I'm sad."

This is her bottom, her ground of being. As she speaks, her eyes fill with light, and I understand that so long as, frightened at the prospect of pain, she numbs her heart and makes it empty, she breaks her aware connection to both the power chakra of the solar plexus and the *hara* or bodily center in the belly. This numbing of the heart breaks a person in two pieces—the computer and the zombie, a thinking machine and a moving machine. The avoidance of emotion blocks confidence, for in avoiding emotions we sever our connection to our center: the fountain of self-renewing inner vitality which the Japanese call the *hara* and the Chinese call the *tan tien*, the field of heaven. It is the avoidance of suffering, ancient and contemporary, that removes people from the irrefutable solidity and certainty of existence that allows confidence in one's here-and-now experience.

[I worked with the dream of endless falling in a recent and very different group, a training group for professional mental health workers. In this group, I ask the woman who reports the dream to create a bottom for herself. When she says, "I can't," I reply, "Of course you can. You chose not to." And then she admits that on first hearing the question, she had seen a town. This stunning shift to truth and self-responsibility is the turning point in her work. In that moment, she decides to trust herself, as well as me and the others in the group, and in trusting she finds a ground for her being.

When she falls into the town, she says she feels like she's flying, and when she wanders through the town, she delights in its variety. When she stops working, another woman says that, in childhood, she had a similar dream. She weeps as she tells how the image of the town touches her, and when I suggest she talk to the town, she greets it with the immense relief of a traveler returning home from a long journey.

At the end of her work, she says she feels refreshed— *sukkiri*, a word Japanese people often use when they discover something new. Fritz Perls said, "Learning is discovery," and it is among the joys and purposes of human existence. In this workshop I learn that a person can resolve the dilemma of the missing ground with an image discovered by another. The falling dream and the ungrounded state it signifies is likely a statement about our difficulty finding a place for ourselves, our real selves, in our families of origin and in the larger society in which each must somehow contrive to live.]

The members of the women's group are young and distressed. Living in a literally man-made world, where they are by definition inferior and at fault, they are disconnected from their inner power. One of the women says, "I am like a cockroach. No one would care if I live or die. I come to groups like this instead of sitting in my messy room." Nevertheless, the human spirit is indomitable: she does come to groups like this, and, like the phoenix, she rises from the ashes of her socially imposed destruction so long as she continues to seek out places of safety where she can touch the ground of being—which, in nearly every instance, will first be experienced as pain.

"I am this one who suffers," is perhaps the first glimmer of self-affirmation that many people (men as well as women) feel as they discover their true vocation: self-creation from the ashes of a blasted childhood. "I cry, therefore, I am."

Before we finish, I speak briefly about touching the Earth, finding what they might love in nature: trees, ocean, animals, sunsets—it doesn't matter what one chooses to love. It is in loving and seeking out what one loves that we meet ourselves. As I speak I hear the translator translating my words into beautiful Japanese. When I say, "It's great to have a poet for a translator," she hears me say that she is a poor translator, and so the fixed gestalt of low self-esteem among women is poignantly emphasized once again. We laugh at our terrible consistency.

DECEMBER 4, WEDNESDAY, 6:00 A.M.

As I retrace the landscape of pain I have recently traveled, I imagine that what I see and share is not the worst of human suffering; the worst, perhaps, is among militarists, criminals, and those others whose fierce and frantic desperation can no longer be contained in an inner struggle against the self or battles within the family and is, instead, turned outward against strangers.

Ever since 1966, when Charles Whitman, after quarreling with his father, mounted the tower at the University of Texas and shot 23 people he had never met, I have half-seriously defined mental health as killing the person you're mad at. However, even large- scale murder and mayhem bring only temporary relief from internal pressures, for I observe the relentless repetition of acted-out savagery. Such people never stop of their own accord unless they kill themselves, because the true tormentor is within, and their brutality toward others is an evasion—a way to avoid meeting the true aggressor who has become one with their own existence. Adolf Hitler had such unbearable night terrors that someone had to sit by his bed to protect him from his inner tormentor. Long before Macbeth murdered sleep, "chief nourisher in life's feast," tyrants were known for their restless nights. The cruel one within is a nocturnal creature who leaps from the cave of sleep into the dreams of the suspecting sleeper.

No one achieves freedom by blaming people who never harmed them. Do such people suffer less because they act their misery out upon the bodies of others? Does it ease inner pain to torture? Perhaps it does, for otherwise what would be the point of doing it? This is one of the things I will never know, for it is not given to human beings to know the suffering of any other except the one I am here and now—the "me, myself, and I" my friends and I used to talk about in grade school.

I am the only one I know; all else is imagination. All others I will know, in the words of Paul's epistle, "only as I am known." What I can know is how I feel when I face the magnificent courage of people who are willing to sit with themselves and allow the present moment to emerge in their awareness with whatever sensations and emotions it includes. I often feel honored that people allow me to be present with them as they do the courageous and demanding work of self-discovery.

I was recently in a Japanese group with my colleague Lois Brien, when she said, "There are no races, only one race: the human race." A perceptible shudder fluttered through the group as they took in the possibility that this might be so, for if there is such a thing as a Japanese religion, its major tenet is that the Japanese are a unique race. Perhaps the defining myth of Japanese culture is that of "we Japanese." I have heard this phrase on many occasions when it incarnates the speaker's belief that he or she belongs to a unique race with qualities that others do not have and perhaps will never understand.

This usage is an irritant to the many Japanese who do not wish to be included in other people's petty biases: as, for example (and I'm not making this up), "We Japanese wait for the light to change before crossing the street." Funny little manifestations of this belief system show up in the newspapers from time to time, as when one of the government ministers said the Japanese could not import more American beef because their intestines were too short to digest beef easily. I have heard a Japanese acquaintance insist the Japanese brain is particularly well adapted for the enjoyment of insect sounds—which, if it were true, would be a benefit, for in Japan's summer the insects are clamorous.

Another manifestation of the phenomenon is the fantasy that Japanese life and culture are mysterious and difficult to understand. When I mention to a Japanese friend the exclusion of the *Burakumin*, the historical underclass that is still identified and shunned by many Japanese, he or she might respond with, "You know so much," as though unaware that most aspects of Japan's culture have been exhaustively described in books.

The myth of Japanese uniqueness, like all cultural myths, contains a grain of truth, for every culture is a particular people's response to the geography and population of its neighborhood. It is also true that Japan was probably the only country to hold the Americans and Europeans at bay and maintain control of its society while it industrialized. This is a unique achievement, and a definite statement about the vigor of the Japanese cultural tradition.

Included in the Japanese sense of specialness is a finely nuanced sensitivity to other people's feelings and desires, which the Japanese see as essential for members of a large population living in a small space and which encourages them to believe in their telepathic ability to divine what other people are thinking and feeling. When I first came to Japan I was often astonished to have my wishes fulfilled before I was even aware of them myself. The first Christmas my son Lawrence and I were in Japan, people invited us for church services, Christmas dinners, and New Year's celebrations long before we had a chance to feel like strangers.

As an American I am not accustomed to being observed so closely, and sometimes I find Japanese people's anticipation of my needs uncanny. When someone insists on fulfilling a need I don't have, however—as when my landlady insisted on taking me to the police station to retrieve a lost wallet for which I had already made other arrangements, it is intensely intrusive and annoying. Since I'm not Japanese, I can be impolite and get out of the system when it becomes claustrophobic. I can readily imagine how tiresome it would become to be embedded in such a tight system of mutual interaction.

Many people in Japanese groups express fear of other people's eyes. They often stare intently at the floor when they say this and, equally often, are astonished with what they see when, with my encouragement, they actually look at other people in the group. After this little experiment in reality testing, I tell them Fritz's notion that many people give away their eyes, imagining what others see rather than seeing with their own eyes. I encourage them to attend to what they see when they frighten themselves with fantasies of what others see.

In a recent group a man refused my invitation to look at other people and chose, instead, to remain encapsulated in his fearful inventions rather than check out the world beyond his imagination. Perhaps the intense socialization of Japanese childhood teaches people to be as sensitive to their fantasies of others as to the real other people in their environment. This might be another example of the Zen student who watches the pointing finger instead of the moon it designates.

These Zen stories surely have cultural significance, for they didn't hatch full-blown from some philosophical egg. As one who grew up in a West Virginia town of five thousand people, I know the preoccupation with the eyes of others is not unique to the Japanese. Nevertheless, I think that the emphasis on being a member of a special group combined with the necessity of fitting into that group makes disapproval a near equivalent to ostracism, and therefore far more painful than it would be for many Americans.

One of the most important things I teach my Japanese students is the (for Japan) counter-cultural behavior of checking with the other person to discover her or his feeling rather than trusting intuition alone. Regardless of how often I am accurate in my guesses concerning other people's states of mind, they remain guesses, products of my imagination, and it is disrespectful to insist that I know what you are feeling better than you know yourself. No matter how certain one may be that she or he is accurate, saying "I don't believe you"—not an easy thing to say to someone's face—expresses the outer limit of one's certainty.

I can say "I don't believe you" with assurance, because this is a statement about me rather than you. When I feel tempted to contest another's expression of feeling, I do well to heed Oliver Cromwell's advice: "I beseech you, in the bowels of Christ, think it possible you may be mistaken." To insist that you accept my interpretation of your emotional state is a raw assertion of power; I've heard interpretation called a hostile act. A major shortcoming of traditional psychoanalysis is its reliance on interpretation, which teaches the student to accept the expert's authority rather than discover his or her own.

Besides being arrogant and hostile, insisting on the reality of my fantasy in the face of your evidence to the contrary is foolish, for, as Gertrude Stein said, "Knowledge is what you know," and it is impossible to know another person as well as we may, if we have the courage, know ourselves. We are all far better occupied fulfilling Delphi's ancient and apparently eternally valid directive to know one's self than in asserting our illusory knowledge of other people's thoughts and feelings.

While Japanese people often confuse the distinction between their fantasies and other people's emotional states, their language provides them with useful concepts for classifying their awareness of emotional and behavioral states. In addition to *honne* (deep reality) and *tatemae* (surface appearances), the Japanese recognize another important polarity of response in social situations: the one between *giri* (obligation) and *ninjo* (true human feeling). From this point of view, human society is based on *giri*. The chocolate the young women give their bosses on Valentine's Day is forthrightly called *giri-choko* (obligation chocolate), and many Japanese people actually dread receiving expressions of kindness because they entail future obligation.

The Japanese acknowledge, however, that there is more to life than a complex web of social obligations, and *ninjo* is the word for the human interactions based on desire and feeling that come from within each person. It is the contrasting world of *giri* and *ninjo* existing side by side in the tiny islands that account for many of the seeming contradictions of Japanese society: the loving mothers and the draconian schools, the overworked salarymen and the floating word of sex for money. While such divisions occur in all societies, it is a refinement of the Japanese that with their language they perform the healing act of (in Perls's words) "making the implicit explicit." Social demands are less harmful when the person, especially a young person, can see them for the social rituals they are rather than as expressions of an absolute morality that must be followed at any cost.

Perhaps these explicit categories—*giri* and *ninjo*, *honne* and *tatemae*—are concepts we as America'ns can take from the Japanese as we give in exchange our precious regard for the individual person in all his and her distinctive originality; for it is individual human beings that are unique rather than the various groupings in which we arrange ourselves. If, learning from each other, Americans and Japanese will integrate our different cultural priorities, we might achieve a caring and choiceful balancing of the interests of the individual with those of the group. This would be a leap toward personal and community harmony for people of both cultures.

WEDNESDAY, DECEMBER 4, 9:00 A.M.

In the early morning almost any place on Honshu the crows fly overhead announcing their plans for the day; this morning, since I, too, will fly, I mutely submit my own for inclusion in their prophecy. It's my last day in Japan, and I practice Tai Chi by the pond in Yasukuni Shrine. I savor the sweetness of early morning in the silence of this controversial site where some among the Japanese honor those who died in Japan's recent wars.

International war is a recent occurrence here: from the attempted Mongol invasions of the twelfth century until the Sino-Japanese War of 1894, all Japanese wars were feudal conflicts fought among the great families of the islands. I notice that many who come here are from the generation a little ahead of mine—those who fought in World War II. Since it is a rare bit of green in the middle of Tokyo, there are also many families and lovers who, like me, come to enjoy the scenery with no regard for its ritual significance.

Whenever I practice here, I honor the world's war dead with a prayer for peace, a prayer for the souls of both the old men, who sit in safety and plan wars, and the young men, who die as blood sacrifices to the parochial divinities of ideal manhood. I agree with Ford Maddox Ford, who, after surviving the trenches of the first world war, had this to say about the war dead:

> *All these men given into the hands of the most*
> *cynically care-free intriguers in long corridors who*
> *made plots that harrowed the hearts of the world.*
> *All these men toys; all these agonies mere occasions*
> *for picturesque phrases to be put into politicians'*
> *speeches without heart or even intelligence.*

Birds sing in this wooded spot; one of the Tokyo crows, about three times the size of those I've seen in the corn fields of America, flies down and watches me from his perch on a bamboo fence. The maple leaves smolder against the gray sky as I perform the soothing movements of the Tai Chi sets I bring here from San Francisco and Shanghai.

Last night Rieko, Yasuko, and I ate and drank until 2:00 a.m. We remembered Yasuko's father, who died unexpectedly just a few months after we had visited him in Saitama last year. Finishing the evening slightly drunk and entwined together on the floor of Rieko's apartment, we affirmed again the vitality of what my son Lawrence calls "puppy power"—the tendency for people to cuddle together whenever they are given the least encouragement. I often see puppy power in groups, although I usually lack sufficient courage to facilitate its expression.

Before dissolving into puppydom, we decided to name the book we have been working on *Live Now* (*Ima Ikiru*). I like it for the association with Kurosawa's wonderful movie "*Ikiru*," which means "To Live." Yasuko wants me to write a book about the universality of human experience. [Thanks, Yasuko; I hope this is it.]

SAME DAY, NARITA AIRPORT, 6:30 P.M.

People from every continent wait to board the plane to Hong Kong. They bear a vast variety of baggage-satchels of every material ranging from softest leather and finest brocade through Louis Vuitton's expensive plastic and solid American canvas to the red, white, and blue plastic webbing which is the signature of packets from mainland China. We are late in boarding, and the first-class passengers, beckoned from the security of their lounge before the flight is ready, cluster impatiently at the front of the crowd. As a premium frequent flier, I cluster with them, eavesdropping on their conversations.

At the head of the line stands an eerie-looking man with a high balding forehead above narrow eyes squinting behind heavy gold-rimmed lenses that balance his wide, hard mouth stretched over large carnivorous teeth. His sinister appearance is intensified by his traveling companion, an Oliver North type in dark glasses and baseball cap pushed back to fortify the image of good-natured thug.

This is my first time to be aware of someone traveling with a bodyguard, and I feel the flesh stir on the back of my neck. I bypass them carefully and listen as a tall, Hollywood-handsome man with a gold chain as big as a rapper's on one arm and a tastefully hard, well-dressed blonde on the other discusses business in Hong Kong. "I'm in electronics." His conversation partner, an attractive, well-fed man of sixty-something, reports that he is "in toys." They discuss the merits of subcontracting everything to China these days because that is where the "price for labor is right, even though you don't have much control. You have to trust your people."

"Your people" refers to the re-emerging compradore class that profited as their countrymen and -women were impoverished by the Europeans and Americans during the nineteenth and early twentieth centuries—a fate that the Japanese avoided by their intense tribal loyalty. Of this phenomenon Reischauer writes: "When confronted by overwhelming Western economic and military power in the middle of the nineteenth century, no Japanese sought to make common cause with outsiders against their fellow Japanese for their own personal gain. Many of the leaders of other developing countries facing crises and disasters such as the Japanese experienced have built up huge personal fortunes abroad at the expense of their countrymen, but there is no case of a Japanese acting in this way."

This is one reason why, even submitted to the same unequal treaties as the Chinese—treaties which controlled tariffs and left the economy open and vulnerable to the inexpensive machine production of the West, Japan did not collapse as China had done. Further, the Japanese weren't terribly interested in foreign goods, especially opium (of which, more later), while a silk blight in Europe enabled them to sell silk for foreign exchange which financed their own development. The people of nineteenth-century Japan, unlike their Chinese counterparts, were able to maintain their cultural, political, economic, social, and legal integrity—a great accomplishment in the face of the might of the European and American onslaught. Japanese did not become rich while their countrymen and women sank into poverty, nor did they send their money to Swiss banks while their cities became putrid slums.

At the same time, the essentially feudal classes who industrialized Japan did not include the peasantry in the rising standard of living, and this is one reason why the Japanese army was unable to liberate other Asian people from European colonialism. The Asian linguist and scholar Owen Lattimore helped me understand this conundrum by pointing out, in his classic *Inner Asian Frontiers of China*, that in the 1930s and 1940s Japan was forced to keep the standard of living in Manchuria and southeast Asia "even lower than in Japan, because to raise the standard of living of the conquered people without raising that of rural Japan would create uncontrollable discontent among the peasants from whom the Japanese army was recruited and at the same time make impossible the only methods of exploiting Manchurian [and southeast Asian] resources that Japan's social organization allowed." Thus the people whom Japan conquered in World War II came to hate their Asian conquers as much as or more than they hated the Europeans.

Feudalism did not end in Japan until 1945, when the American occupation forced land reform on the feudal landlords who, already weakened by defeat and thoroughly discredited by their alliance with the militarists, had no alternative but to accept the will of their conquers. The Japanese people with whom I have discussed this consider land reform perhaps the most salutary result of the occupation, for it laid the foundation for popular democracy in Japan.

It is curious and rather depressing that land reform is something that only enemies can accomplish. If the American government had been able to convince the Nationalist government to reform the land tenure system of China, it is unlikely that the Communists would have been successful there. To this day, many states friendly to the United States government, e.g. the Philippines and all of central American except Costa Rica, continue to languish under systems of land tenure that make elections essentially meaningless. There is no meaningful democracy when people are hungry, and no one is free when they not only must vote, but must vote a certain way to stay alive.

The conclusion of the conversation on which I'm eavesdropping is that although the Cantonese Chinese do not have the solid skill and work ethic of the Hong Kong Chinese, "they are learning."

When the plane is ready to board, we shuffle along the passageway, the businessmen to their first-class cabin and me to the economy crush. The flight is uneventful, which as far as I'm concerned is the only way to fly. The last thing I want is an exciting flight. All announcements are in three languages, Japanese, Cantonese, and English, and there is a Mandarin-speaking attendant aboard for anyone who might need help in the official language of mainland China and Taiwan.

Chapter 3

China: Hong Kong's expatriates as colonialism ends

> «*The anxieties of those who own china.*»
> —Virginia Woolf

Still December 4, 10:00 P.M.

Riding in the dark through Hong Kong's narrow streets, I welcome its warm confusion into my tired body. If Tokyo's measured crowds surge and crest with a stately rhythm, Hong Kong Kong jitterbugs, to a tuneful pulse totally unlike the solemn Noh drummer of Japan.

The differences between the Cantonese people and the Japanese are created, in part at least, by geography. Hong Kong, on the Tropic of Cancer, borders the tropics, and even in winter people wear soft, loose clothing that flows and flaps about their bodies as, relaxed and rambunctious, they prance through the gaudy streets. In contrast, the Japanese of Tokyo wear tailored suits and structured garments reminiscent of kimonos, and they saunter and stand about in loose flocks, often surrounding someone who holds an elevated position in the omnipresent hierarchy and to whom everyone bows to the precise depth required by the recipient's rank. I've left Tokyo's sharp delineations for Hong Kong's fuzzy abundance, which spills over the city making a pungent and friendly mess.

Hong Kong is the city that opium built. The British, in 1841 and again in 1848, sailed warships half way around the world to persuade the Chinese to buy their opium. British traders, who wanted to purchase tea without paying for it in precious silver and gold, had decided that, since opium was easily grown in their nearby colonies of Burma and India, compelling the Chinese to buy opium was the perfect solution to a difficult cash flow problem. The Opium Wars are analogous to the Mendelian cartel fighting, and winning, a war to force the United States government to accept the importation of cocaine.

The Chinese, earlier and far more completely than the Japanese, lost control of their borders, which is the same as saying that they lost the defining attribute of national identity: their sovereignty. Since Admiral Perry came to Japan with one third of the American Navy, the relatively benevolent "opening of Japan" we study in school was more like the wolf's opening of the little pig's house of sticks. Perry sat offshore with his great guns and chanted the equivalent of "Little pig, little pig, let me come in or I'll huff and I'll puff and I'll blow your house in!"

Japan's rulers, when presented with such an ultimatum, opened the door. However, because they were unified in their opposition to the unequal treaties they had signed at gun point, they were able to get rid of the foreigners far earlier than the Chinese, various factions of whom cooperated with the Europeans and profited from the impoverishment and addiction of their countrymen and -women. China retained its formal sovereignty only because the European powers, unable to agree on how to parcel out the vast territory among themselves, decided it was best to maintain the weak central power of the Manchu dynasty.

For many years the British controlled Chinese import customs—always a major signifier of sovereignty and, before the income tax, a main sources of revenue for all governments—in order to guarantee the collection of the numerous large indemnities the European powers extracted from the Chinese for various malfeasances against foreigners and their commerce. British coercion of the Chinese to accept the opium trade is just one of many examples of the Chinese government's failure to maintain its integrity and protect the people from suffering caused by foreign intrusion.

In 1839, the Chinese Emperor sent Lin Ze Xu as Imperial High Commissioner of the Court of Heaven—nowadays we would call him a drug czar—to Guangzhou (Canton) to stop the flow of opium into the country. Mr. Lin, intent on his job, confiscated 20,000 chests of opium from the British warehouses and threw them into the sea. In retaliation for this act of national self-preservation, British troops and gunboats shot their way up the Pearl River and forced the Chinese to accept the opium trade or be blown to bits by the big guns. Because the Chinese were such recalcitrant consumers of the poison that was wrecking their already weak society, this engagement, brazenly called the First Opium War, was repeated several years later as the Second Opium War. After British troops and warships had made China safe for opium, the opium dealers set up shop on Hong Kong, a sparsely inhabited island in the Pearl River estuary blessed with a supply of fresh water and forcibly leased from the Chinese in perpetuity.

Hong Kong remains Chinese, however, and the British occupation has, like the omnipresent MSG in the food, served to enhance the Chinese flavor of Hong Kong by preserving traditions that have disappeared in the wars and revolutions of the mainland. Hong Kong Chinese continue to observe the traditional lunar New Year, which has been demoted to a spring festival on the mainland, and maintain their local shrines and temples, many containing the colorful Taoist altars where for centuries the inhabitants of the Pearl River delta and the myriad islands of the estuary have prayed to Tien Hou, goddess of the sea.

The dragon boat festival in Hong Kong draws competitors from all over Southeast Asia, who gather to honor a variety of dragons, ancient water deities whom humans must propitiate to prevent their incarceration of sailors within their underwater castles. Over two thousand years ago, when they were still the southern barbarians, the present-day Cantonese and Fukienese were seafaring people, some of whom still resist the colonial government as it tries to force them from their houseboats.

To this day the great mercantile houses like Jardine Matheson, who made their original fortunes in opium. continue to dominate Hong Kong's economic life. (And some among the elders try to tell us that crime doesn't pay!) Similar to the present-day urban ghettos in the United States, China in the middle of the 19th century was a demoralized land filled with hopeless people who used chemical substances as self-medication to ease their suffering. The history and background of the two countries is totally different, and yet their people's recourse to chemical solutions for problems of pain and hopelessness is agonizingly similar. The lesson seems to be that when political and economic systems render people helpless and hopeless of practical solutions to their misery, they will— regardless of the desires and demands of the authorities— seek, and find, chemical relief. Perhaps, given the circumstances, it is an adaptive response to a life void of pleasure—an application of the entirely human tendency to "gather ye rosebuds while ye may." In the case of mid-19th century China, the British were eager to supply the noxious rosebuds regardless of the ultimate consequences for the Chinese people and government.

The role of mood- and mind-altering chemicals in allowing societies to continue amidst unfathomed popular misery is still not recognized by historians or medical people, let alone politicians who, as the British example demonstrates, often cooperate with the dealers and make money from the cycle of despair and dependency. Tobacco and alcohol play a similar role in nearly all industrialized countries. People use mood-altering substances to continue functioning in unfulfilled lives, and these substances are often toxic. Men in present-day Japan and China furiously suck on cigarettes as they move en masse through the huge maze of their modern economic systems, and a common sight in Tokyo's train and subway stations is the splash of somebody's undigested noodles—an after-drink snack refused by an overburdened stomach.

Mind-altering chemicals serve among other uses to comfort individual human beings floundering in the gloom and boredom created by industrialization and the inhuman uses of human beings that the traditional design of industrial processes require. While not necessarily the best solution, it is clear that people will use chemicals to alter their experience so long as, for whatever reasons— ignorance, economic necessity, political powerlessness, "and so on" (to quote Kurt Vonnegut)—they are denied more life-enhancing choices.

Modern Hong Kong is a reformed opium dealer who has gone on to legal and more constructive forms of business activity.

Thursday, December 5, 7:00 p.m.

Doing Tai Chi on the quay in Kowloon, I look over an immense expanse of sky and water accented by a shiny sweep of skyscrapers. Gray clouds glower over the pale pink dawn; the dark water, in which a few boats have begun to move, sloshes in the narrow channel between Hong Kong island and Kowloon, which is on the Asian mainland. Cranes on large flat barges lumber through the strait on their way to the ships moored among the small outer islands, waiting to be unloaded and reloaded in this major center for the transshipping of goods in and out of both China and the other countries of southeast Asia.

It's a gateway, this Asian colony of the British, and just as Tokyo opens into an Americanized sphere of Asia, Hong Kong opens into a district mapped by the U.K. Nevertheless, both Hong Kong and Japan retain their local character, and the foreign influence is just enough to provide the transition zone that allows me tentatively to step through the door without totally loosing orientation and going into a free fall. I come to Asia, like an initiate in a secret society, going through progressive gates of esoterica in my quest for deeper understanding of communities that have become my neighbor after centuries of being the ultimate Other.

Moving through the Tai Chi set, I watch the light come up on the Hong Kong skyline, miles of variation on the theme of window walls. The latest totem of power is the Bank of China building, whose I.M. Pei geometries rise like a bright knife against the charcoal green slopes of the hilly island. The local people say the building is an attempt to destroy the favorable Feng Shui—literally wind and water, the earth forces—of the island, and it conspicuously dominates the skyline, making the other high-rises, each impressive in its own right, seem insignificant in its presence. As I continue my practice, the strait gradually fills with boats of every size and design, from rowboats and classic Chinese junks sheltering families whose drying laundry flaps in the wind, to a dingy cruise ship slipping out to sea on its way to Shanghai. A British warship lies at anchor across the strait at the Admiralty pier, confirming the last remnant of a once formidable Asian empire that is passing into history.

I find it impossible to resist Hong Kong's allure. The most unabashedly and ostentatiously wealthy city in the world, it is a place where visiting Europeans and Americans get to pretend they're rich. The beautiful natural setting combines with the British traditions of elegant service to create an atmosphere of affordable luxury. Being in Hong Kong is like winning at "Queen for a Day," a game that most people are only too eager to play.

No exception, I sit in the Regent Hotel's coffee shop in my Tai Chi clothes, acting out my version of the wealthy American—too eccentric to conform, too rich to care. I read my newspaper while gracious people call me "Madam" and place plates of delicious food before me. I read nonchalantly and pour thick cream into the rich, dark coffee endlessly poured into my cup by slender young men of impeccable poise. With Hong Kong as a backdrop, I watch walkers and joggers from every continent move along the quay. In the water below, I notice two men fishing with a drop line from a small boat which they skillfully maneuver around the pilings with a single stern oar. They pull up a basket containing two or three red and blue crabs, forcing me to remember that I'm in China surrounded by Chinese people quietly living their lives while the foreigners bounce gently on the surface like people riding a tolerant river on a big rubber raft.

Gradually the restaurant fills with men arrayed for the business rituals of the coming day, their costumes as elaborate and rigidly proscribed as those of an aboriginal group preparing to welcome the sun's return at winter solstice. Like the other major patriarchal ceremonies of war and sports, business is something that, traditionally, men do; and it is business that drives Hong Kong's frenzy. I sit and watch as early morning evolves into the work day, its pace transformed by the busy-ness of business as though someone had pushed the fast forward button. When I walk out onto the street, cars fly by and pedestrians step aggressively into the street against the light. Another day of the great game of chicken begins.

I do my bit of business before the polluted air and manic rhythms of the city became frantic and unfriendly. I find a dress for my daughter-in-law Kathleen for $89HK and a blouse for me for $39HK. At HK$7.9 to US$1, these are bargains which quickly satisfy my shopping impulse. For lunch I meet Barry, my Hong Kong Gestalt partner, in the new YMCA dining room, a cool air-conditioned bowl which wraps us in the dingy yellow glow of a sunless sky.

Barry and I discuss our upcoming workshop in Taiwan. Barry is a Hong Kong Chinese whom I met six years ago in San Francisco when he came to the Gestalt Institute for training. We have been working together for three years, since 1989 when I came from China to join him in a residential workshop on the Queen's birthday in June shortly after the massacre in Tienanmen Square. This year we're going to Taiwan for the first time, and we're both suspicious of Harold Tse, who has invited us there. Barry thinks Harold has lied to us about the budget for the groups, that he changes the numbers to suit his own needs, which invariably seem to consist of giving us as little as possible and keeping mysteriously unaccounted-for amounts himself. So far Harold's mathematics have created a series of hassles, the latest of which resulted in a threat to cancel Barry's participation in the workshop.

Harold wants to renege on his agreement to pay a translator from Hong Kong who would translate for Barry from Cantonese to what Americans call Mandarin—truly an anachronistic name for the national Chinese language, called "Chinese" in Taiwan, *Gwokyu* (National Language) in Hong Kong, and *Putongwa* (Common Language) in the People's Republic, and which is a variation of the Beijing dialect imposed upon the people of China by the government.

Perhaps "Mandarin" expresses as well as any single word the exact nature of this language which is taught to millions of children in schools throughout China. At home, except in Beijing, these same children speak a variety of local dialects which are sufficiently different from the national language that an interpreter is required for clear communication. The people who, to many in the United States, all look alike and speak a language called Chinese actually speak a variety of dialects that are so different that one may designate them branches of a family of Chinese languages, just as French, Spanish, Italian, and Rumanian are call Romance languages from their common Latin. The enormous complexities of China emerge in this narrative, and I often find myself wondering if there really is such a place. Often the word, "China," seems to obscure more than it illuminates because the vastness and variety of the entity it pretends to disclose refuse to be enclosed within a single word.

Among Euro-Americans there are two prevailing attitudes toward China. The first exists among those who have never been closer to China than their grandmother's china cabinet or perhaps a foray into one of the Chinatowns in large American cities. They associate China mainly with dishes, both the ceramic cups and plates and the food enclosed therein. The other, and much smaller group, are those who have had direct experience with the wide-ranging geographies, human beings, and historical events subsumed under the word "China." Members of the latter group tend to greet one another with sighs and grimaces accompanied by strange jerks and head noddings as soon as they have identified one another as among those who have "been there," and most especially those who have "done business there."

Among this latter group there tends to be an instant bonding like that among survivors of a fierce storm or an earthquake— which, in many ways, is what present-day China most resembles. I say "present-day" deliberately; for modern China, still in the birth canal, has not yet arrived into our view. The difficulties the Chinese people face in recreating their social, political, economic, and psychological organization after five thousand years of recorded absolutism are probably incomprehensible to outsiders, and nearly so to the vast majority of the Chinese themselves. It is a task of human reconstruction on a scale no one, except perhaps the great spiritual teachers like Jesus and Shakyamuni, has even dared to imagine.

As Barry and I discuss our coming work in Taiwan, I feel slightly queasy. I strongly suspect that Harold is another of the New Age schemers that I had finally learned to recognize and avoid in America. If he's a liar—and it's likely he is, all my denial notwithstanding—the coming workshop will be an ordeal. Since Harold threatened to drop Barry from the program without consulting me, I realize that he's not very smart. I have already faxed him that the option of my coming alone does not exist. Since I've committed myself to going with Barry and Carol, the disputed translator, I'm willing to see the plan through, but I would never consider going without them. I'm willing to check my fantasy about Harold against the reality of working with him—a behavior that Shirley Luthman, one of my teachers, defined as sanity. In addition to the challenge of running a good group, we will have the additional task of preventing Harold from cheating us. My heart pounds lightly as we talk, and I see Barry licking his lips as though anticipating the challenge.

After lunch, I wander the streets of Hong Kong, where, especially in North Point and Yau Ma Tei where the tourists rarely go, I loosen my hold on identity and become Chinese. I love the vibrant street life of these neighborhoods, where bins full of dark, earthy substances spill from the stores over the sidewalk and into the street. I recognize the puffy brown mushrooms and small red beans which the Japanese call azuki, but a wild variety of sticks and stems and pods remain silently unnamed; pure essences of exotic pungency, they fill my senses with mystery and delight. Everything is edible, and I am confident that under the practiced kung fu of a good cook (in China cooks, too, can have kung fu) all are delicious. My stomach and taste buds, true international chameleons who blend with relish into whatever culinary environment I take them, tremble with excitement. Eating in Hong Kong, especially if one is lucky enough to do it with Chinese friends, is a justly famous sensual delight.

I continue down the street under a ceiling of brushes and baskets, past a sheet metal shop emitting the dry, hard smell of solder. A line of stalls filled with clothing and shoes falls off to my left behind a store featuring damp, slippery mounds of pink, gray, and green fish. A tub of turtles rests beside my foot and a pile of fish eyes stare at me, seeming to return my wonder. Could fish eyes ever be good to eat? My imagination pants and strains as I try to include them in my list of acceptable edibles. Threading my way among a group of small tables scattered in the street, I decide to stop for a bowl of *tong mein*, soup noodles; since I know how to pronounce their name, I order with at least a semblance of confidence.

I recall the first time Lawrence and I went to China. Eager to avoid the other tourists, we stayed in a Chinese hotel in Guangzhou, where, for the first time, I encountered a real Chinese menu—the kind that doesn't have English words written under the characters. We nearly starved to death on a steady diet of sweet and sour pork, which everyone seemed to think we wanted whether we ordered it or not. Once we managed to get a plate of chicken whose bony, meatless body filled us with dismay and anger at what we perceived to be an insult, until we realized that this was probably a normal Chinese chicken. There are many ways to be spoiled, and expecting all chickens to be plump is one of them.

Since this adventure took place in 1983, before the economic reforms, there was almost no food for sale on the street. When we did find a bag of pistachios, we grabbed it and rushed to the hotel in a frenzy of expectation, only to discover that they were unroasted and inedible. After three days of this silliness, I ordered a cab and we went to the White Swan Hotel, one of the biggest and best of tourist hotels, where, greatly humbled, we reveled in the spacious dinning room and readable menu.

It has taken a while to feel comfortable eating in the small Chinese restaurants and street stalls of Hong Kong, and each time I do it I feel the satisfaction of small accomplishment. This time the noodles are great, the street a pleasure, and the effort a success.

Friday, December 6, 7:00 a.m.

Relishing my elegant Regency breakfast, I read in the newspaper about 42 kilos of "ice" (methamphetamine crack) found in the Philippines on its way from Hong Kong. The traffic in mood-altering chemicals continues even when much else has changed. In a materialistic society, many must think the distinction between trading in illegal substances and legal ones a pointless one. So long as making money is the prime value and the value of certain substances is enhanced by their declared illegality, there will be prominent people and institutions with vested interests in making and keeping basically worthless substances illegal and, thus, increasing their value.

Rich people telling poor people that there are values more important than money is just not credible. The only people who with credibility and good conscience can say that there are more important things than wealth are the voluntarily poor, who number precious few and who are amazingly quiet when it comes to telling other people how they should live their lives.

Certain people and organizations make a great deal of money on the production, transportation, and marketing of mood-altering chemicals. Some historians have estimated that in the 1850s opium accounted for nearly fifty per cent of the total value of world trade—a stunning figure when one considers that most of this wealth was extracted from a supposedly poor China. If it wasn't poor before the opium trade began, it surely was so by the time the British and the Americans agreed to stop it in 1913.

While there are no accurate estimates of the value of the trade in mood-altering chemicals today, the amount is enormous, especially when tobacco and alcohol are included. The legality of some chemicals and not others tends to emphasize that it is not the mood-changing aspect that is worrisome to national entities so much as the issue of who makes the money on the transactions. While it is acceptable for Seagrams or Philip Morris to profit from mood-altering chemicals, it is unacceptable for the Cali cartel or various Mexican and California producers and distributors to do the same.

Decriminalizing a heretofore illegal substance is a way to wipe out a great deal of wealth, which is probably one reason it is rarely done. I remember reading that by the time Prohibition ended in the United States, the only people in favor of it were the bootleggers and the ministers—the people who made money from it.

Drinking my fourth cup of coffee—another popular and forever legal mood-altering substance, fortunately the "drug" of choice of the

Arabs, presently the richest people in the world— I read another story of smugglers. Smuggling, which probably arrived in human history at the exact instant boundaries were drawn and custom offices established, remains a popular and lucrative activity with many ties, official and unofficial, to big business and big government. This time the smugglers are the "good guys" who helped the young student rebels escape from China after Tienanmen. Ethics in Hong Kong seem to be refracted by mirrors reflecting mirrors, just like Bruce Lee in "Enter the Dragon." Surely it's no accident that the first Chinese artifacts found in Japan were mirrors of polished bronze.

After breakfast, I catch the grungy green Star Ferry for Hong Kong. The ride across is bright and breezy, a sweet moment in the open air before I go to the counseling center where I will work from nine to five.

SAME DAY, 9:00 A.M.

It's the joy of my work that I am privileged to encounter the poetry of people's feelings, and I am aware of this good fortune as I enter the nearly empty group room where I wait while people gather. All the members of this group are counselors and expatriates. Four of the eight are people I have worked with before, and it is good to see familiar faces. New faces are fun, too. Some of both are best, like the song we used to sing at Girl Scout camp:

Make new friends, but keep the old
One is silver and the other gold.

Since everyone speaks English, there is no translator present. I begin with the usual request: "Introduce yourself. Say what you are feeling right now and what you want from the group." During this round Dan, who is Canadian, tells how he had gained enough awareness from his work in the previous group that he could meet his brother in a new and more satisfying way. Beth, too, reports that she had changed as a result of work we did. It is relatively rare for me to hear concrete news of how people have used their increased awareness to change their lives. Usually I see the changes in a face, a demeanor, a new level of grace or liveliness—observable change that is hard to feign. It's good to hear the words sometimes, and I feel gratified and grateful as I listen.

I also learn that two people have had no experience with Gestalt. I observe with interest my own lessening loyalty to Gestalt as a label. I quote Laura Perls, who said, "Gestalt is anything that is existential and experiential," before I say a few sentences about awareness in the here and now.

"Only the present provides orientation. This means literally that it's only in the present that I know which end's up. Since past and future are fantasies, I can make anything happen there. In fantasy I can float to the ceiling or drop through the floor; I can go to Jupiter, or kill my father; but it is only in the present that I have power to see, to move, and to do."

Such simple reminders can sometimes be a compelling realization for someone who has never before envisioned the amazing and simple fact that each one must live her or his life in the present moment or not live at all. I add that in order to be true to the spirit of Gestalt, I have to practice it rather than talk about it and, therefore, I prefer to answer questions about theory and method after we have worked. I notice that while people often express an interest in theory at the beginning of a workshop, they soon lose interest as they become involved in the ongoing process of life unfolding in the moment—which is, of course, far more interesting and engaging than talking about theory. Once the group begins, the poetry and power of feeling and sensation take over and most people lose interest in explanations.

Uma comes forward to work. Her first sentence is, "I write many letters and don't mail them." When I ask her to put herself on the pillow, she asks herself why she didn't mail the letters, and then, on the verge of tears, she answers, "No one wants to hear what I have to say." She immediately becomes aware that it is her father's voice that insists that what she has to say is worthless.

It often happens that as a person develops the dialogue between internally split parts of the self, the demanding, commanding, and sometimes cruel side of the dialogue is recognized as a parental voice.

In Uma's work this happens as soon as she says," No one wants to hear what I have to say." As she struggles to control her feelings, I ask her how she is stopping herself. Again she remembers her father's words: "It's weak to cry. You must be strong, Never show your tears." Coming in a whispered voice from her tear-swollen face, these demands sound woefully absurd, and the violence they have inflicted is obvious—most likely violence that stretches through the generations: as the father did to his daughter, his father surely did to him.

Behavior to children, which is rarely chosen with awareness, is the last link in a long chain that rattles through the generations, imprisoning each of us as we learn often absurdly anachronistic parenting behaviors and imagine them to be natural. The parenting role, with its "ancestral voices prophesying war," is the most unaware and archaic role most of us will ever play, for this voice speaks through ancient masks which cover the scars of wounds inflicted so long ago that many imagine that they represent unchangeable aspects of human existence. Guided by Maria Montessori and Benjamin Spock, who advocated trust in and respect for the immature human being and its innate evolutionary wisdom, we are just beginning to question ancient and unaware parenting behaviors. By leading the way to a more gentle and considerate way of teaching children, Montessori and Spock are benefactors of the human spirit; and just as the Japanese designate certain people as living national treasures, I nominate both of them as planetary human treasures.

When Uma changes from her father's seat, she remembers being ten years old and attending her sister's wedding. Her twenty-year-old sister had been an important caretaker in her childhood, and when she married and left home, Uma had been bereft. When he saw her weeping at the wedding, her father told her not to cry. As she tells this story, she begins to cry. When I suggest she talk to her sister, she does and, after twenty years, expresses her long-held grief at her sister's leaving, a grief that has been sitting inside her like huge rubber stopper, containing and restricting her emotional expression ever since. Uma, an Indian woman, expresses her grief with a soft voice and gentle gestures.

I am uncertain whether she has expressed enough to allow completion of this sorrow. However, after she has told her sister how much she hated to see her leave, she expresses relief, and I can see an easing of her face and body. When she returns to her seat, she says, "Now I can write about more than just the weather and other superficial things."

At the end of her work, which lasted no longer than twenty minutes, Uma exclaims, "Oh, it's over so fast. I imagined sitting here all afternoon while everyone got bored and tired of me."

I laugh and say, "That was your catastrophic fantasy." When others laugh, too, I tell them of the time when, in a moment of love and appreciation, I squeezed Fritz Perls's hand and said, "You know, Fritz, the best thing about you is that you're right." He, of course, loved my acknowledgment, and we laughed together. I still think so. Fritz was right about many things, and the catastrophic fantasy is one of them. Imagining terrible outcomes is an important way people stop themselves from doing what they want to do. The human events that Fritz and Laura described and discussed occur, and from their observations they created an open-ended system, a fluid gestalt process, that is not easily turned into dogma and instead remains a path, a way of discovery and a precious gift for understanding. They, too, were living planetary treasures.

The Perlses called their method—and I believe that Gestalt is a method, for the existential and phenomenological underpinning was created by others—Gestalt Therapy. Although "therapy" has come to have a slightly derogatory connotation, I think it's applicable because, especially since the Industrial Revolution, human beings have inflicted and continue to inflict severe pain and injury on each other. We need the healing which therapy implies and which the Gestalt approach promotes and facilitates.

Werner Heisenberg, the German philosopher who by insisting that the observer becomes part of what she or he observes demolished the myth of objectivity, also wrote that "method and object can no longer be separated." By creating a new method one might hypothesize that the Perlses initiated the creation of new people. Gestalt is radically different from traditional Euro-American forms of healing in that the healing process is demystified and the personal power of the injured person is explicitly evoked as the client becomes both the healer and the healed.

When I recently told my son's roommate about my work, he turned to Lawrence and said, "Your mother is a shaman." Of course, we laughed. I think, however, that he was responding to Gestalt's holistic view of the world—its view of the world as an integrated and living entity within which human beings abide and participate. This worldview differs significantly from the mechanistic and manipulative notions which created the industrial revolution and are reinforced by its success. The Perlses insisted that "organismic self-regulation" maintains the life and health of all forms of life. Our healing task is to learn how we interfere with our own natural processes. Just as a river will cleanse itself once pollution stops, human being heal themselves once they stop their damaging behaviors.

In Uma's work I am impressed once again with how the avoidance of past feelings drains energy and diminishes awareness. The terrible burden of depression, denial, and numbness that unexpressed feelings impose on every waking moment creates fear and avoidance of sleep as well. Repression and avoidance allow what I am avoiding to run my life, turning it into a big "No, I won't," rather than Molly Bloom's joyful, "Yes I will Yes," with which James Joyce ended Ulysses.

Writing this, I recall the work I once did with Jim Simkin at the Esalen Institute. I had been walking with my friend, Tony Rey, enjoying Esalen's beautiful paths and exquisite views, and I entered the group filled with gratitude for the beauty of the Earth and the kind acceptance of Tony's friendship. I came to what Fritz and Jim called the "hot seat" (a term then much in vogue, and, I believe, a symbol of the unconscious sadism that Fritz brought to Gestalt and that many students gleefully perpetrated as part of a Gestalt assault that continued long after Fritz died; adopted by people far less intelligent and skilled than Fritz, this aggressive and confrontational way of working has been damaging to the teaching and learning of Gestalt in the United States). I sat in front of Jim and said, "I'm already working." I was crying at the time, flooded with feelings that I didn't understand; then, remembering Ulysses, which I had read recently, I expressed my appreciation for that book which is (among other things) about saying "Yes." Ulysses ends with the sixty-page sentence of Molly's soliloquy, which concludes: "...then I asked him with my eyes to ask again yes and then he asked me would I yes to say yes my mountain flower and first I put my arms around him yes and drew him down to me so he could feel my breasts all perfume yes and his heart was going like mad and yes I said yes I will Yes."

Ulysses is a monument to saying yes, and, sitting in front of Jim filled with the grandeur of Joyce's affirmation, I took a deep breath and further understood that I could say yes to saying no—that "yes I will Yes" does not preclude saying no, but rather includes "no I won't No," not only for myself but for others as well. It was a revelation to me: that I could say yes to saying no; that acceptance, understanding, and affirmation included everything, even negativity, ignorance, and denial. It was my first tentative step beyond duality into the unity of acceptance.

At the end of Uma's work, Madhuri shares a conversation she recently had with her daughter. Her daughter misses her brother, who is studying in England, and wants him to come home for Christmas. The family can't afford his trip, and since he also had a heavy exam schedule, he won't be returning at all this year. Madhuri is aware of feeling so uncomfortable with her daughter's unhappiness that she tried to talk her out of her feelings, saying, "Oh, it's not so bad. He'll be home soon." As she tells this, she begins to feel her own sorrow at her son's absence and becomes aware that her daughter's plea had made it more difficult for her to deny her own feelings. She had dismissed and minimized her daughter's feelings and desires as a way of avoiding her own.

Parents who deny their feelings will insist that their children deny theirs, too. The parental discomfort in feeling emotions for which they have inadequate internal support leads them to say things like, "Don't cry," "It's not so bad," and "Don't make such a fuss," thus stilling the voice of the organism and perpetuating the chains of denial into another generation. It's difficult to remain present with one's helplessness to ease the suffering of children. When the child expresses her or his pain, the parent is likely to suffer as well, and often will try to suppress the child as a way of protecting herself. Madhuri saw this in Uma's work when the father's harshness was revealed to be related to his own denied grief at his daughter's leaving home.

Next Dan tells of taking his son to Canada for college. As the time came to say good-bye, he says, he felt himself freezing inside. Because he wouldn't express his love and sadness on leaving his son, he withdrew more each day and began having fantasies of dying on the return flight without his son's ever knowing how much he loved him. Dan says that even at the time he knew that if he would express himself, he and his son could experience comfort in joining and sharing their mutual grief instead of the alienation accompanying denied feelings.

Deep primal feelings like grief are among the ways that human beings are most profoundly alike, and sharing them creates comfort in the powerful bonding that reaffirms our communality and connection. The powerful public ritual of grief that Americans shared at the time of John Kennedy's death is a good example of this.

On their last day together, Dan was able to overcome his inner message that men don't cry and tell his son of his love and sadness at leaving. He cries as he tells this—unfinished grief, a process of loss still healing. It's grief that heals the wound of loss and allows new connection. Deadened grief, which is a way of hanging on to the past, guarantees loneliness in the present.

Beth, whose former home is the United Kingdom, comes forward, her face puffy with unshed tears and her cheeks, jaws, and neck rigid with the effort of holding and clenching. She leaps toward me as she sits down and announces she has a terrible headache. Imagining how I might feel if I were holding on as tightly as she is, I'm not at all surprised, and I suggest she pay attention to what she's doing with her face and neck. Ignoring me, she begins to tell how she dreads the arrival of her ten-year-old son from boarding school in England. Speaking to him on the pillow, she expresses fear that he might be changed after being in England for a term. I can see that sending their children abroad to be educated is one of the tolls people pay for the relative luxury of expatriate life in Hong Kong—a hidden cost of empire that never shows up on any balance sheet.

I have her be her son and respond. In his role, resentment at parental anger comes up, and she begins to talk as the child who is bullied by the parent's anger. I remember from our last work that Beth is a person who in response to stress in her original home learned to make contact and create intimacy by fighting. We do unto our children as has been done to us, and our hurt children speak with the voice of our own pain. Without awareness, each person becomes both the abuser and the abused.

I ask Beth to be herself as a child and she begins to fight back energetically, clearly enlivened and vitalized by the fighting which had been her way to stand up to a tyrannical father. She says, "I'm set against you," and "I'm steeling myself against you." These remarks fit perfectly with the rigid posture I observed at the beginning of her work, and demonstrate clearly how her angry unwillingness to bend served her well in maintaining some degree of personal integrity in what must have been a very intrusive and disrespectful home.

After each of these angry outbursts, she subsides into a collapsed, dejected posture, bowing her head and supporting it with her left hand. Beyond a sense of generalized dissatisfaction, she is unaware of the feelings that go with this posture. She repeats the cycle of angry contact and collapsed withdrawal. I don't know the content of her withdrawal although it looks depressive, and I remember Laura Perls's words, "Depression is the opposite of Expression." I don't know what Beth is depressing, although I imagine it is sorrow still too threatening and dangerous to touch. Her angry, fighting self is all she is willing to share, and this work makes her choice dramatically explicit.

Gradually she relaxes and, after a while, looks at me and criticizes her angry way of interacting. When I say, "Anger is okay. It's only a problem when it's the only choice," she continues her self-criticism as though I had never spoken. I interrupt and point out what she has just done. At that moment she seems to snap out of her trance of repetition and hear me for an instant. I repeat, "Anger is okay. Anger is natural. Anger is better than being destroyed by overwhelming force coming from outside, and anger was obviously tolerated in your home." I do my best to facilitate her seeing and respecting the childhood choices she had made. The missing part of this work is hidden in the collapsed posture—sorrow and perhaps despair, emotions which for the present she lacks adequate support to contact. When she returns to her seat, she is far more connected with the group than when she began and she says her headache is gone. It's another step. Awareness and growth will not happen all at once; each bit of denied vitality must be reclaimed and integrated to create support for the next step.

By now it is obvious that Gestalt work is an interaction between two people, one of whom is pledged to remain present and to facilitate or ease the awareness of the other. Many people, once they clear a space from the clutter of the chattering demands of their inner voice, the so-called thinking process, can follow the continuum of their own awareness, at least until they reach the fence posted, "Stop! Do not enter here." The facilitator's job is to ease and encourage the client's experience of the fence and to explore how she is creating it and what purpose it serves in her life. It is only after a person becomes aware of how they are creating barriers to awareness that they can begin to experiment with de-structuring these obstacles whose original creation was an important achievement of survival and growth. Sometimes, as in Uma's work, the barrier is discrete and dramatic; in other cases, as in Madhuri's work, it is built of hundreds or thousands tiny demands not easily or succinctly expressed.

The work of the client—and the client has to do the greatest part of the work—is to remain present with her feelings. When she tries to avoid a feeling, she can still remain aware of the process, the how, of avoidance. From continual practice in being aware of how she stops her experience she will gain the ability to stop stopping, to refrain from the behaviors that avoid and deny her present experience. Since aware existence is intrinsically different from unaware experience, there is no need for a person to work in order to change. With awareness, something new will inevitable emerge—new sensations, new experience, new behavior. So long as an activity is unaware and automatic, a person has no choice and is, in essence, a slave to the past and to the choices that in their ignorance and weakness they made or allowed others to force upon them. These choices were, at the time, the best possible solutions, but, as time and circumstance change, have become problems themselves. I hear my former husband Larry Bloomberg's voice saying, "People don't have problems; they have solutions that no longer work," and I think of the drama of discovery that occurred with the collapse of communism, which many thought was the problem. Only then could we begin to see the enormity of the problems for which communism was a failed solution.

Gestalt work is a path to awareness and awareness allows choice. Freedom—despite the songwriter's depressed insistence that it's "just another word for nothing left to lose"—is really just another word for choice and freedom. In his essay "On Liberty," John Stuart Mill, discusses the other essential element of freedom—a range of alternatives from which to chose. Thus, freedom, perhaps the most human of all pleasures, is the ability to make aware choices from among significant alternatives. Alternatives seem to arise spontaneously as feeling is liberated, for the suppression of feeling inevitably suppresses both imagination and perception. With the liberation of perception and imagination comes awareness of a broader range of possibilities and the recognition that the old choice—the newly recognized fixed gestalt, previously a compulsive response driven by fear—is still available as one choice among many rather than as the only one.

The importance of variety from which to chose is a compelling argument for pluralism of ideas, of environments, of cultures, creeds, nationalities, species—the argument Mill makes so brilliantly in his essay. Awareness, pluralism, and diversity allow the meaningful choice which is freedom: the liberty which Patrick Henry wanted above all else, even life.

Back in the group, Rita presents a dream she dreamed long ago. The dream images had stayed with her and, in fact, had gained new significance from words she had recently heard from a psychologist who is working with a family crisis involving her daughter. She does not tell me what the crisis is, but says, "He told me to get on the boat." Before telling the dream, she says, "I want to get on the boat because I think I can be of more help to my daughter on the boat than in the water, where I am in the dream." This is the dream which I ask her to tell in the present tense in order to bring it into the present, to make it existential and experiential: I am swimming in the harbor from Yauh Ma Tai to Hong Kong. There is much debris in the water, and still I am swimming strongly and comfortably, from time to time pushing the debris away and clearing a path forward for myself. The Star Ferry passes me and I see many people on the boat. They seem to be having a good time although throughout the dream I have no desire to join them. I arrive at Hong Kong and walk up the steps on the dock and out of the water. Then I seem to be awake and I am walking hand in hand with my grandmother in the U.K. She takes me into a shop and buys me some polos. My parents have told me that my grandmother doesn't have much money and I shouldn't let her buy me things. Still the polos are so cheap that I think it's okay and I'm happy leaving the shop with my grandmother.

Rita says that this dream has always been memorable to her and that shortly after she dreamed it, she learned to swim, which was a source of pride for her. She emphasizes that learning to swim taught her to "breathe properly." She had always been content with the dream as it was until the psychologist, without knowing of the dream, told her she needed to get out of the water and into the boat—meaning, she thought, that she was too immersed in her daughter's problem to be helpful

I still don't know what the difficulty with the daughter is, and I don't ask, waiting for her to tell when and if she wants to. Beginning the work, I tell her to go back to the dream and put herself in the water. Closing her eyes, she does this.

As I write these words I am awed with the intensity of the human imagination and our almost magical ability to create situations which evoke a tangible and observable here-and-now response. One has only to attend a workshop such as this one to see the profound impact imagined events, aware and unaware, have on a person's present existence.

People tremble, cry, rage, and scream in response to the events their imaginations bring forward. The particular intensity to the imaginative recreation that I encourage comes from people's expressing live memories, pre-existing structures fixed within the body/mind by events of the past that remain unfinished. Incomplete experiences continue in the timeless realm of the psyche, awaiting an opportunity to emerge imaginatively in the present, where people have power to act and, therefore, to finish them. People create powerful changes in their experience by participating fully in events that emerge from the muscular, visceral, and neurological structures of the body/mind memory.

Imagining herself in the water, Rita says she feels fine and now wants to get on the boat. Working from the Gestalt premise that she is everyone in the dream, I ask her to change seats and be the people on the boat. She indicates the empty cushion (a big overstuffed one now that we're in Hong Kong), and says, "It makes me nervous."

I reply, "Okay, stay where you are and be the people on the boat." She says, "Now there's only one person on the boat. It's a woman. She's very sophisticated. I feel too intimidated to identify with her."

"Okay," I say. "You're in the water. What do you want to do?"

"I want to get on the boat."

"How are you going to do it?"

"I can't. I have a clear wall surrounding me. I can't get past it."

"Be the wall. 'I'm a clear wall.'"

"I'm a clear wall surrounding Rita. I protect her. She can see through me, but she can't get out."

Holding her face and body rigid, she says, "I can't get out." I notice she's contracting her shoulders and upper arms, and I direct her awareness to this behavior. She becomes aware of her tension at once and says, "I see the sun over my left shoulder, and it could dissolve the plastic wall."

"Be the sun and do it."

She allows the wall to melt into the water.

"It's gone."

"How are you going to get into the boat?"

"I can't climb in; it's too high. I need a ladder."

"How can you get a ladder?"

"The woman I know in the boat can give me one."

"Does she?"

"Yes; I'm in the boat now."

"What do you want to do?"

"I want another boat."

"Describe the boat you want."

"A speedboat. A white one that I can drive fast over the water and go wherever I want to go." She is smiling as she speaks.

"Do you have it now?"

"Yes, I'm more in control now. . . . No," she hesitates, "I have more freedom." Visibly softer and more relaxed, she opens her eyes. The dream is over.

She seems relieved and happy as she listens to people's response to her work. The other group members like this work. They respond to my lack of intrusion into Rita's process, to my following and facilitating. Sandra asks me if I know what polos are and I say, "No," feeling embarrassed because it's unusual for me to proceed without understanding what the person is saying. I stopped myself from asking by thinking that, since Rita had already said she wanted to get on the boat, I wasn't going to work on that part of the dream. Sandra (who is also English) tells me that polos is British English for life-savers, a lovely detail and one that perhaps it was just as well I didn't know. Fortunately Rita hadn't needed her grandmother's life-savers to help her get into the boat.

During the response to her work, Rita volunteers that her daughter was a victim of bullying at school, ijime Hong Kong-style. She feels utterly helpless in the face of her daughter's pain. The teacher's intervention had only worsened the situation, and most people advised against moving the 14-year-old girl to another school even though there was one nearby where a family friend was teaching.

Since childhood I have been the one who fights and runs away and lives to fight another day, a tendency reenforced by the philosophy of yielding in Tai Chi, and I encourage Rita to consider changing schools as a solution. Since she is taking responsibility, I suggest she trust her own intuition regarding a solution. She replies that she knows she will be more effective now that she has her own boat. I agree and encourage her to trust her experience.

As we try to navigate the tsunami of information—much of which is lies and disinformation—that pounds our weary rafts of judgment, we often feel adrift without valid criteria for discerning what is true. Since statistics is a process for manufacturing truth, statistical statements are vulnerable to manipulation. Flawed statistical studies (like the one that found women past 35 having a better chance of being struck by lightning than of marrying) remind us that while figures don't lie, liars figure. And their figures are published in supposedly reputable places. Anecdotal evidence is more experiential, and, when it comes from truthful people, is often more revealing of what is so. In some circumstances, learning to trust intuition becomes a possible way to manage the overabundance of material. Does it have the ring of truth? Has the source lied before? People who lie forfeit trust, and people who continue to believe proven liars are like children trying to make mommy and daddy right in order to maintain the illusion of safety in a dangerous world.

After we get Rita safely into her boat, we have lunch— wonderful box lunches of vegetable curry made by an Indian woman in her home and delivered to offices in Hong Kong's Central district. *Hou sihk!* (Cantonese for "Delicious!") After lunch Kate, who is Chinese, begins by saying her heart is pounding. When I ask her what her heart is saying, she says, "It's excited and ready to go on with it."

When I reply, "Okay, let's go," she withdraws and says, "Oh, I thought we were just making rounds."

"No, we've started. What do you want to do?"

She says she wants to work on her tendency to let others go first, to never allow herself to be the first or the best. When I point out to her that she had just done that very thing, she is unwilling to recognize what she has done. Seeing her reluctance, I encourage her to continue. She mentions her insecurity here at the counseling center, saying that there are more administrative tasks in her job than she had realized and she often feels incapable of doing the work. She appears to be holding her mouth and jaw rigid as she talks, and I direct her awareness to her face. After a few seconds, I ask her what her face is saying. She replies, "I'm not sure."

I feel stumped until I remember something I know and had for the moment forgotten: people answer the question. What a person says or does after the question is the answer to the question. A question is another way of directing awareness, and people respond. Sometimes they reject the first answer that comes to mind, and that too is an answer. It's my job to be present so that I may see and hear the answer to the question I have asked. What happens after the question is the answer, even when it is "I'm not sure" or "I don't know," a gesture, or even a frozen silence.

Fritz Perls answered questions with, "Turn the question into a statement," a response that many found frustrating. He rationalized his response by noting that implicit in every question is a hypothesis or statement, a bit of self that the person might own and integrate by making and taking responsibility for the statement that lies hidden in the question. Fritz, being more than a little paranoid, was sensitive to what he called the "bear trapper," the person who asks a question in order to dispute the answer.

I think this kind of question, the question seeking or pretending to seek information for what Fritz called the "computer, the whore of intelligence," is different from the questions I am discussing. Still, the principle applies, and Fritz, too, always answered the question. His answer, the one implicit in "Turn the question into a statement," was, "You already know the answer." I, too, almost invariably have a hypothesis when I ask a question; nevertheless, it is my job to encourage people to speak for themselves, to tell the truth of their own existence.

This time I catch my mistake quickly and point it out to the group so they can understand what I'm doing. We return to "I'm not sure," and when I ask Kate to say it again, it fits. Yes, her face is saying, "I'm not sure." She immediately adds, "I often don't know what I'm doing," another sentence expressing her sense of uncertainty and insecurity.

As she talks about her insecurity, I have a strong suspicion that she's angry. After a few moments, she says, "You reassured me too much," and smacks her hands against her legs. This is an expression of retroflected anger, and I ask her to put her hands on the pillow while she talks.

Hands are truthful. When people are encouraged to express with their hands, they usually do so in an immediate and personal way. I ask Kate to put her hands on the pillow so that her energy might flow more easily outward into aggression rather than backward in retroflection. She grabs the pillow, and when I ask her what she feels, she says, "The right hand is numb and weak, and the left hand is warm and strong."

The internal splits that people create to protect themselves are often expressed in differences between the right and left sides of the body, including the face. Most people notice this when they see the well-known crooked grin where one side of the face smiles and the other does not. Though some think it's cute, the crooked grin is, in fact, a statement of a lack of integration and likely to be a sign of evasion. We also use the descriptive idiom "talk out of both sides of the mouth," which indicates an awareness that the person who is split inside represents a menace to others. These splits, and they are myriad, are of the greatest significance, both personally and politically, because they are the expression of an internal war, one which the split person can never win, for she is both parties to the conflict as well as the battlefield on which the struggle takes place.

The Gestalt dialogue seeks integration of the splits rather than domination of one side or the other, for it is impossible to quash essential parts of one's self. The internal splitting explains the violent encounters among people: fascism, sexism, ethnic warfare, the Cold War, World Wars I and II, all wars since the beginning of history. Further, they answer James Baldwin's profound question, "Why do they need a nigger?" People need a nigger because they harbor a despised and disowned self within.

Most people, following the guidelines they were given in childhood, hate the attributes which their parents and teachers, peers and preachers insisted were dirty and bad. Since it is intolerable to accept the me they say is bad, I deny the despised attributes and imaginatively place them outside my boundaries where they become the "not-me," the other. The profound discomfort of living with the despised inner self requires one to objectify and externalize the rejected parts of the self in order to relieve some of the pressure and pain of the war within.

The outward objectification of the disowned, denied, and rejected parts of the self is projection, which is the psychological mechanism that creates the nigger, the whitey, the kike, etc. In the real world there are no such people; they are imaginary characters like the Easter bunny, and the people who believe in them are actually telling us about and their own inner conflict. People who hate, hate themselves first.

The process is universal, although far more harsh and violent in some families and groups than in others. A person like David Duke spends his entire life creating movements that allow him to project and denigrate his disowned self in the company of others who share his demons. It is all the life he has, for should he stop he would have to face his inner pain and anger: he would have to become another person, and he does not have the courage or support to do that. As Fritz reminded us, "To lose one's life and be born again is not easy." Until such a one is willing to give up the old way and take the existential leap into the abyss, all that remains is to hate and fear the projected self and join with the same desire in others.

Despite the social and political havoc it creates, projection is a tool for individual survival. Children disown themselves to avoid the despair of rejection and self-loathing. People hate their neighbors because it is an alternative to destroying themselves. They cannot be talked out of their hatred because the imaginary enemy is a stand-in for their own despised selves, and irrational feelings cannot be changed by rational arguments. As Andrea Dworkin observed, "Changes of attitude or opinions do not change systems of power fueled by hate."

These systems can be moderated by social disapproval; thus, anti-Semitism is less dangerous in a social system that condemns scapegoating than in one like Nazi Germany that encourages it. With gossip, law, and punishment, communities can discourage and limit behavior based on inner rage, but they cannot abolish it. Communities can protect people from themselves and each other by recognizing hate for the psychological solution it is, rather than validating it as the solution to a real problem. We need to speak out more about the reality of projection and the innocence of those the projectors force to take on the qualities and characteristics of their disowned selves.

The community can protect people from themselves by naming projected hatred, calling it mental illness, sin, immaturity, wrong headedness, or confusion, depending upon community standards. It's destructive to pretend that it is just a matter of opinion whether women are bitches and Jews run the world, for surely it is horribly damaging to one's spirit to be vindictive against innocent people who never did one any harm. To succeed as either punishment or release, revenge must be accurate and specific. Punishing groups doesn't work, nor does attacking the descendants of those who hurt your ancestors. The feelings of rage, misery, and desperation that drive people to hate crimes can only be changed by a gradual reintegration of the split, alienated, and horribly damaged self, first within itself and then with the world in which it has its being.

Perhaps men are more violent than women because their conditioning rejects expression of powerful elements of the instinctual self—especially the tender emotions of pain, sorrow, delicacy, despair, sensitivity, receptivity, and quiet. The traditional definers of manhood have judged these emotional states sissy and wimpy and ordered that they be crushed—often brutally and often before a boy is five. The refusal of patriarchy to accept men's tears—which expel toxins from the body and are as routinely useful as going to the toilet—deprives the organism of its natural expression of pain and sorrow and assures that boys and men will be unable to experience and express the pain that drives them unless they are willing to risk their male identity.

To the extent that gender identity is socially constructed rather than received with the DNA, both men and women are vulnerable to manipulation by those who wish to control them through rules of how they should be. Without tears boys can never become men, for without tears there is no way to finish childhood's unfinished business.

A cruel upbringing often creates a violent and dependent person who needs to join with others to feel any semblance of self-acceptance and who needs to hate, and perhaps to kill, to ward off the despised inner self. Of course, even this extreme behavior doesn't bring peace or satisfaction. The inner self—no matter how crushed, denied, battered, and abused—cannot be destroyed, and given the opportunity it will emerge from its own ashes and express the awesome pain it continues to experience until truthful expression is allowed. Then, and only then, will healing begin.

My goal in working with these splits is integration: there is no way one part of a person can win while another loses, no way to make part of the self garbage and throw it away— regardless of how desirable this solution may seem to some people. The illusion of domination exists in victory parades and lynchings, but it is a brief and unreal triumph that vanishes when the individuals leave the crowds and go to bed, where they must, once again, face themselves in the solitude of sleep. Chemical dependence, while it is a problem, might more accurately be described as the solution to the necessity of avoiding the miserable, disintegrated, and disowned self who stirs to life in natural sleep. Chemicals that induce sleep smother dreams, one of the vehicles the past uses to enter the lives of those who don't remember.

In Kate's work, I encourage a dialogue between the right and left hands. "What does the right hand say?"

"I'm cold and weak. I can't protect myself."

"The left?"

"I'm holding on. I'm strong and I'm holding on."

"What does the right hand want from the left hand?"

"Help me. I'm weak and can't protect myself."

Now she enters the dialogue and, speaking as the left hand, responds, "I can't help you. I'm so busy holding on I can't help you. I'm afraid to let go."

Writing this, I recognize that a good question might have been,

"What are you holding on to?" At the time, I directed her attention back to the man she had been talking to, the one she felt had encouraged her dependency by being too supportive.

She speaks to him. "I resent your making me dependent." Then she says to me, "I feel like I'm not taking responsibility by blaming him." Here's a New Age introjection, a recent rationalization for an old behavior. By telling herself "I should take responsibility for my feelings," she conveniently reinforces extremely Old Age rules forbidding women's anger, especially against men, and most especially against men in positions of authority.

Regarding responsibility, one can choose from among a wide range of attitudes, including that of Sir Edward Seymour, the commander of the relief expedition to Peking during the Boxer Rebellion, who once wrote, "I could never understand why anyone minds responsibility. You have only to do what seems proper, and if it turns out badly it is the fault of Nature for not having made you cleverer." Even if Kate finds Sir Edward's rather smug sense of responsibility unacceptable, she cannot achieve responsibility for her feelings by turning her desire to do so into a "should." "Should" is irrelevant; she either takes responsibility for what she does or she doesn't.

The process of shoulding is a distraction that does little more than generate good excuses for refusing responsibility, and it inevitably creates an inner dialogue similar to this one: "You should take responsibility." "I know I should, but..."

Taking responsibility is not something one "should do" but an effortless understanding that comes with awareness of one's freedom to choose. It is an existential event that occurs with the recognition of the luminously obvious fact that I do what I do. Prior to that time I can take responsibility as a discipline; this is, however, quite different from telling myself I should. I think the act of taking responsibility for what one does is one of the few times when will may be a useful tool for self-discovery. If I willingly take responsibility for my actions and attend to what happens next, I may be able to experience my existence in a more complete and integrated way.

By assuming a position where the desire to remain silent, regardless of how she may rationalize her choice, cancels her wish to express, Kate balances elegantly on the knife-edge of her impasse. Since she suffers when she continues the old (and now maladaptive) behavior and lacks adequate support to experiment with something new, she is stuck. I observe this in her frozen quietude as she sits before me—barely breathing, eyes fixed on the floor.

At a time like this, I encourage the person to move quickly back and forth between the polarities: in this case, "I resent..." and "I shouldn't resent..." Rapid movement between the two statements allows Kate to become aware that she is creating the conflict and, like wiggling a pole-digger stuck in heavy soil, allows her to loosen the impasse and give herself room to become aware of the range of previously unimagined choices that dwell in the space between the polarities. Gradually she allows herself to become aware of and express some of the anger and pain she feels. Now she understands that the manipulative warmth and reassurance she experienced is seduction: a behavior which, without consideration for Kate, elicits a dependence which the seducer desires.

It's always painful to recognize that one has been seduced—manipulated by one's most tender and trusting feelings—and Kate expresses both anger and pain as she acknowledges that her desire for affection has been used and her trust violated. At the end of this work, one woman in the group is sobbing audibly. Another is furious. I invite the second one to express her fury, and she does, hitting the pillow and saying her angry words: "I hate you. How could you betray me this way?" This is both a release and an accomplishment for her. The crying woman passionately tells her story of betrayal and abandonment. Both feel refreshed after their expression.

Afterwards we talk about trust, the betrayal of trust, and the difficulty in reestablishing trust after it has been violated. Trust is one of the most basic human needs, for without it we are utterly alone in an unpredictable world. Since the people in the group counsel couples, they encounter the problem of trust in their clinical work, and are especially concerned with how trust might be reestablished once it is lost. I suggest that there is no easy way to do this: only consistently trustworthy actions can establish trust which has been betrayed. Those who rush to trust after deception are protecting the other person rather than themselves, much as a child protects the parents. Because the child has nowhere to go, his or her denial of the parent's perfidy is protection from events too frightening to consider. Adults, however, are free to leave a dishonest relationship and find trustworthy people elsewhere.

In their personal lives several group members have had an experience of listening to friends who refused to reciprocate when they wanted attention for their concerns. This is not unusual among helping professionals, who are self-selected from among those who have played the role of helper and listener in their families and who are often unwilling to assert their right to be heard. Any behavior, even the rare and wonderful gift of listening, becomes a problem when it is a fixed gestalt, when it is compulsive and automatic rather than chosen and free.

As we discuss their professional concerns, I encourage them to form a support group and give each other what they give their clients. I am bewildered by how people in the helping professions stop themselves from using their skills to help each other. How do they avoid creating therapeutic communities? What stops them from sharing their pain and facilitating healing within their own group? I know from my own experience that many do. Is it a disgrace to be on the receiving end of one's own skills? What is the catastrophic fantasy? Is it about protecting a self-image? Clearly many people would rather suffer alone than join with others to heal and grow. It's not a problem I share, and in Japan I have found co-workers who are willing to share the healing, helping colleagueship that I have sought for so long.

The last person to work is Madhuri, the women who had briefly explored her discomfort with her children's feeling after Uma's work. Both Uma and Madhuri are Indian, and this is my first experience working with Indian people. I have a feeling of excitement and gratitude when people from other cultures trust me enough to explore their inner world in my presence. I experience their trust as an exciting gift, and I am delighted. All experiential exploration of the self involves trust, for clearly no one can safely go deeper than their trust, in both themselves and the facilitator they are working with. I take my responsibility seriously and do my best to deserve the trust that people place in me.

Madhuri begins telling how she feels guilty when she's angry and abusive with her children. She's aware of becoming, in her judgment, "irrationally angry" when they won't do what she wants. "Just like my father." she says. When I ask her to play the children they are mild and logical: "Mommy, just wait. I'll do it when I have time." Playing her father, she becomes angry with her childhood self just as she is with her own children: "Why don't you do what I ask? Nobody listens to me."

The last sentence grabs my attention, and, probably because her dialogue with the pillow lacks energy, I have her talk to people in the room. I suggest she begin each statement with, "Listen to me." She does this with one person, expressing her regret that she had not been more forthcoming when the two of them were in a training group together. Then she says that outside her family she is afraid to express herself because "I don't have anything to say"—the other side of the coin of "Nobody listens to me."

I ask her if she has anything she wants to say right now. After she speaks to several people in a similar tone, she again turns to me and says that she only feels comfortable when she listens. Since she rarely expresses herself or talks about her own experience, she is embarrassed as she explores this new behavior, and I tell her about the inevitability of embarrassment when one does something new. Gradually she comes to see how this inhibition against speaking outside the family contributes to her explosions with her children. Since she refuses to express the feelings that emerge in her life outside the family to people who are not family, she brings everything home, where she has learned from her father that it is all right to explode. Hence the anger and frustrations of her life become focused within the family, the only place where expression is permissible.

Even as she comes to see the pattern, she says again, "I should only listen," and the thick blanket of suppression that her culture and her family of origin have laid on her becomes palpable. Uma expresses her similar experience: "Don't express what you want or what you feel. Submit to the needs of others. Listen. Listen. Only listen."

These messages are both culture- and (perhaps more emphatically) gender generated. Other women in the group had received similar orders, both explicitly and implicitly. I remember my mother's precaution, "You have to put other people first," and the response I wailed at her: "If I don't put myself first, who will?" Of course, I found her vague answer totally disheartening.

Through the centuries adults have, by subtle and not-so-subtle words, gestures, and silent looks and glances, laid down rules and proscriptions compelling young girls to accept a secondary role. They have done this in the name of love, in the belief that they were protecting the girls from danger and harm, and often they were. Women who take their daughters for clitoridectomies believe the same thing. I recently had a dream in which my mother said, "It is my success that I got you to adulthood alive," and I have had the same thoughts about my own children.

After we become adults, our parents' work is over and we're on our own. If we don't like what they've taught us, we can unlearn it and open ourselves to new teachers. Karen Horney commented, "After all, life is the best therapist," and the more open we are the more we can learn from this great teacher.

The suppression of females is a matter of fact: a cultural reality that lies across Europe, Asia, Africa, and the Americans with a majestic impartiality, perhaps the most common element of the major world cultures. It is the culture of patriarchy, and such diverse ideologies as Chinese Communism, Roman Catholicism, Protestantism, Islam, Hinduism, and institutional secular humanism are all simply variations on its theme of male domination. This unanimity was confirmed at the 1995 United Nations Conference on Women in Beijing, when the Pope joined with the Islamic fundamentalists to discourage women's control of their bodies. (The pope might do better by creating a fund backed by the full faith and credit of the immensely wealthy Catholic Church guaranteeing a loan of $100,000 to every man who fathers a child. The bank or lending agency could pay out the money in appropriate yearly payments to the mother and child—or to the father, mother, and child, depending upon the arrangement the parents make for rearing the child. Once they have pledged their willingness to support the children they so ardently wish to see born, I think the Catholic Church can in good conscience oppose abortion. Until then, I agree with Surgeon General Jocelyn Elders that the opinion of celibate men is enormously beside the point in any discussion of reproduction.)

My son Lawrence taught me an important lesson about patriarchy when one day, in response to my angry "Why do men always need to feel superior?" he informed me in all seriousness that men's struggle is not for superiority, but for adequacy. This revelation has the ring of truth, and might explain the ferocity of male assertions, which certainly lack the gentle persuasion of a confident superior speaking to a person of lower status. If frightened and insecure men are striving for adequacy, it makes the violence of patriarchy far more understandable.

Is it possible that the elaborate "men-only" structures of church and state exist to insure that men will not have to experience their inadequacy? Beyond the common inadequacy of both men and women to live forever, what is men's special inadequacy that frightens them so? In the United States, it could be their inability to live up to the impossibly strict standards of acceptable masculinity, but more broadly, it is probably their inability to reproduce. Since it is not difficult to find a sperm donor, it would seem that a man needs a woman far more than she needs him in order to have power and influence in the reproductive process.

The transient male involvement in mammalian sex and reproduction could partially explain why sexuality is degraded and feared by people who seek control in order to disguise their fear and helplessness. Like death, sexuality is an aspect of existence that human beings, male or female, can never fully control—which perhaps makes the potential of women's management of reproduction even more terrifying. Like death, sexuality has an existence that is beyond the purely human; it is a constant reminder that we are part of a larger whole that we will never control, and that ultimately controls us. These are facts of life that many people find enormously threatening and strive to deny—the truths that often come in bed, the reminders that someday each one will lie down forever.

The hypothesis of male inadequacy would explain the incredible hubris underlying patriarchy, a system in which men "master space" and "harness rivers." When someone struggles to the top of Sargamatha—the mother of mountains which Europeans and Americans call Mt. Everest after a European who measured its height—and scrambles down, frostbitten and dehydrated but still alive, patriarchal language claims s/he has "conquered" the mountain. Is this some kind of joke or what? Would that it were, for it is such language that makes acceptable the objectification and abuse of the mother's body in all its manifestations: mother earth, the mother of one's own children, and even, through economic deprivation, all mothers including one's own. No one who truly loved their own mother would objectify, abuse, or deprive women. Its emphasis on domination and assertions of superiority reveals patriarchy as an attempt to place men outside nature, and therefore outside themselves. Outside nature is a place like the Oakland Gertrude Stein described when she said, "There's no there there." People who desire to live in a nonexistent land are lost in a lonely fiction without grounding or orientation, without connection or solace from others like themselves. Such a fantasy, even more terrifying because it is shared with others, creates in its true believers hysteria and desperation: to wrench from emptiness some semblance of identity and selfhood; to own and control the imaginary which can never be possessed; and to receive recognition and respect, which, for the person detached from his or her source, can only come from the fickle opinions of others. Hysteria and desperation both describe and explain the orgy of weapons accumulation and the feeding frenzy of consumption that men are creating in the modern industrial world. They will inevitably be hysterical so long as they maintain the delusion that they are outside the natural world in which they are embedded. If, to maintain patriarchy, we are all expected to sacrifice ourselves to this lie, it is no wonder we are having a transformation of gender roles, and the sooner the better.

Madhuri's work ends with an awareness that she has expressed herself quite completely. I encourage everyone present both to talk with and listen to each other. Fixed behavior and set responses, rather than any particular behavior or response, are what creates difficulties in people's lives. One can't say it's good to listen and bad to talk, or visa versa; one can only observe that the person who has no choice as to when to talk and when to listen is stuck and unable to respond to the present moment. A person in this position is highly unlikely to feel satisfied with her or his life. The fixed gestalt, the unchanging pattern, is the barrier to spontaneous and energetic living.

Sharing the ways we limit our self-expression is a good way to complete the group because it's a universal experience. Everyone has something to say because everyone limits themselves in one way or another, and speaking out about one's lack of self-expression in and of itself is a change of behavior. In becoming aware and taking responsibility for our part in limiting ourselves, we empower ourselves and each other.

The unmarried man in the group says that in his experience Asian women are more constrained than European and American women. While I agree that this may be statistically so, there is a tremendous muting of the self among women worldwide, because limiting and denigrating women's self-expression is clearly one of the essentials of patriarchy, which requires male dominance to maintain male adequacy. I observe that by forbidding the expression of emotions in boys and young men the enforcers of patriarchy enhance their feelings of inadequacy rather than decrease it. Further, they make it impossible for men to mature, for maturity requires leaving the helplessness, fear, and resentment of childhood behind, and the only way to do this is to express it fully so that one may complete the gestalts of childhood and set the organismic energy free for aware response to the ever-changing present which includes one's maturing self.

People who are afraid to express the full range of human feelings will never become adults. Those who remain dependent and blaming do not accept their maturity in a world where there are no parents and where each one must face an unknown future, act without guaranteed outcomes, and take responsibility for what they do. People stuck in childhood's unfinished business will search for parents, both on earth and in heaven, who tell them what to do and relieve them of responsibility for their existence and the inevitable mistakes that human beings make. In their immaturity, such people run from freedom, and because they can not tolerate it for themselves, they are unable to tolerate it in others. They do not do these things because they are evil, although evil is often the outcome of their actions: they do them because they are scared. Because they imagine they are still helpless children, they seek someone to rescue them from life's dilemmas. When no one does, they blame and rage against others as helpless as themselves.

The group ended with a burst of responsive and appreciative energy, on which I float out the door and down the elevator into Hong Kong's evening rush hour. I walk through a haze of automobile exhaust into the greenery of the park surrounding St. John's Cathedral and on toward the American Consulate to meet my friend who works as a secretary there. Walking through Hong Kong's Central district, which manages to be both lush and urban at the same time, I think about the interpenetrating cultures that modern Hong Kong represents; once again, I'm the water bug skittering over the surface of a vastness that I cannot pretend to comprehend. The high-rise landscape of Hong Kong Central has an inhuman scale that reinforces my feeling of being a very small part of something enormous, most of which is happening beyond my ken. It's not a bother, just a fact of life, like knowing the universe stretches light years in every direction. At this moment, I'm satisfied with the lucidity of my own subjectivity as I greet the guard who politely takes my pack and camera before I'm allowed to enter my nation's consulate.

SATURDAY, DECEMBER 7, 10:00 P.M.

Today is my Tai Chi birthday, and I've just learned that December 8, which in Japan is the date of the Pearl Harbor attack, is the traditional celebration of the Buddha's ascent into heaven: surely another coincidence the unconscious arranged. I don't fully understand how this practice that I have done nearly every day for sixteen years has affected me. Gertrude Stein writes that we only understand things when they are over. Since my Tai Chi practice won't be finished until I am, I am willing to continue with the partial understanding that comes from time to time.

I know that Tai Chi has taught me patience. I know I love the soft, slow patterns I weave as I create the familiar set every day, day after day: always the same, always different. Such a gift, this gradual unfolding of time or space, this meeting with a seamless experience of eternity that is both me and not me.

I have just returned from a Christmas party in the apartment next door. I'm staying with my friend Marylee who works in the U.S. consulate and is housed in an modern apartment complex overlooking Deep Water Bay, one of the many convolutions in the shore of Hong Kong island. The party is my first encounter with the American community here. I first came to Hong Kong to work in June of 1989. I had been teaching at Fudan University in Shanghai for ten months when the Chinese government attacked the students and other activists in Tienanmen square in Beijing. I arrived in Hong Kong with my son Lawrence just in time to read headlines announcing the Chinese government's denial that they had killed anyone—headlines the Hong Kong journalists dramatically juxtaposed with photographs of blood spattered sheets covering mounds of bodies stacked in the streets and hospitals of Beijing. Shocked and anguished, Lawrence and I bonded with the Chinese people we met as we raged and grieved together over events in China—the same China that is to take over Hong Kong in 1997. Until tonight my social experiences in Hong Kong have been with the young Chinese social workers I met then and with whom I usually work.

At the party, I had a long conversation with a young American women who in the fall of 1989 had gone to China to work at a university in Shenyang in northern China. I was surprised she had chosen to go to China in 1989, but then she hadn't been there in June. When I left the U.S. in August of 1988, the CAAC (Chinese Airline Always Cancels, or Crashes, depending on your level of bitterness on any given day) plane stayed in San Francisco airport for an extra six hours to accommodate a similar young woman who abruptly and hysterically decided, just as the ramp was withdrawn from the door, that she did not want to return to China. In her frenzy not to return she nearly stepped out of the 747 into the empty air—no small step, as I could see from my seat three stories above the runway. I never considered not going, although at the time I wondered at her desperation.

The young woman at the party had gone and left before her term was up. The scene in the plane in San Francisco flashed across my memory as she told me her tale of Shenyang, a city in northern China which as a result of the Japanese occupation has been heavily industrialized since the 1930s. Now the plants are old and dirty, filling the air, water, and soil with highly toxic industrial wastes. When she became ill, a local physician told the young American woman she was suffering from pollution poisoning, a common ailment in the area.

Shanghai, too, was disastrously polluted. A viscous, smelly, black river ran through the campus of Fudan and inspired one of my colleagues to remark, "Now I understand what it means to be up shit's creek without a paddle." Riding by a small factory when it released a cloud of fine metal grit into the air, I got a metal particle in my eye which was a red, teary mess for three months as I made the rounds of hospitals and clinics seeking a person who would help me heal myself. When the last word is written about process of forced industrialization we call communism in the twentieth century, perhaps its greatest evil will be the ferocity of its disregard for people and planet in its frantic rush toward heavy industry (which, of course, is only a euphemism for weapons production and personal power for a few people at the expense of everyone else).

Talking with the woman at the party, I felt like the old China hand who loiters on China's borders swapping stories with others who strive to share and understand the unique experience of China. I noticed that I stuck by her as soon as I overheard her telling someone else about her experiences in China. After we began talking about the mainland, everyone else drifted away, as we created a cocoon with our China stories.

Sometimes I think China's not a country, but an obsession—endlessly fascinating if you have it, endlessly boring if you don't.

The school where she taught was down the road from the barracks that housed the troops who finally crushed the student demonstrations in Beijing. These troops, who had taken part in China's war on the Vietnam border as well as the repressions in Tibet, had been sent to Beijing to save the army's face after the local troops had refused to fire on the student protesters. She said everyone in Shenyang was frightened of these battle-hardened troops: strangers who did not speak the local dialect and, therefore, were more like an invading army than local soldiers.

I remembered being plenty paranoid in Shanghai after the massacre when, even though we were nowhere near such units, there were rumors the army was coming to rid the university of "bourgeois liberals," a label which definitely includes me. In Shanghai I learned that in the absence of reliable information people generate rumors to solace their ignorance: in our desperation to know, even false information is apparently better than none. It was not counter-intuitive to imagine that the Chinese army would come to Fudan, for after they had crushed the students of Tienanmen with tanks, no one could predict what they would do next. Lawrence, twenty at the time, was with me, and his presence reinforced my determination to get away safely and soon. On Monday, June 7. we evacuated ourselves by bicycle through the barricaded city to the Shanghai Hilton, which felt like another world and served as a way station on our way to the airport. That night in the Hilton we watched CNN and became even more frightened when we watched silent black and white pictures of the massacre until they vanished abruptly from the screen. There was no announcement, nothing. Just a grainy blank screen buzzing in a forlornly luxurious hotel room.

Living conditions were worse in Shenyang than in Shanghai. My acquaintance said everything was terrible except the students who, seeing her as their only lifeline to the outside world, wept when she left. We agreed on the dilemmas of observing China: while criticism seems ethnocentric and insensitive, acceptance betrays the fear and frustration of one's own experience. It was good for me to retrieve a bit of my life in China, for I had pretty much put it out of my mind as soon as I got away safely. Since there are few among my acquaintances who are interested in hearing me talk about China, my time there remains unintegrated, and talking with this young woman was helpful.

When she asked me if I had been locked into my living quarters in Shanghai, I had a flashback of standing inside the front door of the comfortable guest house where I and the other foreign staff lived. It's 5:30 a.m. and I am furiously shaking the locked door, which makes an ugly metallic racket intended to awaken someone—anyone—to let me out. The tousled young man who shuffles out in his underwear lets me out without making eye contact as I stand aside, shamefaced at having awakened him and furious at having been locked in. Between the compound and the street, there is another gate which, I discover, opens earlier than the one in the guest house. Henceforth, with the help of a well-placed chair, I climb through a window to escape into Shanghai's early morning pageant where people play Tai Chi and Chi Qong on every flat open surface, sing Beijing opera in the park, sit and smoke under trees filled with cages of singing birds, collect night soil into buckets hung from shoulder poles, and walk leisurely or ride bicycles wildly in every direction. I hated being locked in, and yet, as the young woman from Shenyang reminded me, it was accepted practice in China, a country of walls, and walls around walls.

Riding in a bus to Huang Shan, the famous and lovely Yellow Mountain in Anhui province, I remember watching the walls flash by and thinking, "Someday they'll build a wall around the whole country." Pause. "Oh, yeah, they've already done that." I laughed out loud at my tardy realization. Owen Lattimore suggests that a stable and exact frontier, a Great Wall enclosing the walls of smaller units like a skin enclosing clusters of cells, was an inherent part of China's development, which required the rigid separation of what could be included from what must be excluded.

In Fudan's new foreign languages building, the administration assigned a single floor to offices for foreign teachers. On this floor, unlike the others, the door to the stairs was permanently locked "for our own good," supposedly to protect us from thieves. When I complained that there was no way we could get out in case of fire, all I ever got was the prevalent, "*Mei ban fa*" (It can't be helped), as though the door were eternally sealed by some supernatural agency. I know bullshit when I hear it, even in Chinese, and since I take responsibility for myself, there was no way I was going to lock myself in a place where the only exit was a heat-seeking elevator. I was in my office only once during my ten months in Shanghai. Lattimore again makes this behavior understandable: "The very act of drawing a boundary is an acknowledgement that the peoples excluded are not under control and cannot be ruled by command. They must be dealt with by negotiation." As foreigners we fit the definition of those who cannot be controlled by command, and, therefore, the door was locked and the boundary set: a miniature wall.

I had forgotten these events until the young woman from Shenyang reminded me. Nevertheless, the China where I lived in 1988-89 was amazingly open until the massacre on June 6. My students and I discussed both Chinese and American politics without fear or reservation. They had been children during the Cultural Revolution, and said they had liked it because, as a young man explained, "We often got to leave school to march and do this." He stabbed his fist in the air as he spoke, and I could imagine the pleasure of six- and seven-year-olds in such a demonstration. They remembered drawing pictures of Deng Xiao Peng first as a demon and then as a hero.

When I first met them, they asked me how they were different from their counterparts in the U.S., and I told them that as far I could see they were far less knowledgeable about sex. When several students suggested I enlighten them, I told them that I didn't know them well enough yet to talk about sex with them, but that when I did I would. In the second semester, I gave three or four lectures with lots of English vocabulary for functions and body parts most had never heard discussed in any language. I remember ending one graphic and explicit talk on human reproduction with these sentences: "And that's how we all got here. It's how I got here. It's how you got here. It's how Mao Zedong and Deng Xiao Peng got here. There's no other way to get here." One of the students in the first row looked at me with tears in her eyes and said, "It's a miracle." Of course, I agreed. It's our miracle, and it was a privilege to acquaint those eighteen- and nineteen-year-old people with their birthright: the story of their beginning.

When I asked them why there was so much secrecy about sex in China, they said that there was a lot of shame about the body and no one ever talked about it. I found that interesting: I had always associated the Puritanism of my culture with Christianity, and here the prohibitions of puritanism were just as strong if not stronger, in a culture and society that was emphatically not Christian. China and Japan are sometimes called shame societies by people who contrast them to Europe and the Americas, which are said by these same people to be controlled by guilt. I'm not sure I agree with this division, not even sure I know what shame is. Guilt is, I think, retroflected anger: aggressive energy directed toward the self rather than outward toward the one who is interfering with one's actions and desires.

When my students told me how they had been taught, most nonverbally, to be ashamed of their bodies, I remembered Dorothy Dinnerstein's observation that all shame is shame of the body. This might be an explanation of the reluctance many parents, Chinese and non-Chinese, feel in talking with their children about sex and reproduction. The real shame is that one is taught to be ashamed of her or his body: the physical manifestation and concrete reality of one's existence If the body is evil, then everything else must be too, and this is a very depressing way to view the world.

Despite this freedom to teach, the walls remained. A colleague teaching at another university had told me about a collection of videos that the American consulate in Shanghai had given Fudan. When I asked about them, the first response was, "How do you know about that?" Since I was teaching American culture, I persisted, and when I discovered one of them was of Robert Frost reading his poetry, I persevered. First, no one knew where they were; then, someone let me look at a catalog. Finally I was allowed to wait two hours in an empty room with mysterious footprints on the wall, footprints I fully understood by the time someone reluctantly allowed to me to fill out the forms necessary to receive the image and voice of Robert Frost. The student who had expressed his admiration for Frost's work was delighted. I was both pleased with my success and bewildered that so simple a project had been convoluted into a full-scale quest.

This trip to Hong Kong has been unusual in that I have not worked with a group of Chinese people. I really can't write about the Pacific Rim without telling of the varieties of Chinese experience that exist on this boundary, where the Hong Kong Chinese share one of the most unusual and dramatic of Pacific Rim stories. Hostages of the British colonialism that began with the first Opium War, they will, in 1997, be turned over by their colonial mentors to the Chinese government, with their only protection the guarantees of the Basic Law, a contract between Great Britain and China, a political entity that neither recognizes nor understands the rule of law.

A recent article in Hong Kong's South China Morning Post reported the establishment of an on-line consultation service offered jointly by the Legislative Affairs Bureau under China's State Council and the University of Hong Kong, from which Internet users will be able to request an official interpretation of any laws in which they are interested. The manager of the Law-On-Line Database Project, JoJo Tam, said, "It is difficult for Hong Kong to get the most up-to-date version of Chinese laws because mainland legislation changes all the time."

Traditional Confucian ethics valued rule by good and properly educated men, believing them to be more trustworthy than less able men bound by law. While this is a logical and defensible position, Anglo-American political theory has been shaped by the convictions that power tends to corrupt those who have it and that laws which bind everyone, including those in the most powerful positions, offer people their best protection from arbitrary uses of power. This system works, however imperfectly. as Richard Nixon's resignation demonstrated.

Free speech and a free press are important elements in power's limitations; both exist in Hong Kong now. Neither does in China. The limitation of state power in the lives of ordinary people is a dream quite alien to Chinese history, where traditionally conscripted labor has been an essential element in the construction and maintenance of incredible infrastructure: the Great Wall and all the lesser walls as well as equally immense water projects for irrigation, flood control, and transportation. Forced labor was not incidental to traditional Chinese society; it was one of the defining aspects, absolutely essential for the organization of a vast land empire based on intensive agriculture. One of the functions of the Great Wall was to define the separation of settled and organized Chinese society from the mobility of people beyond the area where Chinese-style agriculture was possible.

While the Chinese emphasis on the moral and capable person could be integrated with the Euro-American emphasis on law, this has not happened yet, and I readily understand the flight of the Hong Kong Chinese from their coming inclusion in China. With the appearance of an orderly and well-planned modern diaspora, theirs is an unprecedented escape from a well-planned transfer of sovereignty that comes about not as a result of war, but by mutual agreement between the governments of the United Kingdom and China in which they, the Chinese people of Hong Kong, are treated more like buildings and dock facilities than like people. With their wealth and with English as their second language, they flee to Canada, Australia, and New Zealand—refugees with cash and education who are accepted as assets by their host countries. When a Canadian official said he hoped the Hong Kong Chinese would find a better life in Canada, he was reminded that Canada was receiving some of the richest people in the world seeking not a better life but "a better passport."

The passport is one of those human constructions that, because it embodies the power of the state, may assume life-and-death significance in people's lives. A small book of blank pages containing a photograph and a brief personal history and awaiting stamps and seals of various kinds, it comes to resemble a natural phenomenon. Like a storm or an earthquake, it determines who can go where on this planet we at least theoretically share, although George Orwell got it right in Animal Farm when he noted that "some pigs are more equal than others." Some are certainly more free to travel than others, and I am grateful for the good fortune that grants me a passport from the United States which allows me to go almost everywhere, often without the hassle of a visa.

In the early 1930s, Chiune Sugihara—the Japanese consul in Lithuania—with the help of his wife Yukiko worked day and night to sign and register 300 visas a day on the passports of Jews escaping the Nazis. The Sugiharas, in defiance of the orders of the consul's superiors, made 3000 of these simple imprints saying that Japan would accept the bearers, thus allowing the fleeing Jews to travel through the USSR. Many of the people he helped spent the war in Shanghai, and most survived. When Sugihara returned to Japan in 1947, the Japanese government, even though it was controlled by the U.S. Occupation forces, fired him from the foreign service. Before his death he received the honor "Righteous Among Nations" from the Vad Vshem Martyrs Remembrance Authority in Jerusalem, and said, "I think that my decision was humanely correct." Such goodness happens when the right person controls the stamps and seals.

Regardless of the profound European and American influences on the lands and peoples of the western Pacific Rim, it remains essentially Asian, which inevitably means profoundly marked by the five-thousand-year-old historical entity subsumed under the term "China." During the millennia preceding the coming of the British gunboats, the court in Beijing recognized foreigners only as bearers of tribute who were allowed to remain within the kingdom so long as they showed the proper respect. This respect was demonstrated by the most obsequious behaviors including multiple kowtows (a form of bowing where one touches her or his head to the ground before the honored person). The British began their confrontation with the Chinese government by refusing to allow their envoys to kowtow, thus rejecting the traditional relationship between the Chinese government and the rest of the world.

As a hybrid on the perimeter of this extraordinary historical entity, Hong Kong is unique, and as a partial fusion of European and Chinese cultures, it is a path into the enormous complexity designated by the simple word "China." It is in Hong Kong that I, and many others from the United States and Europe, first encounter the varieties of Chinese experience.

Sunday, December 8, 6:30 a.m.,
on a balcony overlooking Deep Water Bay on Hong Kong Island

Lying on Marylee's balcony, I watch the clouds fill the sky erasing the horizon which fades into a cloudy continuity, a blue-gray blur of sea and sky. Two green mounds of land rest on the water so softly I half expect them to float away in the light breeze. A bird makes a high sound that trills and then drops slowly into the rustling undertones of the dense vegetation on the hillside, so near the balcony I can almost reach out and touch the mass of deep green quivering there. A helicopter appears, the pitch of its clatter dopplers high as it passes overhead and then vanishes into the emptiness. I watch as a large soaring bird breaks from the green and carves a soundless arc in the gleaming white sky. The wind turns the page of my book, and, experiencing the deep stillness that rests behind all sound and motion, I float free in time.

Chapter 4

China: The Hong Kong Chinese, the Coming of 1997, and Becoming Authentic

«The Chinese are the bearers of the most important living culture that can be traced back in unbroken derivation to the Stone Age.»
—Owen Lattimore

June 12, 1992, Thursday, 10:00 p.m.

In the dark liquid heat of Hong Kong's summer, the airport tarmac sizzles through my shoes as I take the half-dozen steps to the air conditioned bus that takes us to the terminal. All flights in and out of Hong Kong are international ones, and I pass quickly through the immigration and customs procedures designed to expedite the movement of the thousands of transients who come here on their way to destinations all over Asia and the South Pacific. I feel lonely as I walk the passageway through the crowd of people waiting to meet their friends and family, and wish someone were here to meet me. Outside in the heat again, I begin to sweat as I walk to another air-conditioned bus, which, for eight Hong Kong dollars (about one U.S.), takes me through the damp commotion of the British Colony to the YMCA on Salisbury Road.

This is the third year I have come to Hong Kong to facilitate a three-day residential workshop over the long weekend holiday in honor of the Queen's birthday. I do this workshop with Barry, my Hong Kong Chinese partner; he makes the arrangements and recruits the young Chinese participants, many of whom are social workers in the large social service system the British and various Christian organizations maintain here.

The first of these workshops was in 1989, when my son Lawrence and I arrived four days after the massacre at Tienanmen Square. Coming from the desperate disorder of Shanghai, we entered a grieving Hong Kong draped in white, the Chinese color for mourning. Large white banners imprinted with the grim black characters for students and death, which sheer repetition forced us to understand, covered doorways and windows memorializing the murdered students of Beijing. Stricken with the guilt of survivors free to escape to Hong Kong while friends and colleagues remained in China, Lawrence and I shared the fear and bewilderment of the Chinese people of Hong Kong as they struggled to reconcile their coming unification with a distant government that murders its young in the night.

Now, two years later, many Hong Kong Chinese have made arrangements to live elsewhere before the Chinese troops arrive in 1997. Many others still search for a solution to the dilemma of being Chinese while fearing to subject themselves to the Chinese government. A billion and a half Chinese people live within and without China's borders and identify themselves as Chinese. To most of them, *Zhongquo*, the Central Country, is the locus of the civilization and culture at the core of the human enterprise. And the center of the center is Beijing, whose dialect is the official language of the whole country and whose single time zone covers a land mass as broad as the United States—an unexpected gift to a visitor in Tibet, where I played Tai Chi amidst a magnificent array of stars in the high-altitude darkness of 3:00 a.m. when the clock said 7:00. Nevertheless, this heavy-handed chronometric imperialism must be a burden to people who are forced to leave their beds and do business in the cold of early morning and go to bed in the light of afternoon.

The conviction that one's own nation is central and superior has a long history in China, and the notion that other nations might be the equals of "the country at the center" is a new one, not yet integrated into the psyche of China's leaders. It is an irrefutable tenet of Confucianism, which has defined Chinese society for over two millennia, that orders go from the center to the periphery rather than vice versa. Those who live outside the center, who are by definition inferiors or barbarians, may not tell the rulers at the center how they should behave. The rulers of China will not tolerate efforts to change this. While there is a horrible irony in the People's Army killing students on the site of the monument to student martyrs of an earlier Chinese Revolution, Tienanmen was an all-too-accurate illustration of the Central Country's guiding ideology.

To the outsider China often seems more myth than reality. The people speak a scramble of dialects that are only understood regionally. Some of these dialects are spoken by enormous numbers of people: eighty-two million people in Southern China, Hong Kong, Singapore, and the United States, speak Cantonese. People in Shanghai speak a dialect which is quite unlike either Cantonese or the modified Beijing dialect Americans call Mandarin. There are many other dialects as well. The entity that English speakers call China has historically been the creation of a written language shared by a land-owning, bureaucratic ruling class that, in the name of the emperor, ruled China for thousands of years. Mastering this language, which the scholar-diplomat Owen Lattimore called a "bureaucratic code," took many years of concentrated study which effectively prohibited upward mobility and created a nearly insurmountable wall between the man of letters and the illiterate peasant.

China's geography varies remarkably as well. From the open steppes of Mongolia and the cold hills of Manchuria through the irrigated river valleys of the Yangtze and Yellow Rivers, which are the source of the ancient systems of agriculture and control, to the tropical forests of Xishuangbanna near the Vietnamese border and Hainan Island in the South China Sea, the variations of land and climate are extreme. Culture, too, ranges from the relative modernity of the coastal cities—the pried-open doors through which European and American influence first entered and continue to pour into the Central Country—and the interior, which remains a traditional peasant culture. It is the traditional millet- and rice-growing Han people who inhabit the great river valleys of central China to whom most of us, including the Chinese themselves, refer when we say Chinese.

In 1949 Mao Zedong stood before Tienanmen, the Gate of Heavenly Peace, in Beijing and declared the People's Republic of China, effectively ending a hundred-year war the Han Chinese fought for control of China. The long, destructive conflict began with the Opium War in 1839. In 1850 came the Taiping Rebellion, a traditional peasant uprising with a new twist in that the leader, Hong Siu-Chuan—who had come under the influence of Christian missionaries— declared himself to be the younger brother of Jesus Christ. This heretical declaration, along with a radical program including equal rights for women and abolition of private property, did little to endear him and his followers to the Europeans and Americans who were beginning to make their influence felt in China and who joined the Manchu dynasty—itself a foreign conqueror—in suppressing the rebellious Chinese and stabilizing the regime. The hundred years' war went on to include the Nien Rebellion; the Moslem Rebellion; another Opium War with Britain; the Boxer Rebellion, an anti-European uprising at the end of the last century; a war with Japan in 1895; the revolution that overthrew the dynasty in 1911; and numerous struggles among warlords after the dynasty collapsed.

The Chinese Communist Party was founded in 1921, and the nationalist and communist Chinese began fighting a civil war that continued through the period of Japanese occupation of the Chinese mainland beginning in 1931. Millions of Chinese people suffered and died throughout the hundred years of chaos that finally ended in 1949, when Chiang Kai-Shek's nationalist armies, unable to consolidate their hold on the mainland after the American defeat of Japan, fled to Taiwan and Mao made his famous declaration, "The Chinese people have stood up."

The war was won by the Han Chinese under the leadership of the Communist Party, and this combination of power has been governing a suffering and battered China ever since. Just forty years later, in the very square where Mao declared the Chinese victory, the same bullets that killed the protesting students chipped and scarred the white marble column whose bas-reliefs depict earlier generations of students, workers, and soldiers struggling for freedom.

During early 1989, before the central government ordered the Tienanmen massacre, there were several months of demonstrations in most of China's major cities, and most of my Shanghai students were happy and excited to be involved. I remember saying to them then, "The test of your commitment to freedom is not what you do now, but what you do in twenty years when you sit in the offices while students gather and speak in the streets below." A student asked about Swiss bank accounts, and when I told her they are secret, she inquired how anyone could know if China's leaders had them or not. Another explained to me the duty the young owe the old and how unsympathetic the older generation is to the aspirations of the young. "They sacrificed for their elders," he said, "and they feel cheated if we don't sacrifice for them." Many understood when I asked them to remember as older people the frustration they felt in 1989 when the government refused to listen.

Beijing, whose peaceful surrender to the Communist armies was more a statement of how Chinese of all ideologies treasure the northern capital than a sign of any cowardice on the part of its defenders, had not been the capital of a united and independent China since 1644, when the Manchus broke out of their northern kingdom beyond the Great Wall and rode south to conquer the Ming rulers and establish the last dynasty of imperial China. The Chinese name for the Manchu dynasty is Qing, and its death throes, complicated enormously by the intrusion of the Europeans and Americans, lasted until 1911, more than half of the hundred years' war. Until 1911, the Manchus reigned, and the Han Chinese were a subject people whose men were forced to wear their hair in the long braided queue as a symbol of their submission. The Manchus refused to allow foot binding among the Manchu women, understanding that foot binding, which began after the Mongol conquest of China in the twelfth century, was an attempt by an oppressed people to maintain masculine pride and prerogative while living under foreign conquest.

Chinese civilization's insistent centrality combined with its historical subjugation to foreign conquerors has created a deep cleavage in the history and psyche of the Chinese people. The contradiction of the superior civilization controlled by outside barbarians is the secret at the heart of China's misery.

As the family therapist Virginia Satir observed, "A sick family is one in which Daddy is short and no one says Daddy is short, and no one says that no one says that Daddy is short." While it requires even more effort to live a lie than to practice the eternal vigilance which is the price of liberty, the shift from denial to awareness to wholeness requires, first, the courage and support to look at what is being denied and, second, a willingness to integrate the denied past into one's present existence.

The denied past dominates the present in ways that an acknowledged and integrated past never can. By experiencing the denied past and the agonizing feelings that inevitably accompany it, both individual people and the collections of people called nations can let go of the disowned misery of their history and live in the present, where choice and responsibility are possible. The denial of the foreign conquests represented by the Mongols and Manchus are one source of the great historical and cultural ambiguities that continue to define the Central Country: the Chinese denial of their subjection and the further denial of this denial are as monumental as that vast past itself. The struggle of the Communist government to get the foreigners out of China continued after 1949 as the Chinese struggled with their great land neighbor, the then Soviet Union. Russian influence in China was gradually reduced during the 1950s. The ability of the Communist government to get the foreigners out of China and regain the territory and government for the Han Chinese will perhaps be remembered as its greatest accomplishment.

I think it is very hard for a person who is not Chinese to understand the magnetic pull of the Central Country on the imagination of its citizens and their descendants living in other lands. Within the Chinese tradition, a Chinese person is one whose father is Chinese, regardless of formal citizenship or professed loyalty. I was in a Chinese class in San Francisco when the teacher, an elderly man of the old school, suddenly asked who the young Chinese-American men in the class would fight for should there be a war between the United States and China. Outraged by his question, I felt sympathy and anger on behalf of the young Americans of Chinese descent who were totally bewildered as their teacher confronted them with the conflict of loyalty that Chinese tradition demands of descendants of immigrants from the Central Country.

Working with Chinese people in British-governed Hong Kong, I see that even among people who share such a powerful and demanding culture as the Chinese, individual differences still shape character and personalty far more than cultural mythology. Nevertheless, cultural mythology, because it is institutionalized everywhere, and most especially in the hearts and minds of the elders, exerts a persistent tug on the Chinese personality, as constant as the moon's influence on the tides. Consequently, as 1997 approaches, I see the ambiguity of pride and fear that their coming inclusion in the Central Country engenders.

Before the Tienanmen massacre most people in Hong Kong were willing to take their chances with China, but now those with high-level skills and education as well as those with lots of money are seeking asylum in other countries. Because insensitive people hold the stamps and seals allowing international travel, the rest have no choice but to stay. The British refused to grant the Hong Kong Chinese British passports in the mistaken fear that they would flood into the U.K.—as though citizens of tropical and prosperous Hong Kong would rush to live in chill, deindustrializing Britain. This decision turned the Hong Kong Chinese into hostages, by removing from them the right to exit that a British passport would have allowed. Now they must leave before the Chinese come or they may never have another chance. With British passports, they could have waited and seen what the Chinese governors would do: how well they would hold up their end of the bargain represented by the Basic Law, which includes an agreement to respect the rights of the Hong Kong people.

Although my partner Barry is planning to leave before 1997, he has rented a new office and discovered that despite the uncertainty of the future, rents in Hong Kong remain high. It is in Barry's new office that I meet with a group of his advanced Gestalt students on the Thursday night before the residential workshop begins.

JUNE 13, FRIDAY, 7:00 P.M.

There are six young Chinese people in the group, all of whom speak English as a second language. I begin the usual way, asking people what they are feeling right now and what they want from the workshop. All but Carol and Barry say they are anxious speaking English, and are relieved when I assure them that I will not grade them on their English grammar. Since Carol is fluently bilingual and can translate, I say that whenever they want to speak Cantonese, they can.

Most of them want to learn more Gestalt and, after several workshops with Barry, want to work with another Gestalt facilitator. I respect this desire because I know from my own training that a variety of facilitators illuminates the practice of Gestalt, which, because it is existential and experiential, is intensely personal and idiosyncratic and inevitably varies with the individual practitioner. A variety of teachers gives students permission to follow their own interests, tracking experience with their own intuition.

The first person to come forward to work says Nancy is her English name. Most of the Hong Kong Chinese have both English and Chinese names. There is a Chinese tradition of having a number of names: a "milk" (baby) name, a student name, a creative or pen name, and, after death, yet another, a Buddhist name. Given this context, an English name is not such an anomaly as one might suppose. I had an Australian colleague in Shanghai who was critical of my calling Chinese people by English names; while I can understand her point of view, it's not mine. Being from San Francisco, I am accustomed to people of Chinese descent having English names, and it's natural and easy for me to use the English name unless the person directly expresses (as some do) the preference that I use her or his Chinese name.

Nancy suffers with a stomach ulcer, and I begin the work by asking, "What does your stomach say?"

"I'm full. I'm uncomfortable." She pauses, and says, "I eat too much." This last sentence I hear as Nancy talking to her stomach, although I don't interrupt her to make this explicit. She continues, "I hate you. I want to kill you. You stuff me with things I don't want."

She switches chairs and becomes herself, saying, "I eat things the doctor tells me not to."

I ask, "What do you want the stomach to do?"

Instantly she replies, "Be obedient."

I see this as the theme of the work, obedience and introjection. Since Nancy does not need to be obedient to do what she wants to do, I know that introjected commands—"shoulds"—underlie this demand for obedience. Her remark, "You stuff me with things I don't want," is an additional marker of a powerful introjective process.

She voices another introject immediately: "I should rely on myself more."

I ask her to say this to someone in the group. She complies in a dull, dispirited manner. Next I ask her what she wants, and unexpectedly, like a person falling through thin ice, she plunges into authenticity and answers, "I want to rely wholly on others."

With these words, Nancy transforms herself, and the automaton becomes a real person. Her eyes brighten and her voice reaches out; it is obvious to everyone in the room that she has spoken the truth. It is completely irrelevant that her truth is immature and impossible to achieve; what is significant is that in this moment Nancy connects with and expresses her deepest and truest desire, regardless of how irrational it may be. By integrating her inner desire with her outer expression, she affirms the solid ground of her being. From this secure base she can begin the process of growth that ceased when she began to deny the reality of her own experience.

Amazed at the sense of liberation she feels, she shakes her head in wonder as she accepts recognition from the group members. Having discovered the underlying truth of her existence, which is her desire to rely on others, she can begin to address the secondary issue: her internalization of the demands of others and the obedience which she hopes will earn approval and acceptance of her dependence. With this awareness, she gains self-understanding that will support her in her daily life as well as the awareness that can allow her to begin, if she wishes, the slow process of aware change.

Excited by Nancy's new awareness, Carol says, "I want to explore how inadequate I feel when people look down on me as a 'dumb Chinese'." She tells us she wants to confront several groups whose criticisms, real and imagined, have been a torment in her life—her grade-school peers, members of her church, students in her counseling class, and colleagues from a former workplace. Beginning, she puts them each group on a different pillow and starts to tell this assortment of people how much she has suffered from their assumptions of superiority. Almost as soon as she changes pillows and begins to play them, she realizes that it is her own internalized messages of inadequacy that made the behavior of these various groups so painful. Of course, people put each other down, but for the put-down to "take," the critical voice has to exist within the victim. Otherwise, she or he will ignore the words and gestures of supremacy, or be puzzled, even amused, at the arrogance and foolish pretensions of the other person. Since most of us have been criticized as children, we often unconsciously assume we are inadequate when we hear a derogatory remark. If we are unaware, we empower the other rather than ourselves and assume they are right and we are wrong.

An interesting exception to this pattern occurs when a person participates in a culture other than the one where she grew up. Since put-down messages are often subtle and subliminal, they gain their power by activating a hologram of inadequacy that remains from childhood; for an outsider, the words and gestures of dominance from a different culture often pass unnoticed. This explains why people often feel more open and free in a culture other than their own.

In China I heard a story of an American woman who, when asked why she preferred to work in Asia, replied that she liked it because in Asia there are three genders—men, women, and foreigners. Since there are two genders in Asia just like everywhere else, it is more likely that, unaware of the signals for dominance and submission in Asian cultures, she could ignore them and even pretend they exist only for the local people—which, to a great extent, they do. An unreceived message exists only for the sender. The inability to read subliminal cultural signals, which is often a problem, is in this case a solution. As a result, in Asia this women experiences herself as gender-free, outside the cultural rituals of male and female in a role she could never achieve in her own culture. (Similarly, I have many Japanese friends who cannot understand why I choose to spend much of my time in Japan, which they find conforming and oppressive. For me, it is not.)

Carol stops working when she realizes that she can free herself from the prejudices of others as soon as she stops reinforcing their judgments with her own relentless self- criticism.

Next Kathryn says she wants to work as a facilitator and asks me to supervise. I agree, and another group member volunteers to be the client. At the beginning of the work Kathryn expresses her anxiety, effectively reducing her own apprehension while reassuring her client that she is both truthful and humanly fallible. With this admission, she creates a trusting relationship that allows the work to proceed successfully. I note that Kathryn is excellent at recognizing her client's nonverbal clues, but less sensitive to significant sentences—for example, "I make myself weaker by trying to appear strong." Later I realize that this may have been because she was working in her second language, where the bell that usually signals "This is important" does not always ring.

During my comments at the end of her session, I point out how crucial Kathryn's honesty about herself was for the success of the work. The most important element in Gestalt is the facilitator's relationship with the client, because integrity in the human connection creates the trust that allows both people to remain aware in the presence of the pain that is an inevitable part of many people's here-and-now experience. Further, no one knows what will happen next, and when people attend to the present moment, this implicit truth becomes blazingly explicit. Uncertainty is absolutely inherent in here-and-now awareness, and it is trust that enables the client to endure uncertainty rather than retreat into the fantasies which are traditionally used to control fear.

Trust in the one with whom I share the present moment strengthens my courage to risk experiencing the dizzying wonder and impermanence of my existence. Even more gratifying, presence in the here and now contains a most amazing paradox: the more completely I am engaged in the present, the less concern I have for my transience; for to be present with the uncertainties of the moment allows one, in William Blake's words, to experience "the universe in a grain of sand, eternity in an hour."

We stop here, and I return to the Y to prepare for the three-day group which begins tomorrow.

June 14, Saturday, 9:00 a.m.

I meet Barry underground in the subway station at Tsim Tsa Tsui and begin the long trip to the Kadoori Agricultural Center in the New Territories. Hong Kong island is but a small bit of the British Colony, which includes a substantial piece of the Asian mainland—the New Territories—as well as the so-called outer islands—including Lantau, which is larger than Hong Kong island itself. In 1842, the Chinese government ceded the island of Hong Kong to the British; it is the lease on the New Territories that expires in 1997. Recognizing that the island without its hinterland was an impossible possession, the British agreed to return the entire colony to China.

To reach the Kadoori Center, we transfer from the subway to a train, gathering group members as we go. For the last lap we squeeze into taxis which carry us through bowers of moisture-laden vegetation among which are scattered gardens and clusters of two-storied houses like the ones across the border in China. The rural areas of the New Territories are identical to the countryside of Guangzhou, a few miles and a few rows of guarded barbed wire away. From time to time the heavy sky unloads the moisture it has been carrying north from the Indian Ocean; everything drips and splatters in the gray mist that occasionally rumbles and flashes with a serious storm. Dropping nearly unnoticed through the humid air, the rains hold us in the wet embrace of the monsoon.

I will always remember the Kadoori Center as I first saw it in 1989. Walking through the large Chinese-style gateway adorned with tiles that charmingly pictured Chinese village life, I saw hanging over the door of the administration building a large white banner announcing death.

The contrast between the gentle pictures and the mournful banner seemed perfectly to mirror my own feelings—my excitement about doing my first Chinese group in Hong Kong and my despair with the China I had just left. For me, the martyred students of Tienanmen continue to haunt the Kadoori Center.

We arrive at 10:30 and go right to work without unpacking, as our rooms will not be ready until noon. There are 24 participants plus me, Barry, and two assistants, Carol and Roberta. We gather in a large auditorium with rows of desks which we move back to make room for us to sit in a circle on the floor.

Group members introduce themselves, most expressing a great deal of anxiety about the necessity of speaking English. As I listen to their uneasiness, I notice that, while there is a definite spectrum of ability, everyone's English is more than adequate for the work we will be doing. I think again that while Japanese people's speech is transformed by the process of translation, in Hong Kong people's verbal expression is limited by their speaking of a second language. Often I hear, "I concern you," a tender example of English expression among the Hong Kong Chinese I work with.

The native language in Hong Kong is *Guangdongwa*: Cantonese, the dialect of the Southern China which is spoken by 82 million people including most of the Chinese in the United States, Canada, Australia, and Singapore. In Singapore there is currently an intense governmental effort to change from *Guangdongwa* to Putongwa, the so-called common language which is a variation of the Beijing dialect. In preparation for 1997 many people in Hong Kong are learning *Putongwa* as well.

In my introductory remarks, I express my gratitude for the group members' willingness to speak English in their work with me. I also assure them that if they want to speak in *Guangdongwa* they can and someone will translate. Doing therapy in a second language has advantages as well as disadvantages. Just as it's easier for many Japanese people today to say *toire*, the Japanese pronunciation of toilet, than *benjo*, which is the traditional word, it is often easier for people to speak of forbidden topics like resentment toward parents in a second language than it would be in their native tongue.

Nevertheless, people express their deepest feelings in their first language, because it is in these sounds that the feelings are bound. I remember watching a session that Laura Perls did with a German woman who was learning English. She was describing a dream in which she had on a metal mask that covered her jaw. Telling the dream in the present tense, she said the metal mask was the German language, and now that she was learning English, she could take it off. After the work, Laura told the woman her own experience of being able to write poetry for the first time as an adult when she lived in South Africa and first began to speak English.

Responding to the group's uneasiness about English, I suggest a non-verbal exercise as a way of getting started. I direct them to walk around and touch each other as I call out, "Hands," "Elbows," "Shoulders," "Knees." Everyone relaxes and laughs as they perform the simple, silly actions. Next we form a circle, and each person makes a gesture accompanied by a sound which the whole group imitates. Much more relaxed after these games, the participants move good-naturedly into their assigned groups as Barry reads out their names. Group A will start with Barry and Group B with me. Each group has an assistant, one of Barry's advanced students, who stays with them to give them some continuity of leadership as they move back and forth for two sessions with each of us.

By the time the participants become acquainted in their small groups, it is time for lunch—which, hungry after a long morning, I devour eagerly. The rain stops during the afternoon, leaving the green park of the Kadoori Center bright and steaming in the sunlight as we spread out over the shining hillside toward the guest houses we'll be living in for the weekend.

SATURDAY, 2:00 P.M.

As soon as we come together Amy wants to work. Grateful to be spared the cautious task of building trust among strangers, I am pleased she feels safe enough to begin. Her first words are, "I want to cry and I can't." After saying this she sits silently before me, holding her hands and arms in a rigid oval. She is barely breathing, and I imagine she requires all her courage to remain present with her fear. She says she is aware of two voices:

I want to cry.

I want to control myself.

I ask her to exaggerate her control. She complies and contracts the muscles of her arms and shoulders. I feel myself becoming tense as I watch her bind herself with the piano wire of her inhibition. At the very moment that she seems completely immobilized, she begins to cry.

By exaggerating what she was doing, she had become aware of how she was stopping her crying, and, with awareness, she gained the option of stopping the interruption. As soon as she stopped interrupting herself, she could express herself naturally, which for her at that moment was to cry. People don't have to learn to be authentic and expressive: they are born knowing how to do this. They have to learn how they interrupt themselves, how they deny their authenticity and stop their expression. Inhibiting expression is a learned response, and what has been learned can be unlearned. Becoming aware of how one stops oneself allows the choice: either to continue the interruption or to stop. By becoming aware of what I am doing I can choose to respond to the present situation, rather than producing a learned response that has become unaware and that may or may not express who I am and what I want right now. Choosing authentic expression is one of the many choices that an aware person can make.

The next woman who comes forward emphasizes that her English name is Diane; she tells us she wants to talk with a friend. She puts her friend on the pillow and begins talking in an extremely rational, controlled manner. She says, "You shouldn't have talked about me to others, but I can understand," and "You hurt my feelings, but I don't think you meant to." I stop her after the third "but," and talk to the group about the function of "but," whose Chinese and Japanese equivalents I often hear.

The Japanese, whose particular moral delicacy often values vagueness, have several ways of saying "but" and use it often to soften a request or a description: it is difficult to speak polite Japanese without using some form of "but." Moreover, "but," and the various words in these languages that are translated as "but," are more than just words. They are indicators of a process that is especially powerful and insidious in interpersonal and intrapersonal dialogues. Since Eric Berne, the founder of Transactional Analysis, named the now famous game, "Yes, but...", many people have become sensitized to this usage and to the frustration it invariably poses for both speaker and listener; saying "but" in this way disguises a split within the person and simultaneously discounts both the speaker and the listener with a single movement of the palate. More than a word, it is the marker for the process of giving with one hand and taking away with the other. Like pretending illness, it is a socially acceptable way to express one's refusal without taking responsibility.

One of Fritz Perls's techniques for working with the process signaled by "but" was to change the "but" to "and"—which, despite its apparent simplicity, is a powerful intervention. "And" is an inclusive word, a statement of relationship which serves to link, to level, and to connect. "And" is nonjudgmental and inclusive, allowing human beings to express the variety and choice inherent in their lives. I have seen people burst into tears when they say "and" instead of "but." I have also seen people stop cold, refusing to say "and" as they experience the power of the inner transition that simply saying the word signifies. Substituting "and" for "but" is more than a substitution of one word for another; it is a transformation of one's potential for living. When I change "I want to see the world, but I'm too busy" into "I want to see the word and I'm too busy," I include both options and may realize that these statements are not mutually exclusive. Saying "and" instead of "but" is the first step toward having one's cake and eating it too, for it opens me to the realization that I can have and do the things I want. Only she who acknowledges that freedom is possible can be free, and only he who admits what he wants will ever get it.

Recently I have been working with "but" by having the speakers change pillows each time they say it. Changing pillows makes explicit the inner split that "but" denotes, and asking people to move their bodies as they say it enhances awareness of the proccss of disintegration that "but" signals. In the course of this work people often experience how they move forward and backward within a single sentence, and demonstrate their awareness with a hand gesture of cutting or breaking. As with everything in Gestalt, there are many ways to approach the stop\go process marked by "but," "*dannhaih*" (Cantonese), "*kedo*," "*demo*,"and "*ga*" (Japanese).

So I suggest to Diane that she say "and" instead of "but," and she has just begun to taste the difference when another group member jumps in and expresses frustration at how Diane is stopping her feelings. Diane avoids both herself and the other person by looking around the group and saying to Jennifer, "You look sad."

Jennifer replies, "I'm sad for you because you stopped your feelings."

Someone says to Jennifer, "Take responsibility for your own sadness."

I suggest that Jennifer talk to the friend Diane has been addressing. When she expresses her sorrow at how the friend is treating Diane, she moves her left arm from the elbow in a small, stiff chopping gesture. When I propose she move the arm from her shoulder, she does, and immediately begins to cry. Still her right side remains immobile. I ask where she is stopping herself, and she says in her throat. I ask what she wants to do, and she raises both hands and brings them down on the pillow with a loud smack. Then she stops.

Although her expression was incomplete, it is sufficient to give her a feeling of relief and she seems satisfied. I'm not, however, and as a coda to the work I ask her to make wide circles with both arms. Immediately she becomes aware of the contrast with her usual posture and says, "When I move this way I feel domineering and aggressive." I suggest she say something as she swings her arms, and she says, "I feel strange," and laughs in a cute and lively way as she experiences a lost fragment of herself.

When one of the group members asks if she may hug her, Jennifer says, "Yes," and then cries in her arms. Joanne, who is sitting beside the hugging pair, begins sobbing audibly. When someone points to her sorrow, she says, "I always cry when I see people hugging."

Someone else says, "Chinese don't hug. Especially in public."

I ask Joanne if I may hug her, and she agrees. It is a full, warm time. To conclude, I say a few words about loving one's self. I emphasize that this does not meaning loving one's image. Narcissus did not fall in love with himself, but with his image, and that makes all the difference. One does not need a mirror to love one's self; all one needs is to experience the wonder of one's here-and-now existence. The experienced self, the self known from within, is more present and more fully integrated with surrounding people, places, and things than the crisp, sharp image seen in a mirror. The experienced self is embedded in the universe and is aware it does not exist separate from contact and connection.

We have done enough, felt enough, been enough.

JUNE 15, SUNDAY, 8:00 P.M.

From my balcony on the hillside, I look out over miles of countryside where fields and villages perch among the vegetation like birds scattered in the foliage of a large tree. I spot the long, dark line of a small airstrip, from which planes, tiny as dragonflies, rise silently. Far away one of the new towns displays its vertical towers, a hallmark of the New Territories, where clusters of high-rise buildings leap up, unexpectedly forming islands of concrete in the lush landscape. When the setting sun breaks through the cloud banks on the horizon, a small rainbow arches over the miniature towers beside the flat golden water.

The group is meeting next door in a little parlor between Barry's and my rooms. I hear lively sounds of Cantonese as he facilitates an art therapy session there, and although it is my choice not to work in the evenings, I feel a twinge of loneliness, like a child who has not been invited to a party. Of course, I have my book and the lovely evening; nevertheless, this feeling of being an outsider is a familiar one. It is not something I have found here, but part of the baggage I bring to Asia.

When I first considered coming to Asia to work, I remember thinking that I would surely feel alienated living outside my own culture. After all, I am such an American enthusiast. I love the traditions of the United States and the magnificence of North America, which I cherish as my home. But in 1985, surrounded by the surprising success of Ronald Reagan's supporters in convincing the American people that the only problem that could be cured by "throwing money at it" was "national security," with the amazing corollary that the military recipients of these huge sums of money were not part of the government, I felt like the child who notices the emperor has no clothes. And since it was real life instead of a story, most people were insisting that the garments were lovely, and wondering what was wrong with those of us who didn't see them. Feeling entirely alienated from the horrendous waste of talent and treasure that the massive military spending of the national security state permits, I leapt at the chance to go to Japan. I imagined that I would feel more comfortable there as a foreigner, more able to accept my alienation there than I could in the United States, where I expected to feel at home.

My fantasy of being content where people recognize me as a foreigner has proven to be true; on the whole, I have been comfortable in Asia, where I have been less different and more accepted than I had dared to hope. Of course, there are times, like now, when I feel left out. Nevertheless, I am fully aware that if I wished to include myself, the young Chinese in the other room would be glad to welcome me into their gathering.

Realizing that I am only marginally different from the Chinese people I work with and it is I who am leaving myself out, I accept that I am creating any pain that accompanies my quiet evening alone. I remember Fritz saying, "Loneliness is solitude plus bullshit," and I laugh at the me who makes myself lonely as I stand on this beautiful hillside watching the sun set over the South China Sea.

June 15, Sunday, 6:00 a.m.

I leap out of bed to turn off the air conditioner, a constant companion in the Hong Kong summer, and am immediately rewarded with the chatter of invisible birds beginning their day. I quickly dress and leave, turning the infernal machine on as I go out the door so that I can turn it off again when I return. I congratulate myself for remembering how to live in the tropics.

The outdoors is warm and damp under piles of gray clouds as I walk up a road that leads through the park and gardens of the Kadoori Center. Along the road, guesthouses of gray stone hug the hillside like cave dwellings, surrounded by tall, dark hedges covered with mysterious yellow and white flowers, bright and furry as large moths. While trying to photograph one of the flowers, I inadvertently break it from its stem. Apologetically, I place the blossom back on the bush, and the heavy sweet fragrance remains on my hand.

Walking around the hillside, I find a wide place where I do my Tai Chi, surrounded by a tangle of unfamiliar leaves and flowers. In the background, a rolling hillside rises in great sweeps of green, totally empty of human habitation. Playing the familiar movements, I sing Garcia Lorca's paean, "Green, how much I love you, green," over and over to myself like a mantra until I finish my practice as empty and clear as the hillside. I'm ready to work.

Sunday, 10:00 a.m.

This morning I am meeting with a new group, and we take some time to get acquainted. Since they know each other from yesterday's work with Barry, I'm the only outsider. Nevertheless, I see they are ready to trust me, and even during the check-in period they put in their names to work.

First is Karl, a young man who tells us about an unfinished relationship with a former girlfriend. This content swiftly disappears as his here-and-now tension increases dramatically. Almost as soon as he begins to talk, he becomes stiff and says that he wants to lie down. The group has gathered quite close to him and now opens a space; he lies down on the floor. I ask him if I may touch him, and he says, "Yes." When I take his hand, he begins to tremble. I put my hand on his diaphragm and, with gentle pressure, encourage him to continue breathing. He releases several desperate cries telling us of his despair in a wordless story of intense suffering contained and denied. Everyone in the room knows they are witnessing the expression of heretofore inexpressible misery that Karl has, at last, found the safety to disclose. It's a sweet moment when he sits up and shows us his shining face, relieved and relaxed after the work he has done.

The group shares their joy at Karl's release. Annette comes forward and, before she begins, asks two of the women for support. They agree and come to sit on either side of her. I am touched by her courage in asking for support and by their simple acceptance of her request.

I understand from Annette's opening that her agenda is to talk to her co-workers and also her clients. I encourage her to do this. To the clients she says, "I am threatened by you. Also I pity you."

As the clients she responds, "You don't accept me."

Since she seems stuck here, I join in and play her, saying, "I don't accept you because I don't accept myself."

When she hears this, she says, "I hear a voice that says, 'You should always be successful.'" This is an interruption; however, in the spirit of not interrupting the interruption, I remain silent. She continues, "It also says that I should always accept others." She says all of this very quickly, skimming the intellectual surface of her process without touching the feelings that go with the words. Then she says she wants to stop.

Of course, I agree. I believe the power to stop, to exit from the interaction, is absolute and belongs to everyone. Then she says she wants to hold my hands. I agree, and as we hold hands, she says she feels like running away because, holding my hands, she feels "a pain she has felt before."

After we disengage, I talk about unfinished business, especially unexpressed suffering, and how it emerges in the present at times of intimacy. When I am intimate with another person I am being intimate with myself, and at such moments I will feel the inner distress that I have been avoiding. Trying to avoid the pain associated with intimate contact, many of us avoid closeness altogether. Annette seems to understood exactly what I am saying, yet I'm uncertain about her ability to integrate what she has done because she has guarded her feelings so closely. I feel compassion, for she is clearly a distressed person who lacks the support and security she needs to meet her pain, her past, and herself.

Next, Martha wants to work on a dream. She tells of a brief scene in which a car flies over a V-shaped gap. When I ask her to play the gap, she begins to show some sadness, which she dissipates by talking about dreams and other work she has done. I ask her what she feels now, and she says she is blank and numb. I suggest she stand up and act out the V-shaped gap with her body. She gets up, holds up her arms, and says, "I can touch this side and this side," and then, breaking into deep sobs, she drops to the floor in front of me. She sobs until she begins to feel cramps in her legs.

Cramping sometimes accompanies the rush of adrenaline that comes when powerful feelings are released. Some people are time bombs, waiting for the support and safety they need to explode into the vigorous emotions they have held hidden away for years, emotions whose intensity threaten the equilibrium of the personalities they've constructed to contain their passion and to survive everyday life. Expressing their suppressed emotions is a necessary part of integrating the personality with the available energy of the present moment.

Suppression is expensive energetically, for in addition to the energy lost in the unexpressed feelings, even more energy is required to hold them down. Thus some people are exhausted with their inner struggle before they even begin to do anything else. In a safe environment where explosions of feeling are facilitated and well supported, the person may begin nourishing the coping personality, which is often running on a nearly empty tank, with the vital and renewable energy of the living organism.

A personality founded on suppressed emotion is limited in its development because suppressed suffering divides the deepest springs of vitality from the thoughts and actions of everyday life. This separation underlies the robotic personalities so common in industrial societies, as well as the growing number of depressed people who exhaust themselves avoiding the suffering they do not have adequate support to meet.

The open heart is the channel which connects the thinking self and the instinctual energy of the body's center: the *hara* or *tan tien*, which is the place where we experience our affiliation with life. The long period of socialization required for membership in most human societies far too often encapsulates in fear and misery the delight that lies at the center of our existence, disengaging it from present awareness. The consequent suppression and denial of feeling divides the person so that she or he is unable to touch the original joy in living that is each one's birthright. It is disintegration created by the separation of the socialized self from the instinctual self that creates the inner split that the Perlses labeled "top dog" and "bottom dog."

Until the 1950s pleasure was rarely discussed in psychology. Then James Olds and his colleagues began a series of experiments on rats that, according to Lewis Thomas, "should have changed everything about our view of the mind, but hasn't yet." Olds intended to follow up on the work of Magoum, who had discovered sleep and wakefulness centers. "By a stroke of luck, and an instrument bent slightly out of shape, his electrode ended up in a narrow bundle of fibers near the midline, long known to neuroanatomists as the medial forebrain bundle." After this bundle was stimulated, the rats who were free to run kept returning to the exact area where this charge had been delivered. Olds set up further experiments, including a conventional maze, and the rats always learned how to receive the stimulation. "They would climb heights, circumvent blockades and cross electrified grates that were painful enough to keep away ordinary rats in search of food. Finally, Olds adapted a Skinner box to permit his rats to stimulate their own brains by pressing a treadle."

Once the duration and magnitude of the electrical current had been arranged to its satisfaction, a rat would push the treadle continuously and would choose it over food and water. This impulse to receive pleasure was unrelated to hunger and thirst and sexual arousal, and did not cause an addiction, for "when the source of current was switched off the animals usually would try the lever a few times, then simply give it up and go to sleep." Olds and Milner, his colleague, called the area being stimulated in their experiments the "pleasure center." Each species tested seems to have one. As Thomas summarizes, "The range of animals possessing a pleasure center is already broad enough to allow the generalization that it is a property built into all vertebrate brains."

Perhaps because the notion of a pleasure center is just too outlandish in a society where enjoyment is seen as morally suspect, the phenomenon was renamed ICSS, Intracranial Self-Stimulation, and, according to Thomas, has now disappeared from the field of neurobiology. Thomas likes it this way, "for it has raised, it seems to me, one of the loveliest of all the possibilities raised by biological science in memory....Namely, there is such a thing as pure pleasure, and there is a mechanism for mediating it alive in our brains." It is Thomas's hypothesis that "the medial forebrain bundle carries the impulses, coming from cells all over the body, bearing the news that they are alive." He continues, "The sense of being alive should exist, even if it proves not to when the work has moved further along. Pleasure in being alive ought to exist as a special, independent, autonomous sense."

I believe we are endowed with precisely this sense and that many of us experience it from time to time. We see its fullest expression in small children and animals as they play for the sheer joy of the moment, in fish as they leap from the water in early summer, and in birds as they do the lovely, useless things that birds often do. Surely this is the phenomenon that inspired Wilhelm Reich to intuit that all anxiety is pleasure anxiety, the uneasiness that people who have learned that they must suffer to be worthy feel when life's pleasurable excitement stirs within them.

We become separate from our profound joy in living when our caretakers break our hearts, when those we depend on in our helplessness hurt us rather than help us. Maria Montessori says the essence of the child is love—a profound idea, for it asserts that since we were all children once, our human essence is love. Yet if this is so, how can we grow so distant from our beginning? The small, loving human being knows when it is betrayed. He or she knows, grieves, denies, rages, and denies some more before giving up. Then, on top of the misery of betrayal, most of us—though not all—live on to construct an existence that endures.

Children who cannot deny their despair kill themselves, and more and more are doing so every year. The pain that accompanies the realization of betrayal is often too great to experience, and so is suppressed. But hiding and denying pain does not heal the heart; instead, it allows the wounded person to continue existence as a paltry wisp of his or her original design and potential.

The heart is healed when one finds a person or people who will love them. Love means to stay with a person while they suffer and rage, and to accept and respect their emotions as an essential part of who they are. According to Carl Jung: "Where love rules there is no will to power, and where power predominates, there love is lacking. The one is the shadow of the other."

This dynamic is true both within the self and in our feelings and actions toward others. So long as we try only to infuse ourselves with power, we will never be whole. We will never be successful in controlling ourselves either, for the deep energies that drive behavior are beyond the reach of our will.

To love, one must be present and disinterested—the Buddhists say unattached—which means that one cares for the other without requiring any special behaviors in return. If we love, we trust others to know what is best for themselves and even trust them to make mistakes and to learn from their mistakes. Frightened people do not trust easily or quickly, which is entirely natural, as trust once betrayed is not wisely given in haste.

Lovers are patient people who can sit with others with no particular goal except to be together. The one who finds such a person, or preferably a group of such people, can begin to heal her or his broken heart and to touch the place within that says, "I'm here now and I feel good to be alive." Once the heart opens, a person will experience his or her spot within the web of existence. Aware or not, we are part of Earth's living, and our awareness of this connection frees us to live with fearless delight in the experienced certainty that we are part of a larger whole from which we will never, even in death, be separated.

The broken heart is a metaphor that is increasingly present in my thinking. When disappointment and betrayal break the heart, we lose the connection between the center and the brain; thus, the subvocal talking which we call thinking becomes separated from here-and-now existence, with its firm grounding in the Earth's present. Ungroundedness creates people who are not only stupid but dangerous as well, for they indulge in detached, pseudo-rational thought.

I will never forget watching the scenes in the movie "Hearts and Minds" in which General Westmoreland, his elegant white hair topping a sturdy masculinity of craggy features and impeccable uniform, tells the world that Asians do not feel sorrow when their loved ones die. Intercut with his speech were pictures of Asian people passionately mourning at gravesides, which revealed Westmoreland's performance for what it was: a stunning presentation of how people whose hearts are broken think and live. The general's exterior was perfect, and the inner self was absent. He was the hollow man. It is not unusual for the hollow man to obscure his own anguish by threatening others, so that instead of pitying him, people will view him with fear and thus allow him the illusion of fully dimensional existence: "You fear me, therefore I am."

Trust returns in unexpected ways. Recently a woman in a different group began her work by saying to herself on the cushion, "You have no right to be." When she changed pillows, she was aware that she did not trust this voice. She experienced her distrust with absolute certainty, and it was from this paradoxical certainty that she began to ground her being and to build her life. She found this alone and essentially unaided. I did not have the imaginative power to formulate such a basis for trust until she showed me how.

Now, in Hong Kong, the next woman whispers that she wants to work. I have to strain to hear the tiny voice coming from the small person who sits with her head lowered and her back hunched. She resembles an invalid child. She wants me to use her Chinese name, which, of course, I do. She tells of her relationship with her mother, a nightmare of entanglement and dependency. "I can't leave home until my mother says it's okay."

From what she says, she seems willing to give up her own life to make her mother happy and accepts her mother's criticism for her inevitable failure to accomplish this task. She continues to love and serve her mother regardless of how her mother treats her, and says, "I can't be happy until my mother is happy." On the other hand, in a lifeless and unsupported voice, she says again and again, "I'm lost. I'm lost."

I work with her in tiny increments of awareness that lead no further than enabling her dimly to experience her profound pain and her blocking of further expression. I finally ask her if it is all right to stop. She agrees. We both feel helpless and frustrated. I tell her that she needs intensive on-going therapy. I hope she finds it.

Everyone in the group is tired after an emotional morning. We're more than ready to quit for lunch.

SUNDAY, 2:00 P.M.

I'm back with the group I met with yesterday. They have joined together in a supportive and understanding fellowship, energized and ready to work.

The first woman, Christine, wants to work with a skin disease. I ask her to talk to the disease and she does, saying, "I hate you. You take away my freedom. You take away my money." When I ask her to play the disease, she says, "I'm very weak," and she slumps forward as though unable to support her own weight. I see her effort simply to keep herself sitting and again am struck with the power of imagination as she creates the states that go with the various roles in her inner psychic drama. She becomes the disease. Without acting in any aware sense, she presents her weakness, a heretofore hidden and unconsciously expressed aspect of herself. I ask her what she wants, and she says support.

I ask another member to sit back to back with her to give her the support she has requested. (As I write this, I see that this was a mistake, for I could have encouraged her to ask for support herself.) Feeling more supported in her now explicit weakness, she continues expressing her frailty while receiving the warmth and encouragement she needs to become aware of her sorrow. After she expresses her sadness, she switches and plays her parents, who show their love by being critical and demanding, by enrolling their daughter in a strict school, and by often "scolding" her. When she becomes the disease again, she is aware of feeling angry toward her parents. After she expresses her anger, she feels much stronger than before.

Next Christine becomes angry at herself for internalizing her parents' demands. She recognizes that by making more and more demands on herself, she has driven her non-verbal self to say, "I rebel." This silenced and now inarticulate part of her being has spoken out in the only way it knows how, which in this case is as a skin disease. When she switches again and plays herself, she tells the weak self that she drove her to work hard because it was the only way she knew how to be.

Now I sit on the cushion and play the weak self, saying, "If you don't take care of me, I will torture you."

When she hears this, she becomes rigid, and says, "I know I have to take care of you, and I can't move." For a few seconds she sits perfectly still, holding her head in her hands. Then she says, "Of course I don't know how to nurture you. My parents nurtured me by feeding me lots of food and medicine, taking me to the doctor, scolding me and putting me in hard schools. I don't know how to nurture you."

As she says this, I have the fantasy of a little girl holding a baby doll. I pick up the pillow which stands for the weak, sick self; cradling it like a baby, I say, "This is little Christine. Would you like to hold her?"

She says, "Yes," and takes the pillow, which she begins to stroke softly. She says, "I don't know where my feelings are."

I reply, "Just let your hands talk. There's no right way to do this."

She holds the pillow awkwardly for a minute or so and then puts it on the floor and gently strokes it for a few seconds. Then she stands it on its end as though it has become a toddler. She takes it in her arms again and cradles it like a baby. I caress her head while she caresses the pillow. Everyone in the group is crying, including me. As I participate in this quiet scene, I have the clear understanding that none of us have been nurtured very well, and so barely know how to nurture either ourselves or each other. I stop myself from sobbing out loud as with the others in group I meet my own deprivation. Later I will think of our wounded planet—scarred and mutilated by this specie that has apparently forgotten how to cherish its young, its home, its resources, and itself.

We take a break after this work, and I walk onto the balcony into the noonday heat thinking about how to resume. In the vast sky between the hillside and the horizon the clouds hang in soft clusters.

It is clear that people do not create illness in any concrete and aware way; nevertheless, aside from infectious bacteria and viruses, it is the totality of the organism that is generating the disease. Of course this is not a useful concept if it is used to make people feel guilty; no concept is. The distinction between taking responsibility and blaming oneself is a very important one, and I am still not clear exactly how to shape this boundary. I can see, through this work and other work that people have done with me, that there is great power in playing the role of the symptom, speaking as the symptom, saying "I am" to the symptom. Taking responsibility is not self-blame; it is coming to know what I am doing, what I am expressing, what I am saying.

For those who have difficultly taking responsibility for illness, it might be useful to approach the notion of taking responsibility as a healing fiction. Maybe it's so; maybe it's not. Nevertheless, by entering into the existential mode of identifying with the symptom rather than denying my role in its creation, I may gain perspective and expand my awareness of what I am doing and how I am doing it as opposed to suffering passively. Blaming is a moralistic mode of judgment and evaluation, a narrowing rather than a broadening of the possibility for change.

I know that the distinction between blaming and taking responsibility is a difficult issue for many people who encounter Gestalt, and I would like to clarify it as much as possible. I really don't know the extent to which any of us creates his or her own illness, yet I have observed that some people have been able to heal themselves by taking responsibility for their illness, even though this is a difficult thing to do and one which requires great trust both in oneself and in the facilitator.

I also want to comment on the role of the pillow or the empty chair in Gestalt work. The human imagination is so powerful, especially when strong unfinished emotion comes forward, that the pillow takes on the identity and attributes of the projected self in an almost magical way. I have had people say, "I can't say that to my mother; it would hurt her too much." When I have remind them that it's just a pillow and their mother won't hear what they say, they hear my remark as a revelation; they have configured their mother so powerfully in their imagination that, for them at that moment, she is present in the room.

This mighty ability to evoke the powers of one's life is also a healing power. I can speak my unfinished emotion to people who are dead. I can learn from my childhood self and comfort her as well. When Christine holds the pillow and caresses it like a baby, she is giving herself something that she missed, and soothing the pain of her deprivation. There's no doubt that it's better to have received the comforting caresses as a child. There's equally no doubt that rather than denying our misery for a lifetime, we are better off becoming aware of how we have been deprived, and how we might begin to fulfill some of these unfulfilled needs in the present.

One reason Gestalt works is that the adult has resources that the child lacked and so can express what was impossible for the dependent child, who had no place to go if she broke the family rules by speaking the unspeakable. When we adults become aware of how our actions perpetuate the deprivations of the past, we become free to chose alternatives to the deprivation and solace for the trauma that the helpless child could only endure. On the other hand, the suppressed child has attributes adults lack. Often I have observed that forgiveness, acceptance, and creativity are more likely to emerge in the child's voice. Both child and adult are essential; both must be included for a person to become whole.

When we reconvene, Adam wants to work. I ask him to come forward and sit in front of me, a relatively recent change I have made in response to my declining vision, rather than a desire to replicate the "hot seat" popularized by Fritz Perls.Adam is a slight, elusive young man who presents us with a tight bundle of dilemmas that are effectively paralyzing him. His process goes roughly like this: I have to be number one and I have to do hard jobs, and I have to have lots of money to prove that I am number one. This pursuit takes all my time and I never do what I like to do. In fact I don't even know what I want to do because I am so preoccupied with what I should do that I never have an opportunity to discover what I like.

This series of double binds has been reinforced by humiliation, by various people telling Adam that if he does not fulfill the impossible task of always being number one, he is worthless. He expresses the impossibility of his situation poignantly as he says, "I have no confidence. I am always trying to get people to tell me they approve of me. When they do, I feel contempt for them because I know I have manipulated them."

When I ask him what he feels as he says this, he replies, "Despair." He pauses and then adds, "Humiliation. No matter what I do, I don't respect myself." He lowers his head, and his voice disappears into his chest.

We sit silently for a minute or so. Then I ask him to look around at the people in the group. He does, and then looks at me. "What do you see?" I ask, and he says, "I see warmth." He looks again. "Understanding."

"How do you feel now?"

He smiles a shy smile. "Better."

I point out that his awareness of his despair allows him to stop humiliating himself and to do something different. Now he is able to see the people here in the room instead of the ones who denied and humiliated him in the past. He seems surprised to hear this.

I suggest that he begin to pay attention to what he wants each moment, to his smallest desires, as a practice that could gradually lead to his reclaiming his lost self. Then I ask, "What do you want to do right now?"

"Go back to my seat and listen to the other group members," he replies.

We exchange smiles as he returns to his seat.

This work is a telling example of how young men are often hollowed out by their socialization. Humiliated as a child by those who promote an institutional masculinity that denies significant aspects of his spontaneous vitality, the young boy experiences consistent ridicule of the people and activities he enjoys, especially if these are of a gentle sort that the overactive patriarchal imagination might label feminine. He is expected from an early age to live up to demands that he become rigid and unfeeling—a state that many regard as "strong"—so he loses his confidence, which is another word for his center and the source of his real strength. As he learns to deny his experience and deprecate his choices based on genuine preference, he becomes hollow and forfeits the security that comes from trusting one's self and one's own authentic desires. Adults teach him that he will find satisfaction in the approval of others, and in seeking this recognition from others he becomes obedient, obsequious, and empty. He stops doing the things he loves and instead does the things that he has been taught will bring approval, especially from those—often older—men whose approval is infused with social value.

A man who is doing what he loves does not care whether others approve or not; his reward is in the doing, and the approval of others is a non-essential bonus. People who do what they enjoy doing inevitably become proficient because they are motivated by the sheer pleasure of the activity and so they do it over and over again. Such a person is not easily manipulated and controlled; because he knows what he likes, which is a fundamental ingredient of knowing who one is.

The man whose inner self is crushed by humiliation and disapproval desperately seeks from others the satisfaction that can come only from gratifying his own deepest self, so he is never satisfied. Such individuals are very useful in mass societies, which need a lot of people to perform tasks that no one in their right mind would ever do by choice. And so the rigid enforcement of the masculine ideal, which is essentially a life-denying ethic of competition and conformity, ensures a steady supply of broken young men and women who strive to please.

Vital and dissatisfied young men are potentially dangerous because unless they are sent away to war they present a threat to the peace of the community, as anyone who watches television can observe. Seeking the identity that was dismantled by the caretakers' disapproval, they are encouraged to believe they will find it by satisfying some other authority figure.

The problems of men are the great ones of our time. Who are all these people with guns and poison gas? Who are the muggers and rapists? The overwhelming majority are young men who, with their violence, draw our attention to their personal suffering. The violence of young men is, like so many so-called problems, a failed solution to the real problem of socialization by humiliation. As well-meaning elders try to shape boys and young men into an idealized image of manhood, they destroy sense and feeling. While this rigid definition of masculinity may have been justified in times when war was necessary to protect the community, or when it was a dangerous but enjoyable pastime for men of all ages, now that nuclear wars mean suicide for our entire specie and ecosystem it is an unacceptable menace.

Fortunately the inner self is indestructible, and through the kind of work Adam is doing, men of all ages can discover and nurture the damaged selves their elders humiliated into silence. They can begin the lifelong integration of desire and energy that allows them to avoid the fate that Gertrude Stein so poignantly articulated when she asked, "What's the use of being a little boy if one has to grow up to be a man?" People with massive unfinished business cannot mature because they are stuck in the loop of the repetition compulsion, the fixed gestalten; and they strive again and again to complete what they could not finish in childhood. Helping male people face their real problems and learn to live with the dilemmas of their existence is not altruism: it is self-preservation.

We stop after Adam's work. I feel tired and satisfied, ready to let the young people party while I go off by myself.

JUNE 16, MONDAY, 10:00 A.M.

It's the last day of the workshop. We meet for two hours in working groups, and then the two groups will come together for a session completing the workshop.

Annette feels dissatisfied with the work she has begun earlier. This is unfinished business; and, while not always possible, it is infinitely desirable that no one leave a Gestalt workshop with more unfinished business than she or he originally brought in. I am not surprised when Annette begins to cry. She is expressing the feelings that she had blocked during her work on the first day, and I am happy to sit with her and hold her hand again while she weeps. She is good at getting the support she needs, and I feel good seeing her touch the feelings that, just the day before yesterday, had been too threatening for her to experience. Her work gives a strong sense of completion to her group.

We go into the large group in good spirits, although Annette is still very vulnerable and sits with her two friends, quietly crying throughout the ensuing expressions of appreciation and resentment. I welcome resentment, because it's important not to create a goody-goody atmosphere in the groups, and it's helpful for everyone to see that expressing anger or other negative feelings is possible, not just in the work but in the here and now, which is far more challenging and dangerous.

We end in time for lunch and walk into the hot day, brighter and drier now that the sky has cleared. There's even a light breeze on the hillside, which brushes softly against my skin as we walk together to the dining hall.

The group is over, and we all find our way back to the site of our individual enterprises. I return to Deep Water Bay, where my friend and hostess, Marylee, has prepared spaghetti with pesto which I love. I feel befriended and content as I go to sleep in the soft hum of the discreet air conditioner in her wonderful apartment.

TUESDAY, JUNE 17, 8:00 P.M.

This is the second of two evening groups I am doing with Barry's advanced trainees. I enjoy being back in a small group of familiar faces after the large group of mostly new people that I worked with over the weekend. I am accustomed to meeting roomsful of new people and offering concentrated attention to their present behavior. At time I find it tiring; at other times, I am awed at my own presumption. How can I possibly know someone after being in their presence for only a few minutes? Of course, the answer is: I can't. Yet people are, as Gertrude Stein observed, "always repeating the whole of them"; and for one who is willing to tune in to this repetition, which varies enormously from person to person in its periodicity and not at all in its veracity, the essence of each person is here and now. Everyone is always repeating the whole of them: it's only because most of us don't pay attention and often want to be fooled, for one reason or another, that everyone is not fully unmasked at every minute.

I am at ease in the familiar group—sensitive, as I was not over the weekend, to the prim precision with which the group members speak English as they check in with what they want.

Martha wants to work. She is a young Chinese woman in her late twenties who has been working with Barry for the past few years. I have worked with her several times and know something of her painful history. We begin with her here-and-now experience. She reports that her body is hot and her fingertips are cold. She touches her back for emphasis as she says, "I m cold and I'm hot."

I suggest she add to her sentence, "And this is part of my existence."

She repeats, "I'm cold and I'm hot and this is part of my existence." Then she says, "I feel resentment to myself for these extremes."

I say, "Martha, say it to me. 'I resent you for making me aware of the extremes of my existence.'"

She hesitates. Coaxing her a bit, I say, "Do it as an experiment."

She says to me, "I resent you for making me aware of my extremes." She says it again and again with increasing power and emphasis. She begins to sob deep sobs, seizes my hands in hers, and says, "I'm on a threshold." And then, with immense passion and energy, "I want my life to be more than the pain it has been in the past."

I hold her hands and remain silent with her for some seconds. Then I encourage her to say this sentence to others in the group, people who have been her friends and colleagues for years. They have seen her through changes that might otherwise seem astonishing, and yet within the context of an ongoing and committed Gestalt community are not surprising at all. Martha very concisely says to each person, "I want my life to be more than the pain it has been in the past." Each one recognizes that Martha is accepting her past, which allows the opening of her future, and this is an accomplishment to rejoice. Those of us who do not fully experience the past are the ones who endlessly and senselessly repeat it. They have seen Martha cross the lonely valley, the one you have to cross by yourself because "ain't nobody gonna cross it for you." And she did it!

Now we are welcoming her on the other side. Spontaneously, the group forms a circle around her. We stand with our arms around each other. Martha is home, aware in the present where she has been all along and where she at last has the safety, courage, and support to authentically experience. T. S. Eliot knew:

> *We shall not cease from exploration*
> *And the end of all our exploring*
> *Will be to arrive where we started*
> *And know the place for the first time.*

Among the Chinese, the constraints of pleasing and satisfying the demands of the older generation continue far longer into adulthood than among Japanese or Americans. I have heard Hong Kong Chinese young adults say, "I can't leave home until my parents are happy," or "If I leave home, my parents will get a divorce." Such statements reveal an encasement in the family of origin that creates horrendous stress for the young adult seeking to find his or her own life. It is quite a stunning attitude to Americans, who are likely to be focused on what their parents owe them rather than vice versa. For the youth of the various

Chinas, the expectations of the elders is a large and often impossible burden: young people cannot make their parent's marriage work, nor can they guarantee their parents' happiness.

The idea that we can make others happy is one of the great myths underlying all systems, both personal and political, that try to manipulate people through guilt. One can do what another asks, but that will not make them happy. A person who demands that others make them happy is insatiable and, as soon as one demand is satisfied, will make another, and another, and another. Anyone who has tried to make another person happy knows what a futile task it is; people have to make themselves happy.

Among mental health professionals the U.S.-style independence from the family of origin is tellingly called "emancipation," and is often consciously sought by therapists and social workers as a solution to conflicts between parents and young adults. In the Chinese family, however, "emancipation" is a superfluous concept: unnecessary, undesirable, and basically disruptive of the natural order of things as defined by Confucianism with its emphasis on serving the elders. In the Confucian tradition time runs backward, from future to past, with the young living to serve the old; it's been doing this for over two thousand years. Since in Confucian morality one is expected to serve not only the parents, but the parents' parents, and all the ancestors stretching back to the beginning of time, the notion of an independent, mature human being is quite extraneous and disruptive to the system. Everyone is forever a child serving the elders, and it is only when one dies that one becomes a true adult.

Unlike the Japanese, who are expected to mature into loyalty to an organization like the company, which is larger than the family, Chinese young people in Hong Kong are expected to retain their primary loyalty to the family that bore and raised them. This cohesion of the family of origin creates painful struggles as the young Hong Kong adults, strongly influenced by American popular culture, try to find their way toward a satisfying sense of self within, not distinct from, the family.

Since the children are responsible for the parents, the precept of filial piety also justifies child labor. In a recent group in Hong Kong, several young people remembered making plastic flowers (*qua fa*) as children. Susan mentioned the endlessness of the work: counting 12 flowers, 12 batches of 12, and then starting over again. It seemed to last forever, she said. Remembering the urgency of childhood—the eons between Thanksgiving and Christmas, the unbearably long wait for a few minutes before being allowed to go for ice cream—I shivered at the eternity of misery and boredom that child labor represents, wholly apart from the deprivation of intellectual and social development it demands. For one member of the group, John, it was the separation from friends and the loss of after school play that continued to rankle as he remembered the mother who could only see her little boy as a source of income, a possession rather than a precious individual revealing himself for her enlightenment and joy. To be able to do so was outside her imagination, for no one had ever seen her that way.

I think we are coming to the end of the grand illusion of wealth, an illusion which could not become explicit until we experienced the democratization of greed. Behaviors like greedy acquisition and killing in anger, which may be tolerable in a few, become unacceptably destructive to the social and ecological order when everyone does them. From an international perspective it seems clear that as people in the United States become richer, they become more miserable and mean-spirited. Their frenzy of greed fuels the crime of murder as well as the spiritual death expressed in the desperately angry fanaticism that some claim as religion. In the name of wealth, children in poor countries suffer the death of their childhood, while in the richest country in the world children murder each other. In a culture of winning, for the spiritually dead murder is the only way to win, for I win only when I make you deader than I feel.

Qing is a male social worker in a center for what he calls "youth at risk." He presents himself by saying that he doesn't like these young men, whom he considers juvenile delinquents. He tells of two boys, about 15, who recently came into his center and began miming sexual intercourse.

He became furious and told them to leave, and they did. His conflict was between his rage and the ethics of acceptance and understanding he had been taught in social work school.

Feeling himself inadequate as a social worker, Qing thought it might be better if he became a policeman, because, in his words, "sometimes violence must be used." He frames his description of violence in the language of irresponsibility, saying several times, "I have no choice." He says he has friends who are policemen, and he is clearly attracted to this mode of interaction, especially as he experiences what he perceives as his inadequacy as a social worker.

I ask him to dialogue with the "youth at risk," and then with the ideal social worker. In neither dialogue is he able to convincingly express his anger. He was clearly outraged by the young men's miming of the sex act, and he wanted to exclude them from the human race. A group member asks, "Weren't you able to get them to leave the center without violence?" He ignores the question until I draw his attention to his refusal. Keenly aware that I value non-violence, I focus on his unwillingness to take responsibility for his desire for violent solutions.

As I write this, I imagine that his denial of responsibility is the expression of his ambivalence, and that the real issue is his inability to see any middle ground between the compassionate acceptance of the social worker and the routine violence of the policeman. Since this dilemma is a social as well as a personal one, Qing will have to touch his deep individualism and creativity to learn how to manage it. As the member of the Danish defense ministry said recently, while discussing the existence of a counter-culture community in Copenhagen, "You know, a dilemma is not the same thing as a problem. You can solve a problem. You cannot solve a dilemma. You have to manage it." By taking responsibility for his feelings when he considers violence, Qing might begin managing the dilemma of confronting violence without becoming violent himself.

And so, within their distinct variety of Chinese culture, the Chinese people of Hong Kong struggle with the same issues of self-awareness and self-expression that people face everywhere. Their

Gestalt work is very much like the work Japanese or Americans do. The issues of individuation, self-trust, vitality and growth being blocked by repressed pain and anger, troubled relations with friends and lovers, resolving dependency on parents and other authority figures—all these change little from culture to culture. Culture is a costume—often strikingly beautiful and colorful, and sometimes very heavy—drawn on over the basic human realities: birth, childhood dependence, extended socialization, initiation into the larger group, gender indoctrination, sex, procreation, care for the young, work, community, care for the sick, old age, illness, death.

Regardless of how our cultures try to regulate these significant universal processes, they can only elaborate them with ribbons and jewels. And while some people place a high value on their jewelry, it is within each person that excitement stirs and awareness emerges; it is individual human beings who learn, feel sexual attraction, meet death. Nothing will change this basic fact of life.

The difficulty of controlling the essential happenings in our lives is only made more emphatic by the insistent demands and commands of culture, which do not so much change the nature of our living as distract us so that we become less aware of the essential elements of our living and dying here at home on Earth. The faithful world of nature is with us always, both within and without, and if we refuse to be distracted by the bright colors and flamboyant gestures of the social magicians, we can constantly confirm the biological heritage of billions of years of evolution which is the essence of our human condition, the home from which no one can evicts us. Knowing we are the Earth and the Earth is us, we can be at peace with ourselves and our surroundings. This relation is unchangeable, and the aware certainty of this profound truth is available to every person who is secure enough to experience her or his present existence.

Feelings of isolation and abandonment come when we suspend awareness of our immersion in the Earth's living processes: our most fundamental certainty. We are part of a web of existence, both human and nonhuman; and the essence of our humanity resides in the choices we make regarding the quality of our inevitable relatedness.

Certainly the choice we make regarding our relationship to our aware self is vital to how we will relate to others— people, places, and things. If I treat myself as a machine, a way to earn money or satisfy the expectations of others, I will treat everyone else the same way. I may mask my use of others with caring words and seductive phrases; nevertheless, I will sense what I'm doing and experience the emptiness of a life that misses the true living that comes with authentic meeting.

We can choose to relate in the I-It mode, making others, people and objects, depersonalized things to be used and manipulated without respect or caring. Or we can choose to place ourselves in relationships of mutuality, honoring everything and everybody as part of a respected reality in which we experience our own existence. Then everything becomes support. This is our choice, our area of free will. We do not have the choice to avoid relationship, which is an inevitable condition of our existence; it is, however, from the choices we make regarding the quality of relationships that we create the morality of our existence.

Chapter 5

China: Taiwan's uneasy mix of Confucianism and modernity

«Life is a public performance on the violin, in which you must learn the instrument as you go along.»
—E. M. Forester

Tuesday, December 10, 8:00 p.m.

Today I arrived in Taipei, where I immediately embarrassed myself by popping out of the restricted customs area without my passport. I missed it at once, and, sheepishly confessing my error to the small group waiting for me in the airport, immediately disabused them all of any exalted expectations they might have had concerning the wisdom and infallibility of the foreign teacher.

My Chinese companions courteously retrieved the passport with an absence of wisecracks that was downright un-American—yet another useful reminder that I'm not in Kansas. The seven of us got into a van which James, the driver, had parked illegally in front of the air terminal. As he left the airport grounds and merged the loaded van skillfully into Taipei's infamous turmoil of traffic and air pollution, I felt the completion of my arrival. I was in Taipei, and on my way to new adventures.

The seven in the van include Ellen, who will be my translator in the group here, and James, driver and guide through the intricacies of Taipei.

Both are staff members of LTB, Vitality, Inc., who are arranging the workshop. LTB stands for Life, Truth, and Beauty; we'll see how well they live up to their name.

There are also four people from Hong Kong who arrived on an earlier flight: Barry; his wife Marilyn; their two-year-old daughter He Ling; and Carol, the trilingual translator (Mandarin, Cantonese, and English) who is also an advanced student of Gestalt. It is Carol's fare and expenses that Harold Tse, the president of LTB, Vitality, Inc., didn't want to pay and over which he threatened to cancel Barry's participation in the workshop. I am the solitary American and, since we have three generations, also the grandmother of the group. To these two roles, I add my favorite, the traveler, as, vibrating with excitement, I eagerly embrace the fascination of a new land unfolding before me.

With its streets and freeways jammed full of dusty cars driven on the right side of the road, Taiwan resembles the United States more than does either Hong Kong or Tokyo. This is not surprising: since well before World War II the United States has sponsored and supported the Kuomintang—the Chinese political party whose army invaded Taiwan and took over the government there after the Communists defeated them on the mainland in 1949. The U.S. military shield has enabled Taiwan to develop under the control of the leadership of the Kuomintang: an authoritarian party which, in its early enthusiasm to make Taiwan the one true China, forced the people to speak Mandarin and forbade the Taiwanese the public use of their native dialect, a variation of the dialect of Fukin province, a hundred miles of water away on the mainland.

There was a time, not too long ago, when the local people who dared to speak their native tongue in public were arrested. The Taiwanese have for nearly two centuries been controlled by outsiders—first the Dutch, then the Japanese, and now the Chinese—and must be quite accustomed to this kind of arbitrariness. Still, I imagine it's not a taste one ever acquires, and must inevitably leave bitterness in the mouths of people subjected to such relentless domination.

At first glance, Taipei looks like an American city with all the signs in Chinese and no auto emission controls. The majority of the cars, in distinct contrast to those in Tokyo, are American-made and encrusted with dust and grime; so far as I could see during my first drive, the streets are paved. The air here is putrid and lies in noxious clouds over the jammed traffic inching through the streets and over the elaborate labyrinth of freeways. If Hong Kong is China with a British flair, Taipei is China with an American accent.

While I am contemplating the new environment, James maneuvers us through the congestion and into the surrounding hills to the Methodist retreat center where we will be staying. We pull up before a cluster of nondescript buildings in the plain, earnest style that I associate with Christianity in China. The center is attended by an equally plain, nondescript woman who escorts us to a row of small bare rooms and announces that the bathroom is on the floor below. Austere accommodations indeed, I muse, as I rub my feet against the rough texture of the concrete floor. Barry appears an instant later, full of loud, angry disapproval about the accommodations which he immediately expresses to James.

My new room is a bright orange shipping container, the kind that giant freighters carry all over the world and the Japanese make into soundproof cubicles for karaoke singing. Barry, Marilyn, and He Ling have their own box, and so does Carol; all three rooms open onto a small patch of greenery, which gives us the feeling of being a small community in the hills. My box has a bathroom, although from an array of tubes and nozzles worthy of a chemistry lab I can coax no more than a puny stream of tepid water. Still, for now it's home, and I'm grateful for it. We have left the pollution in the valley below, and the green surroundings chant a mantra of freshness that only plants can sing.

In a Spartan dining room, we eat a dismal meal—a genuine rarity in Chinese settings, and as we talk together, preparing for our meeting with Harold and our first full day in Taipei, we chuckle at the primitive accommodations. I recall Fritz Perls's reminder that others, including Harold, are "not in this world to live up to my expectations."

Living would be far less fun if they were, and I'm happy to be here with Barry, Marilyn, Carol, and He Ling. We share our wonder at what we've gotten ourselves into as we walk in the twilight, complaining and laughing together before retiring to our container boxes, thankful to have the privacy and the bathroom that each one encloses.

From our outlook here on the hillside, Taipei steams and seethes in its murky valley, sporadically releasing long plumes of gas into the already destroyed atmosphere like a city on a doomed planet in a 1950s science-fiction movie. As evening approaches, the clouds are outlined bright red against a photogenic display of purple and gray. Pollution creates brilliant sunsets and (as my children once pointed out) green moons. It's a new moon tonight, just a glowing fingernail slipping through the haze, too small to show any particular shade of green.

Alone in my box, I realize that I am spoiled by the generous and respectful Japanese people who sponsor my work. It won't hurt me to rough it in Taiwan, and less TLC in Taiwan will, in fact, encourage me to be more sensitive and appreciative of people's kindness in Japan and Hong Kong. My son Lawrence always tells me that the Japanese spoil me, and now I know he's right. It's good luck to be valued and well-cared for, and spoiled to imagine that it's one's due. Many people confuse good fortune with ability, and I don't want to be among them.

Earlier, when he proposed collaborating, Harold, the President of LTB, had sent me a financial statement announcing that he had grossed US$800,000 last year. In my naiveté (which my colleague Abe Levetsky once told me was denied aggression), I am puzzled that he is so tight with our accommodations when he is making so much money. This is a man who during our first phone conversation asked me to create a three-year training program for his company. I have consistently held him off, viewing his offer as something like a marriage proposal on the first date. In the tradition of "getting to know you better," I told him that we have to do this workshop first and see how we work together. Barry is very suspicious of Harold, his claims, and his numbers, and as I review the hassle over accommodations I'm coming to share his skepticism.

Just now, at ease in my shipping container, the whole process strikes me as slightly ridiculous. I dismiss it easily as I turn off the light and gratefully drop into sleep's warm chute.

WEDNESDAY, DECEMBER 11, EARLY MORNING

Last night I dreamed I was with Pop and Frank, two of my beloved dead. I'm always happy when I see them in my dreams, where from time to time they come alive and we can be together again. They leave, and I join Martha, a high-school friend. As we walk toward a new workplace, the ground caves in under our feet and we plunge into a deep hole, where the ground continues collapsing so rapidly that I become frightened that it will bury us. Then the cave-in stops; exercising great care, we climb out of the hole and continue—taking a wide detour around the unstable area. We find our new workplace, but it is closed. As we contemplate entering the building through a window in the basement, a small African boy discovers us and calls to someone to let us in. The people there know about the subsidence, and they give me writing materials and postage so that I can notify the owners, who will close the area and repair the damage.

This dream dangles in my consciousness as I dress for my early morning explorations. It is one of my joys to explore a new place in the delicious purity of the new day being born. In the early morning Taipei looks calm. A distant mountain, its base obscured by haze, floats above the city like a gentle guardian whose soft contours contrast cordially with the sharp angles of the angry nest of human edifices humming beneath its silence. Before the sun comes to heat and catalyze the various emissions, the city looks distinct and clean resting in its sweeping valley.

I dread the hassle of working with someone I don't trust, and begin to wonder at the wisdom of the choice to come here. I knew Harold was a risk from the moment I met him in Hong Kong: in fact, I knew even earlier, when in his second fax to me he asked me to work for $200 a day after bragging about his $800,000 gross. Nevertheless, I'm here now, and I tell myself that there's nothing to do but make the best of it. My dream says that at least I won't be buried.

Elections are being held in Taiwan. For many years I didn't want to come here because it was a police state. Chiang Kai-shek, the general who, even with massive aid from the United States, was defeated by the Communists in 1949, was never willing to relinquish dictatorial power in Taiwan. He did, however, produce a son, Chiang Ching-kuo, who in 1986 allowed elections. To no one's surprise, he handily won. Nevertheless, when he died in 1989, his preparation spared Taiwan the chaos that so often accompanies generational change in authoritarian societies.

I can think of only three other men—George Washington, Sun Yat-sen, and Mikhail Gorbachev—who, possessing virtually unlimited power, remained sufficiently honest and clear-headed to arrange an orderly transfer of authority. I consider this a rare and remarkable accomplishment, for if ever there has been an accurate description of human tendencies, it's Lord Acton's brilliant observation of power's tendency to currupt. " Impressed by Chiang Ching-kuo's decision to allow elections, I give the father credit for raising such a son.

Taiwan was governed by the Japanese from 1885 to 1945. During their time here, the Japanese constructed railroads, universities, and a telecommunications system, just as they did in Korea and Manchuria. For three years after Japan's defeat, the island was self-governing; then, in 1949, Chiang and his Kuomintang army invaded the island; crushing the Taiwanese independence movement, they set themselves up as the Republic of China, in opposition to the government of the People's Republic of China on the mainland.

Unlike the French Bourbons, who were reputed to forget nothing and learn nothing, Chiang and the Kuomintang seemed to have learned from their experience in China, where their alliance with the landed gentry and their unwillingness to implement land redistribution brought about their ultimate defeat by making it impossible for them to win the support of the peasants who comprise over ninety per cent of the Chinese population. Since the Kuomintang were conquerors in Taiwan, they felt free to dispossess the landowners, and instituted a land reform that created a class of small-and medium-sized land holders who developed the independence and know how to become owners and operators of small- and medium-sized businesses.

Under the Kuomintang, whom Chiang had by this time transformed into a thoroughly Confucian party, the Taiwanese were treated as a conquered people. The Confucian ethic stresses obedience to authority in all its forms—rulers, elders, and husbands-and is the absolute antithesis of Thomas Jefferson's suggestion in the Declaration of Independence that we are all endowed with certain inalienable rights beyond the reach of any authority. Yet even in Taiwan, with its long history of conquest, the dream of government by the people flourishes, and elections take place.

Although elections don't guarantee democracy, they can be the beginning of self-government, just as intellectual understanding can be the beginning of self-awareness. Elections have their limitations: they can be manipulated by disinformative political advertising, intimidation, polling times that discriminate against working people, vote buying, and dishonest counting. As Sun Yat-sen said to a Chinese audience nearly seventy-five years ago: "You must realize that Western democratic government does not have any fundamentally good method of application."

While elections are imperfect tools of democracy, they remain the best way we have of selecting people to whom power may be temporarily entrusted, and they offer far and away the best opportunity for ordinary people to "throw the rascals out." Every other way of selecting a government is so much worse that the introduction of elections gives a signal of optimism and hope.

It is amazing to watch countries like the various Chinas and the successor states to the Soviet Union as, in less than a century's time, they leap from feudalism to democracy. For Europeans and Americans who have devoted centuries to this process, these developments allow the salutary experience of watching a historical video run fast-forward before our astonished eyes.

Breakfast is good—juhk, the rice porridge that the British call congee, with thousand-year old eggs and other mysterious bits and pieces of things that taste good mixed in. A van from the offices of LTB arrives at 9:15, and after an hour of creeping through the vapors of Taipei's morning rush hour, the five of us arrive at the office in central Taipei. The staff greet us warmly, offer coffee, and show us the group rooms, large and carpeted with lots of pillows for sitting and support. The LTB office itself is one large room where everyone works together except Harold, the boss, who has his own space with a large desk and—on a small table resembling an altar—a copiously churning fax machine. Harold greets us in an Esalen T-shirt, thus establishing his credentials as a human-potential insider.

LTB, Vitality, Inc., is modeled on Werner Erhart's EST—a human-potential seminar program with lots of control and structure and a minimum of personal contact, most of which is with unpaid volunteers. The programs tend to be expensive, and the "trainers" float aloof above the ordinary people who pay the money and receive the teaching. When I earlier expressed criticism of Vitality, which has programs in other countries, Harold said that he had no connection with them except the name. He has changed his story so many times that I am beginning to wonder if he is capable of telling the truth.

Aside from this underlying mistrust, the meeting goes fairly well—a drama of good behavior, very Confucian and inexplicit in view of all that has gone on before. Business completed for the day, we leave the office and begin to find our way to the Palace Museum, one of the objects of my visit to Taiwan.

The streets of Taipei are so toxic that two-year-old He Ling vomits every time we get in and out of a taxicab. Still, on a side street, a friendly vendor sells us sweet, crispy fried fritters, which we wash down with snowy coconut milk sipped from straws inserted into soft transparent pouches. After taking a combination of cabs and buses, we arrive at the museum, a gleaming white miniature of the palaces of Beijing's Forbidden City set on a dark green hillside on the outskirts of town. Refusing to be awed by hierarchy's use of magnificence to overwhelm, I immediately christen it "Beijing in the jungle."

What does impress me is the ability of the pyramidal form of social and political organization to capture people's imagination. Something about this (to me) boring political arrangement is so compelling that men have cherished and fostered it for thousands of years. Perhaps its boring predictability is part of what gives hierarchy its power: the power to obscure, if only sporadically, the simple existential truth that none of us knows what will happen next.

Chiang furnished his palace, which he had the grace to open to the public, by packing and bringing to Taiwan tons and tons of Chinese art treasures, many more than can possibly be displayed at any one time. Bringing the Chinese inheritance here was little more than grand larceny; nevertheless, had the artifacts been left in China most of them would likely have been destroyed in the furious rampage that we call the Cultural Revolution (and which, according to a Chinese friend in Shanghai, the Chinese call a catastrophe). Just as Lord Elgin saved the marble treasures on the frieze of the Parthenon by stealing them, Chiang's army preserved a great trove of Chinese art by plundering it.

This paradox seems to say something about the relativity of morality, and reminds me of Prince Matsudaira Fumai, a Japanese master of the tea ceremony, who wrote to his son, "I exhort you to do all the things in the world that are said to be bad." The prince believed that his instruction was the only way to raise an honest man rather than an obedient sycophant. Within the Confucian framework in which he lived, his advice may have been sound, for morality is a far deeper well than the self-righteous would have us believe.

The exhibits of the museum are exquisite. There are masses of Sung and Tang scrolls, beautifully presented with enlarged and illuminated details which lead the viewer breathlessly to marvel at the skill of the hand that held the brush as well as the tenderness of the sensibility that conceived the scene. Cunning treasure boxes designed to hold carefully chosen carvings of plants and animals; intricate cloisonné boxes; tiny cups; wafer-thin vases; and other expensive toys belonging to the mandarins of the Qing dynasty—all are stunning examples of precise craftsmanship. We admire displays of ornately embroidered garments and precious hair ornaments belonging to the imperial concubines; next door are rooms filled with ancient tortoise shells whose inscriptions, cracked in the fires of ancient divination, inspired the design of the poetic and evocative ideographs we see today. The varied and rigorous brushstrokes of antique calligraphy emit a stately joy and wonder that enter my heart directly from my eyes—pure process unmediated by any meaning beyond the flow of ink on paper.

In the objects from the late Qing, like the treasure boxes, I see exactly the same thwarted and convoluted energy I had seen in the carved panels depicting filial piety in a house near Suzhou. Completed in 1911, the year of the first Chinese Revolution; the house, like the boxes, are among the very last emblems of the Chinese imperial system. In this art, the mastery of the Chinese artisans is turned in upon itself in endless complexity and elaboration of traditional formulae, to create outlandish toys like the intricately carved balls-within-balls one may view in shops in the world's Chinatowns. It is execution in the double sense of the word: to do and to die.

Chiang truly created a treasure palace. Even faced with the overbearing statues of the leader on every floor of the museum, with their implicit demand for gratitude, I am grateful.

THURSDAY, DECEMBER 12, 7:00 A.M.

I wake up early and wander around the Methodist camp grounds until I find a spot that looks across a lush valley to a village on the hillside beyond. This is where I do Tai Chi. There is a deep gorge on the property, but it is obscured by vegetation and fenced convincingly; I listen as the water tumbles through the rocks in the mysterious and unreachable territory.

Hungry after my practice, I go to breakfast, only to be informed that since Life, Truth, and Beauty didn't order breakfast for us this morning, there is nothing here to eat. As we are miles from town and the nearest restaurant, there's nothing to do but be hungry for a while.

This visit to Taiwan is becoming a test of my ability to relinquish anticipations, probably a good exercise for a professional existentialist who makes her living teaching people to live in the here and now. Still, no breakfast is a bummer. We catch a bus to town and buy fresh bread and warm soy milk which we eat in a tiny park. Barry sits on a swing and holds He Ling while Marilyn tears off bits of bread and feeds her. I sit on another swing and regain my composure, impatient with myself for being irritated by such a small omission.

After we eat we make our way across town to another center, where we talk about the possibility of doing a Gestalt workshop next year. We meet with a woman named Joan, who takes us out for a pleasant Taiwanese lunch—beef with ginger, tofu, spinach-like greens, crisp shrimp balls, and a fine steamed fish. For dessert, we have a small peanut sweet served on a stick and dark pungent tea poured into tiny earth-colored cups, a tad larger than a thimble, from a matching embossed tea pot. The event is such a striking contrast to Harold's boorish behavior (though he does take us out to dinner later) that my desire to complete the workshop, collect my money, and leave emerges like a ball that had been pressed under water and suddenly released. I see clearly that he is a liar who tries to use other people for his own enrichment and that working with him is a chore. I cross my fingers and hope that I can work well and get away without being cheated.

I ask Joan how best to get to the airport: Harold has offered to drive me, but I know now that I will not trust him for this important favor. I feel an old pattern of panic arise at the very thought of being trapped in Taipei, and sub-vocally shape the words, "I'm afraid you won't let me go." The top dog says, "I don't care what you want. I want you to serve me."

I resist, and insist, "I won't let you control me. I hate you for refusing to care about what I want for myself."

The other voice is adamant: "I want you to do what I want."

The rebel is even more determined: "I won't! You can't make me. I'll do what I want, what I think is best."

This is the vintage dialogue between my mother and me. I remember as a child screaming, "You can't make me," and knowing even as she beat me that she couldn't. Still, the fear remains that for my audacity I'll be imprisoned: confined to my room the way I was in childhood. It's my own unfinished business, and it emerges in Taipei as I realize that I'm working with an unscrupulous person. Fortunately, I'm not alone. My traveling companions—who not only are friends but speak the local language and understand the customs—offer reassurance that they will, of course, help me get out of town.

After lunch we go to the Chiang Kai-shek Memorial, a copy of the Temple of Heaven in Beijing, where the Chinese Emperor in his role as magician performed the rites and rituals that were believed to guarantee the health and wealth of his land and people. Like the Palace Museum, the Memorial is a smaller, brighter, whiter version of the Beijing original, which in its serene grandeur is one of the loveliest buildings in the world. The tall white gates and shining blue tile roofs of the copy stand among soft green shadows and flashy flower beds where multi-colored blossoms form characters glorifying the Republic of China and its dead leader. Everything is brighter and newer than the worn walls of Beijing to which these buildings pay homage with their imitation that is truly the sincerest form of flattery.

China's ancient imperial vision and its revered northern capital continue to ensnare the imagination of Chinese people everywhere and contribute to the unity of China's diffuse totality. Chiang's government will be remembered as a minor dynasty—a remnant like the southern Sung, which continued to exist on the periphery while the vastness of, the Central Country was ruled by others. Chiang, whom the Chinese press called "the super war lord," resembled the traditional founders of Chinese dynasties far more than did his predecessor Sun Yat-sen, the man many call China's George Washington.

The Memorial has a large mural of Chiang and Sun seated together and looking out a train window. Although they are looking in the same direction in the painting, in life they definitely saw two distinct futures; they proved to be an amazingly disparate pair to have been mentor and student. In the painting a fresh young Chiang sits smiling beside a sweetly mature Sun, the revolutionary hero who is honored in both Taipei and Beijing, as well as everywhere else Chinese people live.

When I visited Zhongshan, Sun's native village, I saw a Chinese woman from Canada weeping before his memorial. She stopped crying long enough to tell me, "He was the best of all the Chinese leaders;" and I agreed, for he was a remarkable and noble human being.

A native of the Pearl River delta near Hong Kong, which is the homeland of most of the overseas Chinese, Sun was educated in Hawaii and studied medicine in Hong Kong. From these outposts he absorbed ideas of nationalism and freedom that were to inspire the overthrow of the monarchy and the establishment of China's first republic. Twenty-five years after he had been banned from Hong Kong as a political subversive, he returned, now leader of a successful revolution, to tell an audience at Hong Kong University that the difference between the order and calm of Hong Kong and the arbitrary insecurity of his home in Guangdong Province, only fifty miles away, had been his revolutionary inspiration.

Sun was something new in Chinese history: an educated peasant, taught by the missionaries who destroyed the mandarin monopoly on Chinese education. Sun saw China's salvation in a non-Confucian nationalism that would allow the Chinese self- determination and self-respect after nearly three centuries of foreign domination and five millennia of imperial absolutism.

Sincerely convinced that a strong, modern China would benefit not only the Chinese but the rest of the world as well, Sun became the "traveling salesman of the Chinese Revolution," raising money and recruiting revolutionaries everywhere Chinese people lived. He became internationally prominent in 1896 when he escaped from the Chinese Embassy in London after the Qing authorities kidnapped him with the intention of sending him to Beijing for execution. Totally without imperial pretensions, Sun sought to establish a republic in China where, in his words, "the people—our 400 million—will be king."

When a group of military men who had been won over to the republican cause successfully seized the city of Wuchang in central China on October 10, 1911, the revolution was under way. Sun, who was in Denver, Colorado, at the time, learned of the beginning of his revolution from a local newspaper; instead of rushing home, he began intense diplomatic maneuvering to isolate the Qing and gain recognition for the new republic.

Sun and his followers did not so much create a revolution as ride an evolutionary wave, for Imperial China's time was up. The Manchus would have collapsed during the nineteenth century, perhaps in the Taiping rebellion, if they had not been useful to the Europeans and Americans as accomplices in foreign exploitation of China's resources and people. The revolutionaries did not have to bring down the Chinese government; it collapsed, just as the French and Russian governments had collapsed during the revolutions in those countries.

Those who are called revolutionaries often get exaggerated credit for successes that are the result of luck or, at most, an elegant sense of timing that allows a Tai Chi-like use of energy whereby "four thousand pounds [are] toppled with a trigger force of four ounces." Nevertheless, it was the preparatory work of Sun and his followers that created the republic which emerged after the Qing collapse.

On his return to China after skillfully and successfully protecting the new republic from foreign interference, Sun was elected provisional president of the Republic of China by a near-unanimous vote of the provisional delegates gathered in Shanghai, thus becoming China's George Washington.

There is a tendency now to view Mao and Deng as latter-day emperors; but while I agree that ancient patterns continue to influence events in China, the acceptance by the Chinese intellectuals of the dream of a modern Chinese nation dedicated to Sun's Three Principles—nationalism, democracy, and people's livelihood, which he considered the Chinese equivalent to Lincoln's "government of the people, by the people, and for the people'—was an epochal change. For the Chinese people, the dream's fulfillment is still under way.

An entity as big and old as China will, like a great dragon shedding its skin, transform itself very slowly. In the eventful days of June 1989, I saw the dragon stir as groups of demonstrators—segments of the dragon raucously announcing themselves with bullhorns and banners—

flowed from Nanjing Road onto the wide, waterfront plaza of Shanghai's Bund. The Shanghai Nursing College, the Pharmaceutical College, Fudan University, journalists, doctors, dentists, machinists, metal workers, service people—everyone was on the street that day, either as demonstrators or as part of the dense crowd surrounding them.

From the tenth floor of the Peace Hotel, watching each new group enter the already packed Bund and coil its way through the crowd, I knew I was watching the great dragon spirit of the Chinese people assert itself once again. Down below, the demonstrators on the edge of each group held long loops of plastic string that allowed them to mark their boundary as they moved and melded into the vast crowd.

My fellow foreign teachers and I waited several days before joining in, fearful we would be accused of being the dread "outside agitators." When I finally raised the string and stepped inside, the students cheered; for a long time I walked and watched through tears of nearly overwhelming emotion. Clearly a large and powerful dragon can include everyone, and we had a wonderful walk through the city and into the square in front of city hall, where the hunger strikers lived their protest.

For me, the most touching sight was a small group of students guiding a nearly blind old man: probably a former teacher who had come into the streets to show support. I remember another group of bent, gray-haired men and women in rumpled blue Mao jackets whose coming created a stir and murmurs of "Lai-la, Lai-la" ("They're coming; they're coming") as they painstakingly disembarked from a van and joined the young people. I cherish my days in Shanghai even as I grieve the final outcome of the June demonstrations. I am confident the dragon I saw awaken will never return to its castle on the bottom of the sea.

With his power base in the south, Sun was never able to establish a unified government for all China; and, as part of a deal to assure the peaceful abdication of the Qing rulers and gain financial aid from the Europeans and Americans, he resigned the presidency in favor of Yuan Shih-kai, whom who most of the revolutionaries considered the only man who could save the country from civil war. Yuan, a seasoned and devious northern general who had served the Qing, was inaugurated on

March 10, 1912; the following day Sun promulgated the Provisional Constitution, the first such document in Chinese history.

Yuan turned his final trick when he declared himself emperor in 1915; Sun, leading the group that forced him to abdicate after 82 days, sealed the tomb of China's archaic dynastic system. Henceforward, no matter what happened, China would be a republic: even two republics, although that was far from anyone's fantasy at the time.

Sun, who continued to lecture and write after his abdication, became governor of Guangdong province, which until his death in 1925 was a haven of freedom and progressive creativity for people from all over China and Southeast Asia. In the struggle of warlords that resulted from the collapse of the dynasty and Yuan Shih-kai's unsuccessful bid to become emperor, Chiang Kai-shek, a Christian convert who had studied in Moscow prior to returning to China to create the Kuomintang army, began his rise to prominence.

After Sun's death in 1925, Chiang became the leader of the Kuomintang, the political party that had evolved from the various revolutionary organizations and which, under the fierce pressures of the Japanese invasion and the gradual growth of the Chinese Communist Party, became more and more reactionary. Chiang relied on the Americans to defeat the Japanese in the 1940s, while he saved his own army to destroy the Communists in the civil war he was determined to fight.

Chiang's intransigent refusal to address the needs of the Chinese peasants, whose deepening misery under the traditional landlord class had been intensified by the Japanese occupation, left the Kuomintang with little support among the people. Between 1945 and 1949, the Kuomintang was driven from China, often by Communist armies fighting with captured Americans weapons, for by then the Kuomintang army was so demoralized that entire corps and armies surrendered with all their ordnance intact.

The defeat of Chiang's armies was so complete that they were lucky to get to Taiwan with enough force to establish control of the island. This they did, however; and with continued support from the United States and the boost to their economy from the two wars that the United

States fought in Asia, they not only maintained their power but created a strong economy, based to a large degree on government monopolies in steel, petrochemicals, shipbuilding, and power production.

The Kuomintang's success in Taiwan now supports a gradual movement toward democracy. Sun Yat-sen's dream has been more successful than anyone would have imagined possible in the dreary 1930s and 1940s, when Chinese democracy seemed a lost cause to all but the wishful thinkers of the China Lobby in the United States: the ones who accused the United States State Department of "losing China"—a formulation that rivals "conquering space" for sheer balminess.

By the time he got to Taiwan, Chiang definitely had imperial pretensions. He had declared Confucianism the official religion of China in 1934, even though he himself was a Christian convert. This was a clever way to garner the best of both worlds: using the traditional religion to control the Chinese and the new one to woo the Americans who controlled the money. His violent suppression of the Taiwanese and slavish imitation of Beijing were clear indicators of his continuing commitment to authoritarianism in government. Lacking the historical patina of the originals, Chiang's monuments shout, "See me and tremble," reminding me of the Wizard of Oz—an elaborate facade behind which stands an old man turning wheels and pushing buttons.

To an American, it seems quite old-fashioned to seek domination through awe and grandeur, and it's easy to scoff and dismiss such silly pretentiousness. Still, I know enough history to realize that the Chinese striving for democracy and self-government, which began at least a hundred and eighty years ago with the Taiping rebels, is a pattern of contact and withdrawal, action and reaction, on a time scale beyond the imagination of one who lives in a country whose written history began just three hundred years ago.

It helps maintain perspective to remember that it was not until the early 1920s that the Chinese began writing in the vernacular, an event that began in Europe with Dante and Chaucer nearly five hundred years ago. This Chinese Renaissance, a genuine cultural revolution called the May Fourth Movement, began as a student protest against the Treaty of

Versailles ending World War I. It is a profound statement of the power European and American governments continued to exercise in the Chinese Republic that, from a railroad car in France, diplomats were able to transfer German economic privileges in China to the Japanese. In exchange for a large loan from Tokyo, the elders in Beijing were willing to accept this travesty, but the students, who until this betrayal had looked to Europe and America for inspiration, were outraged.

The May Fourth Movement whose motto was "Overthrow Confucius and Sons," was a young people's movement whose demands included rights for women. An assertion of youth's dignity and passion, the May Fourth Movement stood for the reversal of traditional values, family structure, and political organization. It was dazzlingly successful, generating scores of new publications and changing China's literary establishment and education system forever.

The Chinese Dante is Lu Xun, whose name most Americans have never heard but whose impact on Chinese life and culture is far greater than that of the greedy soldier commemorated with the grandiose memorial I saw today.

While studying medicine in Japan, Lu Xun saw a film of an execution in China and was dismayed by the Chinese audience's passive acceptance of the Manchus' murder of their countrymen. Diagnosing China's malaise as a spiritual one, he quit medicine to become a writer. He was active in the literary movement that replaced the bureaucratic code of the mandarins with a more accessible written version of the spoken language. He edited journals, wrote political essays and polemics, and crafted about twenty short stories: masterpieces of conscience that portray with terrible veracity the misery, torment, superstition, and degradation of the Chinese peasants. Better than anything else ever written, the stories of Lu Xun portray the source of the still ongoing Chinese Revolution.

FRIDAY, DECEMBER 13, 6:00 A.M.

Last night I dreamed:

A man named Henry runs up behind me and hoists me on his shoulders. He makes a deep vibrating sound that resonates in my solar plexus. Together we rise above the ground, vertically, like a helicopter, and fly high in the sky. I'm happy and exhilarated. Then, still in the dream, I awaken and tell another man about the dream; he scoffs, saying my dream sounds very controlled. This man is my adversary, who is always negative and rational; sometimes he wears the garments of a seventeenth- century French courtier. In this dream he has on a blue suit with a white shirt and red patterned tie.

In my second dream I attend a performance by Madonna. She has instructed some of us to come as mothers and others as babies. I am a baby, and wear a pale blue dotted-Swiss nightgown, which I drape over my body using a drawstring. I tell my high-school friends that I bought it just for this occasion as I normally sleep nude, both because I like to and because I think my body needs a chance to breathe. They giggle when I say this, and I nod my head very seriously, and say, "It's really true. You might try it and see."

Today the group begins. Being in Taiwan reminds me of my time in China, for I my present fear and anger is similar to my feelings as I left Shanghai on June 8, 1989. Imperialism and babies: polarities, far apart and seemingly unrelated; and yet in the shadow of sleep I connect them. I think one reason everyone likes Christmas so much is that it's about a baby, which makes it a precious holiday in a world of pretentious grandeur. Christianity began by satisfying the ordinary and everyday in people; then it was taken over by Rome and became imperial—the Roman Catholic Church, the Roman Empire in the twentieth century, still trying to tell everyone what to do. Led by its pater familias, the man in a skirt, the Roman church emphasizes and enforces the power of the center which takes money from poor people to enrich its imperial institutions.

The Chinese government, too, maintains an imperial center in Beijing, placing the whole vast land in a single time zone and forcing everyone to speak its language. And, like Rome, Beijing retains the loyalty of people all over the world. I have often considered loyalty a slave virtue—a demand for undeserved devotion and faithfulness from those who are unrewarded for their trust. When relationships are reciprocal there is no need for loyalty, and it is only with an imbalance of power that it becomes an issue. People usually don't emphasize loyalty during the good times when everyone is satisfied.

My task for the next three days, however, is not to ponder great questions, but to work with Chinese people of Taiwan without losing my center and my integrity. Harold and Barry are both using me. For now, Barry and I recognize our mutual interest. Harold is trying to cheat us both. I need to keep my independence.

The van from LTB comes to our mountain hideaway at 8:45 and drives us to the organization's midtown office. The driver double-parks the van while we eat breakfast: a first course of toast, followed by a glass of Tang (or a Tang substitute, if such a thing can be imagined). Just as I have given breakfast up for lost, however, a very good cup of coffee appears.

We make it to the group at ten, and are greeted by a large room full of people, forty-odd mostly young faces hiding their expectations behind a shy friendliness. Irene, the translator from the staff of LTB, joins me; henceforward we will be rather like Siamese twins as she repeats everything that is said in the group, translating my words into Chinese and the group members' into English. It is a daunting task. When the group splits into two, Carol will translate for Barry from Mandarin or *Putongwa* (which Irene has more than once pointedly called Chinese) into Cantonese and back again. Carol, whose aunt is a nun here in Taipei, is a bright, reassuring member of my Chinese family, and I feel safe and confident as we begin the group together.

I begin with a brief definition of awareness rather like Gertrude Stein's definition of knowledge: "For after all, knowledge is what you know." Awareness is what you're aware of, all those experiences that seem so ordinary and matter-of-fact and that make up the content of your existence. That's your awareness. I also talk a bit about the sources of Gestalt, and Carol writes the hard words like "existentialism" and "experiential" on the board in Chinese. (Harold had promised a handout, but of course it never appears.) I talk about the three zones of awareness:

Outer—sight sound, touch.

Inner—tension, stress, emotion, breath.

Middle—thinking, silent talking. Then I direct the participants' awareness: "Be aware of your back. Of your breathing. Of the gravity holding you to the floor." It is a further attribute of awareness that if I tell you to be aware of your breathing, you will give it at least momentary attention. A purple alligator; an American flag: awareness is suggestible, subject to direction and manipulation from the outside. This is what television and advertising are so expert at doing: directing awareness.

After I direct their awareness for about five minutes or so, I ask the group members to sit in groups of five and share their experience. Barry asks them to introduce themselves and tell their expectations for the group. After this he asks how the awareness experience was, and people report on this for nearly an hour.

I feel my past in my chest.

I almost fall asleep.

I feel a scream.

I feel tension in my back, my shoulders, etc.

I am surprised at how short the time was.

After this the participants start asking questions, indicating that they want to work. After a short break, Martha, who is a member of LTB's staff, comes forward to begin.

Martha begins talking about feeling angry, although her voice and facial expressions remain constricted and unconvincing. She wants to talk to her parents, saying, "You aren't real. You want me to be a traditional woman." Clasping her fists, she hits her knees, a retroflection I ignore at this early stage of the group, and says, "You don't allow me to be genuine. I feel bad when I'm not genuine."

She then begins to criticize herself: "I shouldn't talk to my parents that way." I suggest she change pillows and, as the parents, tell Martha more of what she should do. After she switches, she repeats that she feels better when she is authentic. I ask her if there is someone in the room she wants to be authentic with, and she says, "Yes, there is." She changes to the pillow that represents her authentic self and, addressing Harold, expresses anger to him for being obsequious to foreign teachers, for apologizing for serving us instant coffee. (Like the water strider flitting over the surface of the pond, I hadn't even noticed.)

When I ask her how she feels now that she is being authentic, she says she is feeling guilty, and my hearts sinks. She has tangled herself in the net of a terrible double bind, the "damned if I do and damned if I don't" position of the person whose parents and teachers have exploited their love by using guilt to control. She feels bad when she expresses herself, and she feels bad when she doesn't. Insidious sentences such as, "Mother feels so bad when you do that" are much more harmful for the child than straightforward assertions of power like "You'll do it because I say so." Since it's only too clear to children that adults, with their size and experience, have control, children can give in to assertions of power without damage to their sense of self. They do what they're told and, even though they don't like it, they maintain their integrity.

On the other hand, the clammy and inaccurate insinuation that children are responsible for the parents' feelings will make the children of such parents seek to shape not just their behavior but their very essence, in a futile effort to satisfy the parent. Such a child formulates an inner messages something like: If what I want and who I am destroys my parents' happiness, then there must be something terribly wrong, perhaps even evil, about me.

I direct Martha to switch back to the top dog seat and be the accusing voice which says, "You shouldn't talk to your teacher like that." In this work, I begin to see the complexity of Harold's position with his staff, a risky overlapping of the roles of teacher and boss that offers opportunities for power abuses of which I imagine Harold, from what I know of him, wouldn't hesitate to take advantage. When I invite Martha to be authentic with me, she says, "I don't like you. I don't like foreign teachers. I don't think you're so great."

Since I don't think I'm so great either, I smile and say, "I'm glad you don't. I'm not. I'm a human being just like you."

She responds by telling me she doesn't like being told what to do. This feels genuine and important, so I stop facilitating her and ask her what she wants. She wants to stop and hear from other members of the group, who give her a lot of support for expressing her resentment, both to Harold and to her parents. Many say they had similar feeling toward their parents, and so the morning session ends with work well begun.

Even though her expression was mainly verbal, Martha's work impresses the other participants. The very fact that she could say to her parents, "I don't like your traditional ways," or "I don't want to do what you tell me to" is perceived as courageous by others in the workshop. This is a place where cultural difference is significant; words that to an American seem mild and inconsequential—even natural—are a daring self-assertion to these young people raised in the Confucian tradition where the young are presumed to serve the old and the present to exalt the past. Sometimes in the U.S. we call this attitude ancestor worship; and, if the parents are explicitly included among the ancestors, this designation is not too far off the mark.

We eat lunch in a nearby restaurant, the young Chinese group members sitting at round tables sharing dishes that roll by on a Lazy Susan. It's simple fare: a leafy green vegetable, chicken, cabbage, and pork. Barry's wife and daughter join us, and He Ling's two-year-old presence creates a sweet familiar feeling among the group members.

At times I feel awkward and a bit like a refugee as I travel with my Chinese family. This is culture shock pure and simple, accentuated by the language difference. I am definitely the grandmother figure of the group; and since I've always liked three-generation families, I accept my role gracefully knowing with absolute certainty that I'm lucky to have an opportunity to play, if ever so briefly, the role of Chinese grandmother.

Lunch is a good meal. After eating I leave the group and walk around the narrow neighborhood streets. From a vending machine I buy a can of coffee, which I drink with a piece of sponge cake while sitting on the foundation of an abandoned building in a rubbish-cluttered vacant lot. Happy to find a few dusty green leaves and pale flowering weeds to keep me company in the middle of the city, I share the space with an abandoned car and a pack of scrawny dogs, who tolerate me so long as I don't move too deeply into their territory.

Gathering after lunch, we divide into two groups of about twenty people each. Barry and Carol take their group into the other room, and I feel a little lonely watching them leave. As soon as they're gone Lucy says she wants to work. She has been in several of Harold's classes, and says she is in touch with being angry. As soon as she says, "I'm angry," she clenches everything, refusing to speak or move, and her breathing becomes imperceptibly shallow. When I encourage her to exaggerate the process of stopping, she curls into a tight ball.

As I write this, I think of Fritz's admonition not to interrupt the interruption. Lucy's clenching and holding behaviors are interruptions of her self-expression. After she expresses them fully, she will become free to express what she is avoiding. In other words, the interruption is a form of self-expression as authentic as the original, interrupted impulse.

The more I do this work, the more convinced I am that each bit of revealed existence deserves respect as the solution to a problem whose difficulty is beyond my ken. These are unique problems, locked in each person's past; the solutions displayed before me are the result of the most creative and ingenious effort that this person could make at that time and in that place. What we sometimes call neurosis is a creative response devised in the face of overwhelming power by a small, helpless person with very little life experience and no place to hide. At such times we are forced to live by our wits alone, and any behavior that allows survival in these circumstances is a great accomplishment.

When the solution that served in childhood is no longer life-enhancing, the person begins to seek new solutions for the original problems—among which might be, "How do I express my hurt and anger without injuring myself and others?". Only when I respect each person's ingenuity and tenacity in the face of their childhood dilemmas am

I in a position to facilitate their present awareness and create an environment where the true self—the authentic self, the soul, whatever you want to call the most basic sense of "me-ness" that each one experiences at her or his core—can emerge and discover forms of expression that better serve the present moment.

I encourage Lucy to give the holding-back behavior a voice. She repeats the usual list: Don't say, don't do, don't be. It's the most violent and insistent voice that I have heard since working with people raised by Catholic nuns in New Mexico.

Taiwan was under military law until 1986, and again I observe how the structures of family and government reinforce one another. The family is the government in miniature, as the wily Confucius knew better than anyone; and obversely, government is the family amplified. This is one reason authoritarian people harp on "family values," which in their lingo is a code word for obedience to authority. Respect for the weak and helpless is perhaps the most important of all family values, for without this benevolence there would be no family; nevertheless, in the United States one hears very little about protecting the weak in public discussions of family values.

Authoritarian governments can function only when the patterns of compliance and submission they require have been wired into people's synapses by the teachings of the family. Once the circuit is established, all the government has to do is throw the switch and people will tyrannize themselves and each other. It's impossible to control millions of people by coercion alone; there simply isn't enough force in the world to do it. With the advent of nuclear weapons, there is enough force to kill everyone, but not to control. It is impossible to control fully alive and aware people."

Unless the patterns of domination and submission are firmly in place within the psyche of the great majority of people, those who need to control will be helpless and impotent. This is the state which the founders of the United States of America ardently wished to create: a state where no man or woman could tyrannize the people, even in times when the people, frustrated with the responsibilities of freedom, might actually desire such tyranny. This was the purpose of separating the powers of government in the United States Constitution; as a condition for its ratification, the states demanded the Bill of Rights, which were not part of the original document, to assure people even more protection from arbitrary governmental power.

Those who seek to dominate others never find limitations on state power acceptable, and work incessantly to undermine them; thus the great wisdom of Thomas Jefferson when he said, "Eternal vigilance is the price of liberty." Eternal vigilance is another word for awareness. The family and the government are a continuous loop, as those who fear childhood's fresh perception and originality understand only too well. Confucius (551-479 B.C.), who was among the most ruthless ideologues of state power, understood and articulated this better than most, and Chinese governments and families everywhere have a tendency to emphasize obedience and service to rulers and elders as the essence of morality and good behavior.

So Lucy, brought up in a Confucian home, says, "I'm angry," and immediately curls into a ball of inhibition and shame. When she releases herself from that spasm of control, she becomes aware of moving her left arm, at first in faint, fluttering movements which she follows and expands until she is hitting the pillow with her left hand. The group members rush to pile pillows under her pounding fist so that she doesn't hurt herself. She beats on the pillow relentlessly until she seems so exhausted that I ask her to stop. Because she has used only her left hand and arm, I know her constraint is still very great, and I don't want to encourage her to go beyond her self-support. She can do this easily in the group where the other members are silently supporting her and cheering her on to express their rage as well as her own. Only if she remains within the boundaries of her own support will she be able to integrate this experience and assimilate the newly released energy so that it will be truly a part of herself, available for everyday life and liveliness.

The group members support Lucy's work with their response. Several report feeling soreness in their own bodies as they watched her.

This could be initial awareness of patterns of holding which, having been denied for years, start to emerge when their participation in Lucy's work begins to sensitize them to their own experience.

Next Cynthia works. She begins by being aware of closing her throat. When I ask her what this sensation is saying, she pauses a long time before replying, "I want to tear it up." Picking up a pad of paper, I take a sheet and pantomime tearing it. She bursts into tears and curls herself into a ball. Curling even her fingers and toes, she seems saturated with a giant surge of "NO." Following her awareness, I work with her a long time: "What are your tears saying? What are your toes saying? Your fingers?" Again and again she makes a statement and then retracts it. "I'm sinful" is the sentence she uses to stop herself. She becomes aware of wanting to kick and then stops herself. "I'm sinful."

[What does sinful mean in this culture? Are the ones who say this Christians? (I'm writing this in the hotel coffee shop trying to ignore "Winter Wonderland" jingling from a speaker lodged in some secret place as I puzzle the meaning of sin in Taiwan.)]

When I suggest she stop, she refuses, saying she would regret not doing something in the workshop. I can see the spasm in her feet and imagine she must be aching all over. It's excruciating to watch her; yet I notice that I trust her completely and am not worried about the outcome. From her curled position she sticks out her right leg and moves it a bit before withdrawing it again. Just when she seems the most tightly withdrawn (I'm assuming that the clamping and holding is a form of withdrawal, which perhaps explains how she is able to come out of it with renewed energy), she says, "I'm squeezing everything."

When I say, "Do it to the pillow," she begins to compress the pillow, pushing and squashing it into an unbelievably tiny and compact ball, putting her knees on it and crushing it unmercifully, just as she had previously been doing to herself.

Fritz said, "Do unto others what you are doing to yourself." Since this is often far too cruel, I have amended the Perls axiom with the Bottome corollary: "Do unto pillows what you do to yourself." Clearly the refrain in both is: Direct your energy outward in the world rather than onto your own delicate viscera.

As I allow myself to comprehend that, for years, Cynthia has been doing this to herself and, furthermore, that originally someone had done it to her, I am awed by the cruelty human beings hide within themselves—cruelty that, under cover of the privacy of family life, is passed on from damaged people to their precious progeny while no one bothers to notice what was and is happening.

Surely this community denial, too, has a purpose which I shall come to understand if I remain alert and accepting. The use of the individual adaptation to abuse is obvious—survival. I imagine it must be the same on the communal level. For any given social, political, and economic system to endure, its members must conspire to ignore the suffering that goes into its maintenance. Most especially, we must never allow ourselves or others to ask the dangerous questions: "Is there a better way?" "Might we do something different?"

Just as Cynthia squeezes the pillow to the limit of her power, she releases a wild cry. It's the scream of the helpless child revealing the terror of her abandonment. She has held this, repressed inside her shattered psyche, until the present instant when, at last, she has found people who will listen. It is a soul-searing sound made tolerable only by my certainty that by articulating it she has begun to heal. She screams and says, "I want to tear you to pieces." I give her the notebook and she tears it frantically. She grabs so much paper that she hurts her finger as she tries to tear it. She stops suddenly, awakened into the here and now by her present pain, and says, "I could hurt myself."

I respond, "I don't want you to hurt yourself," knowing that if she hurts herself she recreates her helplessness and negatively reinforces the deep self-expression she needs for healing. Someone hands her a box of tissues; flowing back into her rage, she tears it up, box and all. Bits of box and paper fly everywhere. Then she leaps to her feet and jumps up and down vigorously, exactly like a toddler having a temper tantrum. It is more than a primal scream: it is a resurrection, a return to the place of injury and abandonment. She has journeyed to the site of annihilation, where, like the phoenix, she now gathers the pieces of her shattered self and, from the dust of her own destruction, creates herself anew.

I remember my mother's telling me of such a tantrum thrown by my son John the day I brought his brother David home from the hospital. No sooner had I arrived than, thoughtlessly, I left again with his father, ignoring the little boy, not yet two, who wanted to be with his mommy. As I sit with this young woman in Taiwan, I grieve my cruelty to my own child and pray that others will help my grown children heal.

Cynthia continues her tantrum for at least fifteen minutes. She shows the rage of childhood betrayal and anger held in abeyance until the holding-in became her living while the anger and hurt moldered in the guarded cave of a denied inner world. Today she enters the cave, where she throws herself about, kicks and screams, and, when she is exhausted there, returns to the present. All we do is provide safety and stay out of her way.

I want to describe her work without making it a journey into darkness, for her destination resembles Aladdin's magic caverns—these caves of childhood where treasures of repressed energy and vitality await each traveler who finds the courage and support to enter. Whoever dares to enter the concealed inner world and experience what has been buried there will be able to bring its treasures of light and its energy forward into the present moment.

It is contact with a living, listening, attentive person that makes this pilgrimage into the self positive and possible. All the people whose work I have described have presented themselves eyes down, seemingly lost in the labyrinth of past experience. Since I will not work without contact, my first task is always to make contact with each one, sometimes almost standing on my head to catch the lowered eyes. Contact with another human being is essential to transform the frozen terror of the past into the excitement of expressive experience in the present. Contact with me and with the other people in the group is the anchor in the here and now for each one person who lowers him or herself on the rope of muscular and visceral memory into the shining caves of childhood.

It is the vivid potency of these suppressed experiences that make them so compelling in controlling the everyday present responses of people's lives. By returning to these caves where they were taught to obliterate themselves, Cynthia and Lucy have begun to substitute the direct expression of their repressed selves for the clenching and clamping that were necessary to survive as children in their particular homes. It is here among the sparkling immediacy of childhood that they can reclaim experience remembered not simply in words and images, but in the muscles and nerves as well. In order successfully to make this journey and claim the wholeness that is their birthright, a person needs to experience the safety and human contact of the present along with the terror and isolation of the past.

The experience of being alive, of being this me who is living now, seems to have a core of constancy that lasts a lifetime. Despite the fact that our cells replace themselves every seven years, we continue to be the same person, accepting the new cells much as we would put on new clothing. Clearly each one is a gestalt, a form and entity defined by an organization that is greater than the sum of its parts.

I see this constancy of identity in Gestalt work whenever the childhood self is allowed to emerge in the present. At such times, the adult usually has great difficulty recognizing, not the self which he or she knows well, but the simultaneous immaturity of that self. The child is so completely and familiarly me that I can easily neglect to notice that she is only three feet tall, cannot answer rational arguments, and doesn't know how properly to hold her eating utensils. People forget how easily victimized such a person can be by bigger and more verbal family members, who may not be more intelligent or deserving of more respect, and whose defining feature is that they are bigger and more powerful.

That I am this small person and her experience is mine overrides all other experience, and often I have to remind adults of the limitations of their three-, five-, nine-, or thirteen-year-old selves. While this constancy of identity may make it difficult for people to accurately evaluate childhood experiences, it is a lovely and profound affirmation of individual existence. At no matter what age, I am I, and I inevitably recognize my self.

Each one of us exists within a sense of self, an identity that does not change with time. In The Fragile Species, Lewis Thomas tells of a friend who, in response to being asked how it felt to be old, replied, "I'm not an old man; I'm a young man with something wrong with me."

After her work, although Cynthia does not want to hear from the group members, I encourage her to select someone whose response she wants so that she may experience her expression within a human community. Of course, the person she selects approves and compliments her for her courage and daring. When Harold then asks a technical question, I sense the group's impatience with him. His high-pressure salesmanship fosters people's dependence and, of course, resentment. I don't let myself be distracted by his question, and stress the importance of the trusting contact in the present to the work Cynthia and I have done together. Once again I say, "The most important element in Gestalt work is the relationship with the client." I think many people understand.

Two members of the group feel angry and uncomfortable after Cynthia's work. Several try to get me to play expert, which is a zero-fun game and always reminds me of Hank Williams's great line: "You only build me up to tear me down." No thanks. Harold has clearly built me up as "great" in order to promote his business, and it is my task gently to make myself known as the all-too-fallible person I know myself to be.

During the response to Cynthia's work, one woman says she is very tense and needs to relax. I tell her we don't have time for her to work, and suggest she stand up. Realizing that everyone is tense and full of feeling from the deep and passionate work, I suggest we all stand up and move about a little. One of the LTB staff members puts on a tape of Taiwanese music, and we dance away some of the tension accumulated during the afternoon. Then, still standing, we do a brief round—one sentence per person.

After some hassle and confusion about our hotel—Barry and I insisted on staying in a downtown hotel once the workshop began—I ride away on the back of James's motor scooter to meet my friend Deborah who lives in Taipei. As James threads through minute spaces between cars scattered about in random patterned traffic jams, we discuss the group, yelling over the traffic noises and ignoring the rank air. He tells me he trusts me and asks if I trust him. Clinging for dear life to his back as he races through the chaos of Taipei traffic, I assure him I do: "If I didn't trust you, I wouldn't be riding through Taipei on the back of your motor scooter." We laugh as the obvious strikes again. (When, a week or so later, I receive James's Christmas card, I am elated to read, "You taught me that the relationship with the other person is the most important thing in Gestalt therapy." Thank you for listening, James.)

I arrive safely at the hotel and meet Deborah, a friend from Shanghai who is in Taipei studying Chinese at the Stanford Center. When I ask her how her Chinese is, she replies, "Comfortable," and tells me she is working for a Chinese company where she uses the language every day. We take a cab to her apartment, where I join a potluck dinner of foreign women, mostly from the U.S., who are studying Chinese in Taipei. They are a bright and engaging group, laughing about life in Taipei and joking about their applications to graduate school.

Deborah says that the application form from Harvard inquired, "How much are you willing to put yourself in debt to attend Harvard?" I laugh and say, "It should ask whether you're willing to bankrupt your parents to go to Harvard." Several people giggle when one woman says, "We already did that with undergraduate school." It's fun to be among Americans for a while before returning early to the hotel for a good sleep in preparation for what will definitely be a hard tomorrow.

Saturday morning, December 14, 10;00 a.m.

In the morning session, two women work on their unhappy marriages. Crystal, the first to come forward, reports feeling strong and capable at both work and home, except when she "faces my husband." Then she feels inadequate. She doesn't work on this so much as talk about her feelings and express some of her pain. Joan, the second woman expresses anger, much of which she directs toward herself in a virulent outburst of self-hatred. She speaks with much choking and gagging, which is, I imagine, an expression of disgust.

Self-hatred, which is a learned attitude rather than a natural response to life, is forced upon the child by making her swallow, or introject, false judgments about herself. In order to accept the unwholesome lies the adults forced her to swallow—her body is dirty, she is inferior, she doesn't really belong to the family, etc.—Joan deadens her disgust reaction: the gag reflex in the throat and mouth which says, "I don't want to swallow this shit."

The emphasis on food in traditional Chinese culture is well known, and the connection between eating and introjection, which is a kind of forced feeding, is a bit of the obvious which the Perlses noticed early in their formulation of the Gestalt approach and discussed extensively in their first book, *Ego, Hunger, and Aggression*. I observe a lot of introjection in all the cultures where I work; however, I have never seen and heard so much choking, gagging, and spitting as in Taiwan.

Each time Joan begins to express her anger outward, she collapses and brings it back onto her self. She is clearly suffering, and at the end of her work, one of the men in the group shrieks a deep and mournful cry that seems to express the profound misery at the core of this woman's existence, as well as his own. I experience a room full of people saturated with pain whose expression moves instantaneously from one person to another. I am tired and helpless as I sit with their suffering and deprivation.

Neither of these women has done decisive work. Both, by touching their own deep self-denial and self-hatred, have begun a long and painful process that, should they pursue it, will lead to rebirth and self-renewal. "To lose one's life and be born again is not easy." Their paths of self-discovery will be difficult, although nothing like as painful as their present existence with the thwarted self-expression and mutilating self-hatred reinforced by relationships that recreate over and over again the original denial and mutilation of their past.

The hatred that the child often must swallow and turn inward toward herself, for survival's sake, will, if it is severe, ultimately kill the adult unless she finds support to direct outward toward an image of her abusers the rage which she now retroflects toward herself. She may choose to transform the living memory within her organism into grief at her deprivation which can never be restored and rage toward those who tried to destroy her existence when their job was to welcome her into the world and foster her uniqueness. She may understandably counter a betrayal of this magnitude with life-long hatred, or in the process of existential and experiential remembering she may heal herself.

We take a short break after the group members respond to the women. When the group reconvenes, Mei Ling says she wants to talk to her mother. In a controlled, constricted voice, she begins expressing anger toward her mother while holding her arms tightly against her body. From time to time she interrupts herself by commenting on the sinfulness of hating her parents. After she squeezes out a fine strip of anger, she cries in the same tight, unrelenting way.

She boasts that she has never asked her parents for anything; and when I suggest that she ask for something in the group, she seizes her arms and begins to tremble visibly. She becomes a bundle of vibrating energy within a rigid shell of inhibition. I reach my hand toward her, and for several minutes she struggles with reluctance before she allows herself to touch my hand. When, at last, she does, I take both her hands, and she says she wants me to hold her. I take her in my arms, and for a few minutes she trembles violently before she gradually begins to breathe easily and her trembling stops. Soon afterward she disengages from me and listens as the group members tell her that they, men and women both, identify with her difficulty in reaching out.

One man says he had always been taught to give and never to ask, before expressing his anger and sorrow in a violent fit whose authenticity I don't quite trust. I remind myself that hysteria, too, is an expression of suffering even though the expression is pumped up by the need to perform. In some ways the hysterical person is the most pathetic of all because there is an invisible film between expression and the true self. For the hysterical man or woman it takes much longer to contact and express the misery inside because the demand to perform overwhelms expression, leaving the poor person lost and bewildered in the turmoil of dramatic intensity.

It is a weakness of Gestalt that hysterical people often dominate groups and establish an expectation of dramatic expression that can be intimidating for others. I think the solution to this is to validate all expression, even the most minimal, and most especially the expressions of holding and stopping—the inhibition which is the path to the original feelings that the repression is controlling. I validate hysterical expression, even if it is not completely authentic, because suffering people need recognition and sympathy to allow them to begin the slow process of self-acceptance that permits healing to begin.

I remember thinking that the Chinese pattern of highly ritualized and rationalized child abuse must be very common, and again I recall the carved panels in the late-Qing house near Shanghai. I will not accept the gruesome idea, portrayed there, that children should mutilate themselves to serve their parents. It strains my credulity to believe that anyone seriously entertains such notions; and yet, here in this room, I observe the remnants of this (to me) utterly insane mandate as I listen to people tell of their fierce struggles to wrest some bit of independent life from their parents' urgent and insistent demands upon their behavior.

I feel uneasy as I observe the tip of this ancient culture, which in the nearly static society of China's past must have guaranteed survival just as behaviors learned in childhood do. I understand how respect for elders and their knowledge would be useful in a society that changes slowly, just as suppression of anger can be functional when one is two feet tall. It is characteristic of unfinished business that it prevents one from experiencing the present, and this becomes explicit in groups when present safety allows people experientially to live the terror, misery, and despair they feel inside. Experientially, the unfinished business is happening over and over again; and regardless of how much the present situation changes, the psyche continues its repetitive labor, striving to complete the unfinished gestalt.

The person who is choked with unfinished situations cannot perceive the present and cannot mature. Her or his awareness is preoccupied with the bright holograms of childhood. Thus George Bush can call Al Gore "Ozone Man," because for him the years of environmental degradation have simply not happened; it is still 1945, or 1939, or whenever it was that his efforts to deny his suffering from the demands of a tyrannical father overwhelmed his present awareness. At that point, he stopped responding to the present situation and entered the feedback loop of unfinished business where nothing ever changes.

This phenomenon also accounts for all the out-of-touch remarks that begin, "When I was your age, young man..." and "When I was a girl...." and continue as though the intervening years have simply never happened; to those immersed in unfinished business, they haven't. For such people there is no now, only then; and they simply do not recognize the changes in the external world that have occurred in the years since they lost contact. Not only is now always then for such people, but they remain eternal children, interacting with the word in fixed childhood patterns that can never come out right until enhanced by the expressive power of the organism's language: the long-denied emotions.

Despite my best efforts not to be judgmental and culture-bound, I experience the massive unfinished business of Chinese tradition as perverse. I feel outraged that parents and other adults, themselves embedded in an antiquated ethical system, have forced these young people into convolutions of impotent self-hatred in order to serve the ancient Confucian dream of a continuous ladder of hierarchy extending in an orderly and uninterrupted progression all the way from women and children to an imaginary Son of Heaven. Within such a context, gunning down rebellious students in Tienanmen makes perfect sense, and is, in fact, demanded by the social and cultural imperatives of "filial piety."

As I write about this group, I notice that I make many small mistakes as well as concoct a giant mess for the computer. Often I stop and withdraw from the material. I am baffled by the cruelty of the harsh and rigid "top dog" that Chinese culture creates and glorifies. I hate being judgmental, but at the same time I find traditional Chinese culture, both in Taiwan and on the mainland, too merciless and unrelenting to accept. The cruelty of the culture and of the family system that supports it accounts for the amount of abuse the students at LTB accept from Harold Tse, and for his expectation that Barry and I will accept it as well. Now I'm becoming part of the problem by working for his company.

I'm troubled.

SATURDAY AFTERNOON, DECEMBER 14

This afternoon Barry and I have switched groups, and I'm working with a new group. I'm tired, and the group members are too. One woman becomes seriously out of touch and demonstrates how people use words to drive themselves crazy. "I hate the part of me that hates people," she says, and laughs, expressing amusement at her own suffering. She continues her sadistic self-abuse for a few seconds before becoming obsessed with the black polka dots on the pillow in front of her. She sees them as filth and evil and all those nasty words people often associate with the darkness of their spurned and shadowy selves.

I begin to facilitate her return to the present, which she expedites by her giving herself a leg cramp. The pain of the cramp is very centering because it's a bit of the here and now that she can't deny. Her sensation interrupts her cruel verbal formulas and insists that she pay attention to herself in the present.

The group members are kind as they stroke her and cover her with their coats when she lies down on the pillow. I am comforted as I observe their concern and compassion with her confused and tangled reality. One reason I work in groups is that the compassion of the group's members often far exceeds my own.

The next man announces that he's satisfied and just wants some attention. I feel comfortable with this clear statement until he says, "I want to mess you up." The translator withdraws this wording at once and substitutes "I want to confuse you," reminding me of how much of what I hear is mediated through her decisions.

Neither wording sounds friendly, and, as he continues in this mode, I very quickly tell him I've had enough and send him back to his seat. He seems to appreciate my refusal to tolerate his mess, and the other group members do as well. I really don't understand what he was doing. I just know I don't like it and am happy to get him out of my face.

The last person wants to finish with her father. Aware that she is beating her son just as her father had beaten her, she wants to stop the cruelty she allows to flow through her into her son. Dimly aware of the ancestral voices compelling the sacrifice of the young, she intuits that in Gestalt she has found a way to end the suffering that she transmits to her children. Together we work with all her roles—father, daughter, mother, son. She has passion in each role and, I think, becomes more aware of the sources of her behavior.

The meeting of parent and child in a new parent can be productive, because anyone who is willing to meet their own childhood suffering becomes free to experience both the frustration of the parent and the pain of the child. Sometimes the childhood memories emerge unsought as one lives with one's own children, whose appearance and behavior may evoke repressed memories. If the new family provides adequate support—and often it does—a person may re-experience past feelings and complete the old gestalts.

Sensitivity to the present comes naturally with the ending of repression and the liberation of energy that repression binds away from present awareness. A parent's awareness will protect the child from the family legacy of pain and punishment, for it is the unaware and forgotten suffering that is acted out onto the next generation. If a single generation would willingly and consciously experience the repressed agony and rage of their families of origin, we could begin a process of closure, of completion of both our personal and communal unfinished life. This would be the beginning of our return to the garden.

The meaning of middle age resides in this position between the roles of parent and child, where the person who dares to experience his or own childhood suffering can heal and integrate the family pain. I remember moments of deep satisfaction as, walking between my father and my sons, I realized I was the person in the middle, the Janus-faced one who can see in both directions. It is a powerful place from which the person who dares to resolve her own inner conflicts can experience the richness of human maturity (such as it is, for I am one who thinks we live in the childhood of our species and that even the most mature among us remains a young and immature creature).

I walk back to the hotel alone after we adjourn. The sky over the city glows smoky lavender with pink undertones that soften even the straight lines and right angles of the buildings in the foreground. Watching the colors flare across the sky, I remember reading of a psychologist who suggested his patients look at the sky whenever they felt depressed. I think this is one of the wisest bits of advice I've ever heard. Heeding it, I see the cloud color deepen to a vibrant maroon so lovely that I fix my eyes on it like a sailor seeking to draw the invisible land from the darkening sea. Then the light vanishes, and it is night.

When the acid glow of neon springs into my awareness, I realize I've never seen any of these signs before. I'm lost. After wandering up and down a few unknown streets, I give up and hail a taxi. I show the driver my security card with the name of the hotel written in Chinese characters, and he delivers me there in about three minutes. It's been enough of an adventure to dim the day's work, and I read in bed for a just few minutes before collapsing into my private well of darkness.

Sunday, December 15, 6:00 a.m.

I'm going home tomorrow! I still have to find a way to get to the airport without relying on Harold, who I realize reminds me of another charismatic liar and human-potential entrepreneur I knew in San Francisco. Both men surrounded themselves with people who pay good money for abuse. I'm amazed at the number of people in the world who are vulnerable to the spell that some unscrupulous people cast. How desperate and lonely people must be to submit themselves to the charismatic figures who surface all over the world as the leaders of religious cults, racial cults, national cults, and New-Age cults.

No one is born desiring exploitation and humiliation; people frozen in childhood, however, will seek the parents they never had and offer themselves, their life energy, and their money to false fathers like the Rev. Sun Myung Moon, David Koresh, Shoko Asahara, David Duke, or Harold Tse: men who never deliver even basic human respect, let alone any kind of profound solution to life's misery. I remember sitting in an office in San Francisco where my former husband and his partner set themselves forth as New-Age wise men. It was my last time in their office, for I thought what they were doing was crazy. On my way out, I passed the new recruits coming in: lonely people separated from themselves by denied suffering, who might never mature or touch the home inside where "what seemed abyss becomes the place where true being speaks to us."

On June 23, 1893, George Tyron, Admiral of the British Mediterranean Fleet, hoisted a signal that directed his ships traveling 1200 feet apart to turn inward. The men guiding the ships obeyed the order and ran their ships together, killing 358 sailors. One marvels at the uncritical obedience of everyone down the line to a command that so obviously meant disaster. From the tapes of the squadron that disappeared into the area of the Caribbean called the Bermuda Triangle, it is clear that at least one of the student pilots knew the squadron leader was turned around and was flying out to sea.. Nevertheless, with full knowledge that he was flying to his death, the student did not turn around and fly his plane, over which he had total control, to safety. He chose death rather than disobedience to authority.

These are the actions of hollow men who can imagine no existence outside the hierarchy and for whom obedience to male authority is the only path to manhood. I am reminded of Laura Perls's amusing, and still beguiling, observation that the stiff military posture— shoulders back, chest out, chin tucked in—cuts off the blood supply to the brain. This is my favorite candidate for the single-factor explanation of history.

Thinking of Harold, I am aware that it is time to have a long spoon, which among other things means a way to the airport. No way will I get into a car with him. A taxi ride only costs $900NT, which is $35US and well worth the price to avoid further contact with his machinations.

My inner dialogue with him goes like this:

Paula: I'm afraid you will keep me here against my will. I'm afraid you'll put me in jail.

Harold: Yes, I'll do that if it's the only way I can control you. You won't let me manipulate you, and that frustrates me so much that I want to imprison you.

Paula: I'm afraid of you. I'm afraid you'll hurt me and cheat me.

Harold: I have and I will. You must be very wary. You can never rest or I'll control you. I need control for my own inner peace. I am so frightened and vulnerable that I need the illusion of control to feel secure.

As I write this, I connect it to my mother, a charismatic and insecure woman desperately trying to control a sturdy, headstrong child.

After doing Tai Chi in a parking lot in downtown Taipei, I drink coffee with sweetened condensed milk in a friendly Chinese stall on a main street where the trucks are just beginning to rumble by. The smell of burning petroleum is still faint in the morning air, and I enjoy watching the city stretch and stir in the quiet Sunday daybreak. I return to the totally adequate downtown business hotel to dress. Now, I'm ready to complete the group.

SUNDAY MORNING, 10:00 A.M.

As we sit in the office waiting for the group to begin, a cheerful Harold walks by and greets us saying, "We finish today. I have your checks waiting for you." That's nice, I think, smiling vacuously, for my focus is totally on the participants and what I need to do to complete the gestalt of this particular group.

As soon as Irene and I enter the group room, people begin calling out that they want to work, and we make a list. I put pressure on myself to accommodate everyone who wants to do something in the remaining hours of the group. This means trying to do short work, which is far more difficult than working with the natural flow of contact and withdrawal. In an essay I once wrote on control, I remarked that anyone who imposes time limits is trying to control. I begin this day doing it to myself.

The first person presents a dream of a dismembered baby—a horrible image. Even though I've heard such dreams before, I'm taken aback at such a beginning for what portends to be a long day. I work with her until the baby says, "I exist." I have her repeat those words to several people, and we stop.

Next a weepy, helpless, and very needy woman comes forward. Her first sentence is, "I can't face it." Imagining this to be an important sentence in Chinese culture, I ask her who she doesn't want to face. She says her father, and begins to talk with him. The more she talks the more she hates, and the more she hates the more concern she pretends for her father's well-being. Her impasse is thick as fudge, and I become impatient and tell her so. When I ask her to stand up and observe the process between herself and her father, she says something nondescript; and, giving up with her unfinished business, I bring the present to the rescue and tell her to look at the faces in the room. After looking around, she says, "I wish my family would look at me with such a face." When I tell her our time is up, she says, "I want to talk to my mother." I reply, "Next time," and, reluctantly, she takes her seat.

Next a young teacher expresses some solidly grounded anger to her father, her principal, and her roommates. The variety in this group is astonishing, I think as I move my attention from her to a powerful young man—an oldest son, very constrained by family expectations. He expresses his rage and misery in loud tearless cries forced through a half-opened throat. As always when I work with people, I encourage him not to push or strain, for the process of driving the self is part of the problem and rarely part of the solution.

Eileen, who says she wants to separate from her mother, expresses herself by choking and gagging. Someone brings a trash can, and she spits in it. Again I'm stunned by the magnitude of introjection in this culture. I sit with her, bewildered as she struggles to vomit out some of the introjected elements she has been force-fed. She says a few words to her mother on the pillow, and then chokes again.

Listening as she gags on her self-deprecation, I gain a new appreciation of the role of food in pushing people to choke down the unpalatable roles the elders teach. "Eat, eat," blends into the more abstract cultural message "Learn, Learn," which is in turn strengthened by being joined to the biological necessity of eating. As the child takes in the vitally essential food, she also takes in the culturally essential rules and obligations of the one who feeds her. People who force children to eat may intuit this connection. Both forced feeding and forced identity occur because children's boundaries are weak and their ability to discriminate undeveloped.

In my experience, children know what tastes good to them. By overwhelming the food preferences and gag reflex that protects us from swallowing what we hate, the caretakers expedite the swallowing of food that is *mazui*—a wonderful Japanese word that means "not delicious"—as well as of life-denying "should's."

Introjection and confluence, the inability to distinguish self from others, are themes that preoccupy Eileen, whose boundaries are so weak that she can hardly tell where she stops and her mother begins. I imagine she has integrated some energy for self-support by resensitizing her gag reflex and talking to her mother about her feelings. When I ask her how she feels distancing herself from her mother, she says, "My heart is pounding." When I ask what her heart is saying, she replies, "It's a terrible thing to do." I feel my helplessness rise like a wave and break solidly on the shore of the boundary between her and me. I have done my best and so has she.

This is where we arrive, at this time and this place: partners without power. Perls was right. I am I and you are you. Sometimes we touch and make a difference for each other; sometimes we don't. Still, it's our only hope. I let the conditions softly glow as Eileen and I stop and say goodbye.

Often when people in this group work with their parents they feel guilty afterward, which means they've gone beyond their support and, thus, are unable to integrate what they've done. The coercive strength of the powerful canon of filial piety. shows up in the incredible protectiveness these young people feel for their parents, both when they were children and now, as adults. Often the concern seems to mask hatred and hostility, as it naturally would if one's caring behavior has been coerced and manipulated by the imposition of guilty obligation without concern for one's own wishes and desires.

All my experience indicates that, just as Fritz said, guilt is retroflected anger—anger turned against the self. When I work with guilt, I encourage the person to direct the anger outward toward the pillow, even when he places himself on the pillow. Becoming angry at oneself on the pillow is an outward expression, rather than a retroflection, and will help to release some of the retroflected rage. Of course, it is best if people can become angry at those who have actually hurt them. Here in Taiwan, though, guilt is so deeply embedded that this approach has been relatively ineffective. I would need time and trust before I could work more effectively with the guilty feelings of the people here.

In Eileen's work, her unwillingness to take care of herself creates deprivation, which further reinforces her desperate need to barter consideration for "others" for care and nurturance. The traditional Chinese social system is based upon a mutual dependency which creates a crystalline structure of need and gratification that holds everyone firmly in place. The relative weakness of individuation which is an inevitable concomitant of mutual dependency promotes a social universe whose members are locked together in a rigid structure of helplessness and dependency. The only way to get what one wants is to manipulate those same "others" to whom one must dedicate one's life. This was probably a necessary adaptation in the old China, where nearly everyone was powerless and the only chance for survival was to stick together to assure the continuation of the family or clan, rather than try to cultivate the all too vulnerable individual human being.

I'm exhausted after this session. Remembering that Barry and I will work together in the large group this afternoon, I comfort myself and escape for lunch alone. After lunch I walk the quiet Sunday streets looking at the sky.

SUNDAY AFTERNOON

The group seems huge as everyone comes together again, and three people say they want to work. First is the young man who had shrieked the pain-filled scream in yesterday morning's session. He says that he cannot bear his mother's suffering and cries a while before he begins to experience how angry he is. I recall my son Frank's observations about the tyranny of the weak, as I sit with one of the victims of that despotism. After the young man expresses his anger in a loud, dramatic way, he is satisfied and stops.

Next Barry works with a woman who is furious with, among other people, Harold. (It's no accident that one of the English words for insane is "mad".) She told Barry and Carol about this earlier and said she did not want to identify him in the group. This is no problem, but Barry's provocative way of working with her is. Standing with her in the middle of the group, he holds a pillow and taunts her like a bullfighter enraging a bull. She wants to push and scream. Each time she slows down, Barry says something like, "You can do better than that," and she begins again. I totally lose my nerve and remain quiet—protecting Barry rather than stopping the work, which goes on too long and takes the woman far beyond her ability to integrate it. When they finally stop she is exhausted and leaves the group, remaining in the other room during the following, and last, work of the group.

A pretty young women expresses a great deal of hatred for her husband and father and grieves for her mother, who had died when she was a girl. By now I am numb, self-censorious and barely willing to follow this work, which seems filled with unspoken feelings. Still, she seems to find some release, and the group members are very kind to her when she finishes.

When we gather after the break, the women who had worked with Barry is not with us. When Barry, Carol, Martha, and I go into the other room, she is there huddled in a sobbing heap, and says she doesn't want to join the group. Exhausted and guilty about what she has done, she has clearly gone beyond her support. When we encourage her to rejoin the group, she becomes hysterical and says she can't stand up. I feel frightened—worried about her and concerned for the group. I have never had such a response before.

It is vitally important for Gestalt work to proceed without creating fresh negative reinforcements for the expressive behavior that emerges in the group. Since these feelings and behaviors have already been subjected to disapproval and punishment, healing occurs when a human community recognizes and accepts the hidden and forbidden aspects of the self. The combination of expression and acceptance weakens the repression and allows a wider range of awareness and possible responses the next time. If someone is hurt in the group, she or he is retraumatized, and the repressed behavior becomes even more inaccessible and more difficult to integrate than it was before the work began. I cannot imagine closure with one of the participants weeping alone in a side room.

Completing a group is like docking a huge ocean liner. It takes a steady hand and meticulous attention to bring the variety of feelings and experiences into a whole that people can comfortably walk away from. Feeling tired and uncertain of my ability to create this kind of focus here, I'm anxious about this woman and this group as I work with my colleagues to bring her back to a present where she can feel safe.

After much coaxing and mountains of sensitive and loving support, especially from Carol and Martha, we soothe her until, limp and crying, she goes with us into the other room, where she half sits and half leans between Barry and me as we complete the group. This woman's experience reminds me of Laura's remark that a breakthrough can be a breakdown, and I feel resentful toward Barry for not having known when to stop.

I still wonder at the need of many therapists to create such a heavy impact on people. I have seen it before in the United States, where a facilitator will push someone into a state of depletion and exhaustion rather than stopping after a session has liberated energy that can readily be assimilated and integrated for deeper work next time. I'm critical of Barry, and tell him so later when we are alone. In the group I was cowardly silent and protected him instead of the woman who needed an ally.

Now that we have the group together, Barry encourages people to express appreciations and resentments. Many people express resentment toward Harold for the high cost of the groups. Several people mention feeling addicted to the high they get in groups. There are also those who defend and support Harold, expressing gratitude for what they have learned and experienced with him. The staff members express anger at their low salaries in the face of the high fees the participants pay—a feeling with which I readily identify. I remain an outside observer, although I have resentments I could easily express. By this time I feel scared and compromised, truly humbled by what has happened and by the recognition that I made a mistake in choosing to work with Harold at all, and perhaps by working with Barry as well. I'm willing to take the money and run, for I feel I've earned every penny of it.

After the discussions with Harold about money, the rest of the final statements are appreciations for Barry, Carol, and me. Then LTB stages an EST-type graduation ceremony. I remember thinking when I did EST that cashing in on the feelings and excitement of graduation was a clever ploy. It works just as well in Taiwan, and people seem satisfied. It is good Gestalt practice in that it allows a strong sense of closure for the group; nevertheless, I feel uncomfortable as Irene, the translator, whispers in my ear the names written on the certificates in characters.

I announce each name in a loud voice and give each person a certificate with a handshake and sometimes a hug. The people who greet me as I give them their certificates are happy, and, as we touch, their hands are soft and gentle. It is high-energy time, and I join the general euphoria. I sit in the middle of the group as Martha takes pictures with several cameras, including mine. The prints show a huge mob of people clustered around my small smiling face snuggled close to Barry and Carol. In the far corner, a pudgy Harold is raising his arm to ensure that he is not overlooked.

As we leave the group room and Barry reminds Harold to pay us, I learn that everything up to now has been prologue. Harold doesn't have the checks that he so grandiloquently promised earlier in the day. It seems that by some strange mix-up the checks are with the bookkeeper, and since it's Sunday the bookkeeper is not in the office.

Harold agrees to call the bookkeeper while Barry, Carol, and I exchange glances that say, "Oh, not again!" Irritating as Harold's behavior is, it's also humorous that he is being so true to his dishonorable self. Gertrude Stein is right: Here is Harold, repeating the whole of him, yet one more time.

Barry has a hunch, which he whispers to me as Harold ostentatiously begins tracking down the bookkeeper, that because we made an issue of our payment while the group members and staff are around to witness the show, we will probably get our money. Barry is convinced that Harold, given half a chance, will cheat us out of our fee. Now I, who had never considered this possibility before, agree with him. The path to the little pot of gold at the end of LTB's rainbow is much longer than I imagined.

After bustling about with the phone for a while, Harold announces that the checks are in the bookkeeper's desk. Fine, except the desk is locked. The group participants standing around the office are uncomfortable; they clearly believe we have earned our money and deserve to be paid. People are whispering to each other as Barry and I stand beside the locked desk, supposed repository of the now-mythical checks. Harold tries to usher us into his private office where "we would be more comfortable." We assure him that we will be more comfortable when we are paid and insist on maintaining our post beside the desk. Then he asks if it would be all right if we get the checks tomorrow. It most definitely would not be all right: I have at last realized that it is impossible to be too suspicious of Harold.

Just as I announce, "No, it won't. I'm leaving on a plane tomorrow, and I want to be paid tonight," a locksmith appears. I stand beside the desk with Barry and Carol, and refuse to be moved. Around us Harold and his staff engage in an orgy of paper-shuffling as though their sheer activity will make the checks materialize from the twilight zone into which they have so inconsiderately vanished. By now both the checks and the locksmith, who pokes and jiggles the lock on the desk drawer, have become mythical. In fact, we all have. We're seekers of buried treasure which exists in some mysterious realm far from the grasping hands of simple mortals like ourselves.

I'm committed to getting my money, and it is the sympathy of the group members and staff who have lingered on after the workshop that will ultimately move Harold to produce the money because it will be humiliating not to. He is losing face, and I don't want to create any sympathy for him by giving voice to the rude things that pop to the tip of my tongue.

Of course the checks are not in the desk which the "locksmith" has finally teased open with a tool that resembles a hairpin. Nevertheless, Barry and I continue to insist, and by now it is clear to everyone that we'll never leave without our money. Harold vanishes for a while and returns with the news that his mother has US dollars and he will give us the money in cash. Martha will go get it and bring it to our hotel within the hour.

It is a testament to our trust in Martha that we accept this solution. She seems genuinely embarrassed by Harold's performance and sincere in her desire to pay us. We return to the hotel, still rather dubious; and, sure enough, in less than an hour she appears with a little stack of hundred-dollar bills, enough to fulfill all of Harold's obligation except the hotel bill. Thus we receive our reward for the endless hassle of working with the president of Life, Truth, and Beauty.

After Martha gives us our money, Carol, Barry, and I jokingly congratulate ourselves for our perseverance for a few seconds before returning to our rooms. There, still mentally unfinished with the group, I ponder the meaning of the prodigious spitting, choking, and gagging that I observed these last three days.

Since Chinese Confucianism created a culture that for over seven hundred years required routine crippling for millions of women before they were deemed marriageable, I don't think it is overstating the case to recognize that the paramount value of China's culture was submission to authority. The Confucian ideal of unquestioning obedience is achieved by crushing the spirit with introjects just as the bound foot is smashed by tight bandages. Introjection, which is psychic force-feeding, is facilitated in Chinese culture by the long history of famine and starvation which makes it nearly impossible for anyone, and especially children with their weak boundaries, to refuse whatever is offered.

Even before the European intrusion, the Great Plain of north China was the most densely populated semi-arid area in the world, and Owen Lattimore suggests that overpopulation was deliberately fostered to keep rents high and wages low. Reinforced by Confucian precepts which did not allow women or children to say no, large families were the only social security.

The poverty of the Chinese peasant under the old system is beyond the American imagination. Whenever the government required money, the bureaucrat\land owning class, rather than tax themselves, squeezed additional revenues from the poor, resulting in a kind of cannibalism in which a few families live luxuriously on the starvation of the many.

Recently I read an account of a Chinese peasant woman who prepared rocks, stir-fried with oil and sauce, to flavor her family's solitary food source: rice. Telling the story years later, her son told his grandchildren quite seriously, "They were delicious." Such tales may be juxtaposed with reports of the Empresses eating meals of 127 courses.

Even sucking flavored rocks with rice, however, was not starvation—though that came, too, when even the rice was gone and people ate dirt and tree bark and died by the millions. Lu Xun, who wrote a novella about a man who is convinced that the major motive of traditional Chinese society was to train people to eat one another, has his character cry out, "I am party to a history that counts four thousand years of cannibalism."

The violent reactions of choking, gagging, and spitting in the Taiwan group could be the beginning of resensitizing the delicately receptive areas of the mouth and throat whose stimulation is essential for survival. People's behavior in this group confirmed Perls's recognition that eating is a far more fundamental human activity than sex. The concept of introjection acknowledges that people can be forced to swallow, but not to digest. People who have only flavored rocks to suck on will starve; people who are forced to swallow things they hate will obey the undigestible introjects for a time, and will spit them up at the first opportunity.

People in the group were choking up the social rules they had been forced to swallow—rules that remain as undigestible lumps within their psyches, impossible to integrate into a self-regulating wholeness. While everyone has experienced the force-feeding of introjection, only on Taiwan have I seen it so completely dominate people's efforts at self-expression.

DECEMBER 16, MONDAY

Today I go home. The six days I've been in Taiwan feel like six days on Pluto. In the U.S., today is my son Lawrence's birthday, and since it will still be the morning of December 16 when I arrive in the United States, I'll be there to celebrate with him.

My second thought on awakening is that today I finish my business dealings with Harold Tse! Actually I'm finished already, for the worst he can do now is stick me with the hotel bill, which I can pay and still feel that I've taken care of myself. Part of taking responsibility is taking care of myself; if I let Harold cheat me, I have promoted his dishonesty as well as my own distress. It takes two to cheat, and so I want to be sure he pays the hotel bill, too—for both our sakes. Thoughts of Harold lead to considerations of the way unscrupulous men have been able to exploit the human yearning for community and authenticity to make large amounts of money for themselves. By charging high prices, they transform a natural human desire into an addiction.

James Bradshaw defines addiction as "a relationship with any mood-altering activity, experience, event, or thing that has life-damaging consequences." Yesterday, as the group ended, several people mentioned feeling addicted to their experience in Harold's groups. This is among the damaging aspects of the human potential movement, especially as it has been packaged and popularized by the money-makers, those whom Fritz Perls called the "turner-on-ers".

Exploited by greedy people, the human potential movement has joined the mainstream of activities that one person can use to take advantage of another. As people saw this happening, many became disillusioned with an approach that had initially offered them hope. What an unfortunate and insidious process—and I have cooperated in it by working here in Taiwan with Harold. Ouch! I made a mistake.

Greed in business is self-defeating because, over the long term, business cannot be done on the basis of deceit. While "take-the-money-and-run" operators like Harold can flourish for a time, a serious business requires a long-term commitment to quality and to customer satisfaction. I learned most of what I know about business running a household, and so have always understood that business is not a special category of human activity: it's just the name for money coming in and money going out. People who wish to maintain the flow have to respect the others whose current touches their own, for without respect and mutuality one's sector of the river becomes stagnant. Business will always be with us because it is a part of the constant exchange in which humans, those most social of beings, continuously engage. The liars and cheats ultimately find themselves in a brackish pond full of inedible algae.

Among Harold's staff members I can see the psychological process of the abused child at work. Working for Harold, they get some of what they want in terms of authentic human contact, probably more they would receive in many conventional workplaces. Nevertheless, they are underpaid while Harold makes lots of money. It's another situation in which I have to trust people—trust that they will leave Harold's employ when they are ready, just as I have left situations where people were exploiting and using me for their own purposes. The members of Harold's staff are young, and they will find more satisfying work as soon as they have learned all they can from him. I hope that will include how to protect themselves from people like Harold.

Despite all my complaints, I was moved by the completion of the group. The upsurge of the human spirit comes like a water spout bringing the fresh, living water of pure being to the dingy surface where most of us live. I love these moments, and was happy to have lived through one with the people of Taiwan. I was on such a high that I would have floated out without the money. Barry is a good business partner for me because he is not so easily distracted. Harold did not ruin the group for me.

Another point that came up yesterday at the end of the group (and that I have heard before) is the issue of "real life"— always with the implication that what happens in groups is not real. This is at least in part connected to people's notion that "it has to be hard to be good." It's clear that this kind of puritanical judgment is not rooted in Christianity, for the Chinese most emphatically have the same tendency, and there is no way to call traditional Chinese culture Christian. I feel sad when people have difficulty believing that their experience is real. I also recognize that I'm seeing denial—an operation that is usually sequestered, hidden from the self as well as from others. It is useful to point out to people that they are denying and encourage them to pay attention to how they do it.

Many people are convinced that only pain is real and pleasure some kind of ephemeral dream. Remembering Olds's research on the pleasure center and Reich's insistence that all anxiety is pleasure anxiety, I understand that denial of pleasure is a solution to the problem of being a life-affirming creature in a death-affirming civilization. Many people are shocked to discover that it is possible to rejoice in existence.

Yesterday one of the men in the group said that Barry and I had taken them to hell and brought them back again safely. I think there is something to this analogy, although I was most emphatic in insisting that while I had accompanied him partway, the place he went was his own hell. A more accurate image, I think, is that I hold the rope steady in the present while each one descends into their childhood cave. I remain solid in the now as orientation and navigator to help them return safely with the treasures they left behind years ago.

The hysterical woman who worked with Barry returned from her terror when she saw that we would support her in the present. She is only one who came close to becoming lost in her inner world. I made a therapeutic mistake by not stopping Barry when he encouraged her to go far beyond her support. Dependency is one possible result of this error; breakdown is another. People like Harold—and, judging from yesterday, perhaps Barry, too— discourage self-support. Financially, they have a great deal to gain by fostering dependency. I, on the other hand, imagine that there is plenty of dependency without creating any more.

Eager to finish with Harold and get out of here, I go out on the street and return to yesterday's parking lot for Tai Chi. Afterwards I sit on a stool in a Chinese street stall and watch the working people prepare for their day. They are friendly as we share the small counter and drink the sweet tan-colored coffee.

I have a breakfast meeting with Barry, Carol, and Harold—ostensibly to discuss the training program Harold wants us to do, but in reality to say, "No way!" When we meet in the lobby, I am politely friendly until Harold has paid the hotel bill. Now he wants to take back our hard-earned cash and give us the checks which have reappeared from the Twilight Zone and now rest in his pudgy hands. Barry and I politely refuse, saying we are happy with the way things are. Because of confusion about our travel expenses, the checks are for more than he owes us and would be the source of even further complications; we also fear that he might cancel them as we wing our way homeward. At last we are financially even, and I am relieved.

We go to the coffee shop for breakfast, and immediately Harold announces that I have promised to do a three-year Gestalt training program for him. With some effort, I refrain from laughing in his face as I listen to this assertion, which denies every single conversation we have had on the subject. Barry, who was in Hong Kong where the original agreement was supposed to have been made, backs me up.

I had been scrupulous about insisting that I would not agree to a long-term program until I saw how I felt working with him, and now I tell him that I dislike his way of doing business. I add that, as a person who takes responsibility for what I do, I would feel like a fool if I ever agreed to do business with him again. I tell him that he was dishonest and disrespectful in just about all of our dealings.

He doesn't want to hear this, of course, and asks for explanations. He has a response to everything I say, but the density of his lies increases as his position grows more difficult. He does speak frankly when I push him about his resentment at my insisting that he pay Carol's airfare, and he uses this as an excuse for the poor accommodations and for "forgetting" the checks. Again he suggests that we surrender our cash for the checks, and again we politely decline.

He becomes agitated and tries to convince me that I am indebted to him in some way. He does not want to take no for an answer, and keeps trying to reopen the issue of the money, trying to blame others for the low fee he offered in the first place and for all the ensuing confusion. Barry, Carol, and I, however, are clear about our feelings toward him and only want to get away.

In the group yesterday, members of Harold's staff complained about their low salaries. When I tell him that I don't want to work with someone who charges high fees and pays his staff low salaries, he stares at me and asks, "Why?" "Because I don't like to be cheated," I respond.

He insists again that when we met in Hong Kong I had agreed to open a Gestalt Training Center in Taipei. I don't argue with him, just keep repeating my position: The workshop was far too difficult. I would not put myself through such a process again. The lost checks were a farce. The accommodations were inadequate. I would never consider putting myself again in a situation where he had power in my life.

Finally, angry and fed up with his pushy presumption, I say, "Back off!" in a loud voice. Still he doesn't listen, and for his final performance he cries big tears of angry frustration, which of course he pretends are caused by my cruelty. Like the softie I am, I feel sorry for him, for I know that he's genuinely suffering although I know I'm not the cause. Nevertheless, I have learned the lesson of "Fool me once, shame on you; fool me twice, shame on me." Barry, Carol, and I get up and walk out of the coffee shop leaving him alone at the table, still crying.

I can feel his presence against my back like suction, which I push against as I walk away accompanied by the lilting Muzak rhythms of "Winter Wonderland." I can still see him sitting in the coffee shop crying out his bitterness and self-defeating frustration. There is nothing I want from him at this moment except to get away.

"Sleigh bells ring, are you listening?" Well, as a matter of fact, no. There hasn't been a sleigh without a thousand miles of here since the Ice Age, I think grimly as I lecture myself for sparing an instant's sympathy for Harold's manipulative performance. He was mad as hell at me, and that's the truth of the matter. Throughout our conversation, he ignored Barry and Carol, and acted as though he and I were the only two people at the table. Nevertheless, I was as successful as I was with Harold because I was with them and we supported each other's standing up to his bullying onslaughts. Had I been dependent on him for translation as well as shelter, and orientation, I would have been more vulnerable. Maybe he realized this, which would account for his resistance to their coming and his denial of their presence.

The need to control is a dangerous affliction, for people who must control can never respect other people or any form of spontaneous unfolding, which are inevitably beyond their control. For such people, the enemy is unpredictability and instability I can feel sorry for them, but I will not let them control my life.

After we leave Harold, Carol and Barry say it's the first time they've ever seen me mad. We giggle with relief at being finished with him at last. It was perhaps the hardest money any of us has ever made.

[When I put this story into the computer, I made mistakes that I will never understand—errors such as getting the computer to print out its own language on the screen, using hundreds of pages of memory in the process. I am amazed at my difficulty in writing about my experience in Taiwan: it seems pretty straightforward, and it's hard for me to believe that I have mixed feelings about Harold and all that happened there. Clearly I do, though, or I would not have screwed up so flamboyantly. Thinking about it now, I suppose my conflict is connected to my feelings toward my former husband Larry Bloomberg, who while not as crass as Harold became a human- potential manipulator of some skill and reputation, especially after I left him. I left him because, just as with Harold, I did not want to lend my time and energy to their enterprises. I accept my complicity, insofar as I cooperated with both of them. I am, however, only responsible for what I do, and in no way do I feel guilty for their behavior.]

December 16, 2:00 p.m.

I made it to the airport with no problem. Yesterday Barry's wife Marilyn, sensing my anxiety, discovered how to make the trip by bus. It's simple and cost almost nothing. Carol became worried that I didn't have enough Taiwanese money for emergencies and gave me several hundred dollars at the last minute. I felt sad making my farewells and embracing my Chinese family with whom I'd shared so many adventures.

Now I'm on a plane which is not going anywhere, as workers check the electrical system again and again in search of the bug that prevents switching to the backup system, or so the voice on the loudspeaker says. While I'm waiting, I look up John Bradshaw's definition of addiction as a "relationship that has life-damaging consequences." I give a few moments' thought to concern that people's relationship to my work might be an addiction. Can I distinguish what I do from what Harold does? This is not difficult. I don't use a hard sell, nor do I promote dependency: as the mother of four, I have had more than enough of that.

Hard-sell approaches like Harold's pressure people to make promises and then emphasize the importance of sticking by your word once you have given it. I remember Werner Erhardt quoting someone to the effect that when a person is true to her word, she gains great power. I believe this is true; I also think that the hard-sell process is another kind of lie, and that first to sell by bullying and then to insist on good faith is just another unethical business practice—a way to use a moral principle to exploit people.

The very fact that smooth (or, in Harold's case, not so smooth) operators see the human potential theory and practice as a vehicle for enriching themselves is a validation of the approach. The entrepreneurs study what people want so they can make their fortune supplying it.

People want authenticity and community, and the fact that the existential, experiential group can be packaged and sold for a high price does not diminish its value, any more than expensive restaurants invalidate the importance of eating. People need good existential education, just as they need to be taught nutrition so that they can determine the essence of what they want to eat and be able to resist the distraction of those who package and pander to their secondary desires—status, luxury, glamour, and so forth.

After fours hours on the plane we are unloaded, deprived of our passports, given meal tickets and room keys, and bused to a hotel on the airport grounds. Tomorrow is another day, and United Air Lines promises to *gambaru* (do its best). Feeling vulnerable—internationally naked—without my passport, I surrender to the inevitability of missing my son's birthday and retreat to a pleasant room, where I use my single phone call to wish him a happy one and tell him I'll make it sometime tomorrow.

Fortunately I have a book to read, and my exhaustion guarantees a welcome, early sleep. I go down to the newsstand and buy coffee and a newspaper, grateful for Carol's last-minute gift of money which gives me some freedom during my stranded hours.

DECEMBER 17, TUESDAY, 6:00 A.M.

I awaken early, still in Taipei and still troubled from dreams that echo the past few days of conflict and struggle. I continue to taunt myself trying to understand how Harold, who wanted so much, could have treated me so badly, until I remember Marilyn Monroe's classic remark about men who want a lot in exchange for not very much.

Harold is neurotic in the sense that his behavior was a result of his preoccupation with his unfinished business, which totally obscured the present, including me and the kind of person I am. Perhaps he imagined me to be his long-suffering, all-accepting mother. What's clear is that unfinished business makes people stupid and immature; and Harold, who is capable of intelligence, was stupid in his dealings with me.

During our futile conversation yesterday, he remarked that a Chinese person would not have stood by the desk while he searched for the checks, implying that a Chinese person would have been more polite. Remembering this remark, I feel slightly chagrined until I realize that it's just another of his lies. Barry's a Chinese person, and Barry didn't have any qualms about standing by the desk and asserting his right to be paid for his work. Barry knew all along that Harold was lying and that his budget was filled with fudged figures, like a large fee for a translator who turned out to be a staff member and under salary.

I remember a remark made by Abe Levetsky about one of our colleagues at the San Francisco Gestalt Institute who also lied with nearly every breath. Abe said, "The only way you can talk with such a person is to say, 'That's a lie,' 'That's another one,' "Now you're lying again," and so on for the entire conversation." There is no possibility of dialogue with liars, who by their deception demonstrate an absolute absence of respect—for themselves as well as everyone else.

Lying destroys any possibility for dialogue and is, next to murder, the greatest violation of the human spirit that one person can perpetuate against another. Lying makes genuine human contact impossible and reduces human relations to a mockery. There is no point in talking with someone who is so contemptuous and lacking in good faith that their words communicate nothing beyond their desire to deceive. People who talk with such people turn themselves into shills, marks for the con artist, and damage both themselves and the lying person. This, of course, is not a conversation. At best it's a game; but games require independent scorekeepers to interpret the rules. Without them the game deteriorates into a raw struggle for power and becomes a war.

Everyone is free to choose their involvement with liars. I do my best to minimize mine.

I stretch and do my Tai Chi on the hotel roof, feeling so relieved to be out of Harold's world that I don't even mind being a day late returning home. In fact, I welcome the opportunity to digest some of my experience here so that I don't have to cart all this confusion and resentment back with me. The slow motions of my Tai Chi set are like soft strokes rubbing the mirror of my mind clean of pictures from the last three days and allowing me to experience the pale warm dawn spreading over the airport complex where I am interred without my passport. Even that's okay, I say to myself as I lower my arms, bringing the chi to rest.

December 17, 12:00 noon

This double day, the one that's twice as long as usual to make up for the day I lost going to Asia, is filled with the routine of air travel gone awry. I am peaceful and patient throughout the inconvenience of my return, which begins with a phone call in Taiwan at 10:00 a.m. telling me to be in the lobby at 11:00 for a flight to Tokyo. On the bus, off the bus, pick up tickets and the confiscated passport (bureaucracy's guarantee against the fat chance that I might slip away and disappear into the jungles of Taiwan), and I'm on the regular flight to Tokyo.

Our flight is scheduled to leave Tokyo four hours after our arrival. By careful sign reading and line standing, however, a few of us are able to catch an earlier flight scheduled to arrive in San Francisco at 8:30 a.m. on the 17th after only eight and a half hours in the air—thanks to a strong tail wind, which is usual on flights eastward to the Americas.

Returning in midwinter, we are nearly to San Francisco before the red-rimmed horizon announces the coming sun, which proceeds to melt the opaque blackness into a gray soup that at first appears to be the sea but soon reveals itself as a bed of thick clouds whose shapes emerge gradually with the light. The space above the clouds in which we fly is a pale, pale blue, almost white in its brightness.

The interim day begun in Taipei and abandoned in Tokyo is here to greet me with its uncanny repetition: today is yesterday, and this today is the day I come home. My excitement blends with a slight nausea as the descending plane slips and slides in the lower and more active atmosphere. The mighty machine inspires me with affection and gratitude for the wondrous adventures it allows. The boundary between sky and clouds vibrates faintly golden, and everything beyond the window becomes miraculously brighter. The benediction of dawn joins that of homecoming, and I too brighten and vibrate as I watch the clouds turn coral for an instant before they blaze forth whiter than white as we drop toward then as though to land on their deceptively solid surface.

The window fills with white, and billows of gray which I recognize as fog appear for seconds before disappearing into the whiteness. Once through the clouds, we traverse the loose fog through whose large ragged gaps bits of landscape appear: a mandala of earth, sky. and water. The plane dips and circles into the sun. Clouds splash shadows on the land below. My ears pop as I applaud the beauty revealed through the tiny rectangle of plastic beside me. The plane rumbles more deeply now, and I hear the whine of the massive flaps as their marvelous mechanism draws them out.

A small mountain with a pointed peak appears on the left; rivers and towns, a rough, rambling range of hills, and the long line of a freeway all jump into my vision and vanish again as the plane banks and a bright winter sun turns the settling ponds into shining gold and green mirrors. As we head north toward the airport, the green wall of the coastal range holding the city away from the now-invisible sea slips by on the left. The pitch of the engines rises as we pass over acres of geometric forms in neat rows with small green flames leaping among them, the bland expanse of a golf course with brown kidney-shaped accents, and multitudes of cars slipping by like urgent termites.

We bounce lightly onto the pavement, and the reversing engines announce our safe arrival on the far eastern lip side of the Pacific Rim. Back on earth, the morning sky flickers palest orange behind the shredding fog.

Chapter 6

San Francisco: Completing the circle

«*The country which is nowhere is the real home.*»
—attributed to the
Chinese Master Lu Tzu Li

Tuesday, December 17, 8:30 a.m.

As the pilot moves the plane from the runway toward the San Francisco terminal, I sigh in appreciation of the tiny specks of order we humans manage to create in this tremendous universe that for the most part seems unconcerned with us and our well-being. I breathe a small prayer of thanksgiving to the many skillful and hard-working people who have maintained the pattern long enough to get me to Asia and home again. Looking out the window, I see a tiny being standing, surrounded by the jet's roar, near the edge of the vast concrete prairie. Spiffy in his blue jumpsuit and white gloves with matching white earphones, he motions elegantly, directing the tyrannosaurus of a plane toward its parking space. The plane makes a graceful sweeping turn and stops exactly on the spot he indicates. The pilot cuts the engines. Order prevails. I'm safely home.

The bell sounds, and the seat belt sign disappears. I recover my pack from under the seat and stick my head into the aisle at the exactly the same moment a Japanese woman's very expensive (and, fortunately, very soft) Louis Vuitton handbag slips from the overhead bin. My head and the bag touch softly, accompanied by a flood of apologetic Japanese: "*Sumimasen*" (Excuse me), "*Gomen Nasai*" (I'm sorry). I shake my head and mutter, "*Iie, Iie*" (It's nothing). Oh, yes, I reflect, as, with euphoric acceptance, I look at the pink-faced owner of the bag that has just bopped me: order exists, just not in very large quantities. Still, there was enough to get us here safely, I marvel as, rubbing my head, I enter the line and shuffle down the aisle behind the other passengers with whom I share the inevitable relief of once again being safely on the ground. I have survived another trip to the west and am home—twenty-three hours late and not complaining.

Wednesday, December 18, 6:00 a.m.

When I open my eyes in the barely perceptible brightening of the winter dawn, the first thing I see is the tall, thin pyramid of light which says San Francisco. I stretch, spreading my fingers and toes with the luxurious satisfaction of having once again completed the circle . My son Lawrence is sleeping in the next room, and I am home. As I get up, not from a futon but from an American-style mattress on the floor, I remember reading somewhere of an American politician remarking that he hoped the rising water from global warming would drown all the people who sleep on mattresses on the floor. I smile as I wonder who he is really mad at; I know for sure that, in Bob Dylan's words, "It ain't me, babe," because I never did him any harm.

I do my yoga postures on a blue and coral rug that I brought from Nepal and rejoice, as only the returned traveler can, in the everyday familiarity of my surroundings. After tiptoeing into Lawrence's room to indulge the parental pleasure of watching him sleep, I read a while and await the coming of the light before going outdoors. I am cautious since the dark winter morning almost twenty years ago when a strange man stopped me and asked, "Where is Francisco Street?" It was early—maybe 5:00 a.m.—and dark as midnight. My son John, who lived with us at the time, was studying Shao Lin with my Tai Chi teacher's wife, and we usually walked down Nob Hill together. This morning he had spent the night with a friend, and I was alone. Since I had been walking to Portsmouth Square for many years, I felt perfectly safe in the darkness until the moment, when, just for a second, I took my eyes off the inquiring stranger, and he seized me in a hammerlock around the neck. As he lifted me off the ground, I had the wry thought, "So much for my Kung Fu," before I began screaming for help. In my terror, the image of a Victorian woman lying under a gas street lamp with her long, full skirt spread over the cobblestones flashed in my mind's eye. Hanging by my neck, I clung to the attacker's arms to prevent myself from strangling. As I screamed, he tightened his arms and cut off my air. I went through the whole experience with no thought other than getting out of his grasp alive. He carried me down an alley and, strangling me again, got my sweat pants down around my ankles. Then he lay on top of me and complained because I wouldn't kiss him. When I struggled he strangled me again. Just as I accepted that, even though he wasn't hard, I was going to be raped, he disappeared, vanishing as silently and completely as though I had awakened from a nightmare. Then the sound he must have heard—the metallic click of someone opening a car door—skimmed across the silence, and I leapt to my feet and ran toward it. There I met a man in the brown uniform of the cable car crew on his way to work. I was very frightened and never stopped shaking as I told him my story and asked him to walk with me to Portsmouth Square, which he did with an unassuming kindness. I did my Tai Chi and told one more person about the attempted rape before I rushed home and took a bath. When John came home and I told him what had happened, he burst into tears and we cried together. Both he and Lawrence were gently loving and supportive friends to me as I recovered from the trauma of the attack.

Now I live deeper in Chinatown, and I wait to go out until 7:00, when there's an interlude between the night's terrors and the day's mayhem. It's a good time to be out and about in San Francisco's Chinatown. After Taipei's acrid pollution the cool, rain-washed air of San Francisco is a soothing ambiance, outlining my chin and tickling my face with my hair as it moves about me in small breezy swirls. I walk down

Jackson Street and stand on the corner of Powell as a cable car swings past on the centrifugal force of the curve. In the narrow street, the driver's face passes close to mine, and we smile at each other. I like living near the cable car barn, not only because one of the workers there was my rescuer, but because it's an active place where generally friendly, good-natured men go about their work with pride and pleasure.

The bell clangs out a short, complex rhythm as I cross the street, and the cable car goes on up the hill. I walk past the Chinese hospital, with its old wing and new wing side by side like pictures in a children's book illustrating the modernization of China. The old wing is wood, with a red upturned roof and green trim around the door; the new is grey stone and glass assembled without a trace of curve anywhere. I feel safe with the hospital on my route because there is always someone awake in a hospital. Orangeland, the low-cost produce market on the corner of Stockton and Jackson, isn't open, but Stockton Street itself is wakening as solitary figures glide through the shadows like figures in a Beckett play. The sidewalk is stained with dark spots and an occasional slime of dried mucous, but after seeing the puddles and piles of Shanghai, I am better able to appreciate the relative tidiness of San Francisco's Chinatown.

The Chinese in San Francisco combine with the other Chinese communities of the Pacific Rim—Singapore, Manila, Sydney, Los Angeles, Vancouver—into the conglomerate called the Overseas Chinese, another of the variations on the theme of Chineseness which combine to create China's pentatonic symphony. It was by fundraising among the Overseas Chinese that Sun Yat-sen financed the Chinese Revolution of 1911.

Sun was less a revolutionary plotter than a human-rights visionary, and he came to the United States five times to recruit and raise money among the disenfranchised Chinese who, ineligible for U.S. citizenship at that time, had no other homeland than China. As the first Chinese leader to espouse human values, equality, and liberty, Sun embodied the idealism of the American Chinese, whose dream of equality in the United States seemed, at that time, as impossible as Sun's vision of a democratic China. Sun and his followers, both in China and among the Overseas Chinese, articulated a program of liberation for members of the greatest silent majority of all time: the Chinese peasants.

Money for the 1911 Revolution came (to quote historian Connie Young Yu) from "prune-pickers and professional gamblers alike who donated their dimes and dollars to the cause." Sun traveled to the towns on the Sacramento delta; there, in nearly every Chinese community was a store where his supporters gathered and discussed revolutionary newspapers published in the United States, as well as the steady stream of mail that came from China: "something every day, whether it was letters for the workers in the orchards or a revolutionary newsletter."

Long before the coming of jet planes and fax machines, Sun and the Overseas Chinese traced the outlines of the modern Pacific Rim—including Japan, which during the relatively progressive early decades of this century was a haven for many a the Chinese revolutionary seeking safety beyond the reach of the Manchu executioners.

Sun and his followers did not so much foment revolution as ride an evolutionary wave, for Imperial China's time was up. The Manchus would have collapsed during the nineteenth century, perhaps in the Taiping rebellion, if they had not been useful to the Europeans and Americans as accomplices in their own exploitation of China's resources and people. The revolutionaries did not have to bring down the Chinese government: it collapsed under its own incompetence and corruption, just as the French and Russian governments had. Rather like divorces, revolutions result from the internal workings of the system and are rarely caused by outsiders. Those who are called revolutionaries usually get credit for successes that come from luck or, at best, an elegant sense of timing.

Although he was able to mobilize support among the Chinese worldwide, Sun, who (to his eternal credit) was no Lenin, could not consolidate the Manchu collapse into an effective new government. Knowing his work was incomplete, he exhorted his followers from his deathbed in 1925: "The Revolution is not yet completed. All my comrades must strive on."

Walking through Chinatown, I pass the buildings that house the Chinese family associations where Sun made his pleas and collected the funds for Chinese liberation. Chinese American is my favorite among the varieties of Chinese culture, because it combines the wonders of China's ancient culinary, cultural, and aesthetic accomplishment with the respect for human rights which is the marvel of the United States Constitution. In the United States and Canada, Chinese people have been able to fulfill their culture without sacrificing themselves as individuals, which is the consistent miracle of a pluralist society. Spreading from the intensely Chinese centers in the major urban Chinatowns to assimilation in the suburbs, the Chinese-American culture adds its lively ingredients to the North American mix.

It is the Chinese inclusion in the American mosaic that permitted an eighty-year-old man, born near the Mongolian border of Imperial China, to teach me Tai Chi and push hands for ten years in Portsmouth Square in San Franscisco's Chinatown. I began studying Tai Chi in 1974, when I was living with a six-year-old Lawrence in the Golden Gateway, a high-rise apartment complex a few blocks from Chinatown. The commuter traffic on Battery Street which awakened me every morning at 5:30 was my first teacher: as I lay in bed trying to sleep through its racket, I decided I might as well get up and do something interesting before getting Lawrence off to school. Tai Chi Chuan was part of my human-potential culture, and I knew from a photograph in the newspaper that there was an early morning practice in nearby Portsmouth Square. I decided to check it out.

I was in the studio discussing with a young Chinese woman the details of enrolling when a bald-headed old man in a long black gown entered and flashed me what seemed at the time a slightly demented smile. When she introduced him to me, I heard her say, "This is Seafood," and I remember thinking, "How interesting; I'm going to learn Tai Chi from an old Chinese man named Seafood." Later I learned that his name was Kuo Lin Ying, and *Sifu*, which I had heard incorrectly as "Seafood," is a Chinese title which means father-teacher. Because I'm not one for titles, I always called him Kuo. Since he spoke no more than twenty words of English, our occasional discussions of this matter consisted of his saying, "*Sifu*," and my replying, "Kuo." I never called him *Sifu*, and he never insisted that I do so as a condition of remaining his student. When a later teacher did so insist, I called him *Shifu*, the northern Chinese variant of the title, for as long as I wanted to learn what he taught, but I never loved and respected him as I did Kuo Lin Ying.

Among Kuo's English words, which he usually spoke in pairs, were: "Everyday, everyday," "Beautiful, beautiful," and "Slowly, slowly." I have integrated the last phrase into my own knowledge; and, in addition to reminding myself to go slowly, slowly, I often say it in Japanese, "*Yukkuri, yukkuri*," and Cantonese, "*Mandi la*."

Kuo was in the park from 5:00 to 6:30, everyday, everyday, for the thirteen years I practiced there. His wife, the young woman I had met the first day, did most of the introductory teaching, but as I proved myself by staying around a few years, he began to appear out of the darkness and move my hand an inch or two, turn a leg to a more strongly braced angle, or indicate a certain movement's heretofore unimaginable application.

All the Tai Chi movements have martial applications, and it is these applications that hold the set in place, requiring the hand to be here rather than there and the feet to be placed just so in order to transmit the *chi* energy through the waist into the hand and beyond. While my attraction to Tai Chi is mainly aesthetic, I like the applications for their unexpected efficacy, cunningly using such unexpected body parts as the top of the wrist or the elbow. (The latter is a natural for me, whose elbows sharp as ice picks.)

In his last years, Kuo joined me on the porch of the Holiday Inn across the bridge and pushed hands with me everyday. His hand was soft as a baby's, and he could lead me off balance with absolutely no visible effort and great apparent delight. He was a playmate, as much fun as any I have ever had. From his teaching. I tasted the possibility of toppling four thousand pounds with a force of four ounces—the possibility so often discussed in the traditional literature of Tai Chi Chuan.

I early recognized Kuo Lin Ying as a Chinese version of Fritz Perls: both loved wisdom as well as life and it was my good fortune to have them as teachers. Their uncanny similarity has been a source of self-knowledge as I recognize the attributes of the bad-boy sage who has been willing to teach and from whom I have been willing to learn significant principles of the unity of existence. Both men combined knowledge, competence, and originality with an absolute refusal to clothe themselves in the sham of self-righteousness. Both were independent of the political and social orthodoxy of their time. Fritz and Laura Perls's involvement with Weimar socialism led to their early emigration from the Nazis and saved their lives, while Kuo's willingness to abandon the government in Taiwan after his move to America surely made his life easier, as political pragmatism necessitated the Chinese American community's acceptance of the present government of China.

Both were famous and mischievous *tsukebe* (the Japanese word for "lecher"). Perls, the better-mannered of the two, was a European gentlemen who ungrudgingly took no for an answer and remained a lifelong friend and admirer. Kuo was unrelentingly grabby, which made him a good teacher of self-defense. The last time he tried to cop a feel from me, I knocked him down. I will never forget the thump as his compact body landed on the concrete with such force that I imagined for a moment that he had cracked it. I truly don't know which of us was more surprised. Never one to give up, he lay on his side in the middle of the park and waved his index finger at me in the universal gesture of parental control which I returned; each of us chattered in a language which the other did not understand, and each of us thoroughly understood the other's intent. When I told one of my friends of the incident he said, "Paula, if you had been in old China, all his students would have quit studying with him and followed you"—which made me even more thankful to be in the United States.

Kuo taught me how to develop and use *chi,* and remained my friend even after I used it to dump him. The last time I saw him he was past ninety and preparing to return to China, where he died. Standing about half a block away, he looked at me and, smiling licentiously, formed a circle with his thumb and forefinger and, using the index finger of his other hand, pantomimed a familiar in-and-out motion. He, too, never stopped repeating the whole of him.

My mistrust of goody-goody people, which stems from my West Virginia heritage, has served me well. An intuitive recognition that the pious and self-righteous have a shadow, a hidden polarity, which is made vicious and dangerous by the act of concealment, has led me to trust those who show their faults and, indeed, revel in them. The bad boys and girls of the world more nearly live their wholeness and thus, are more energetic and more trustworthy than those who strive to maintain an image of perfection—or, for that matter, any image. Since I am one, like William Blake, for whom "Energy is eternal delight," I sometimes find the unique and wonderful immaturity of naughty boys and girls utterly endearing.

Approaching Portsmouth Square in the flat light of winter's dawn, I recognize that this is where my connection to the Pacific Rim began. It was here in Portsmouth Square that I unknowingly seized the trapeze that swings me back and forth across the Pacific. Entering the park, I see the usual assortment of homeless people and early-morning practitioners.

My son John once asked me if I thought all Chinese practiced Tai Chi, and sometimes I think it's so. The streets and parks of Shanghai were crowded with people, alone and in groups, exercising in the early light. So are the parks of Hong Kong. I think the Chinese *chi* arts are a genuine folk art, expressing with their extraordinary variety the particular and wide-ranging genius of the people of that vast land, and perhaps supplying one of the elements which along with food and medicine define the nebulous entity called China.

Mrs. Kuo, who after her husband's return to China and death at 92, wisely transformed the honorific *Simu* (mother-teacher) into Simone, is working with a few students. I hear their laughter as I walk across the bridge over Kearny Street and onto the balcony of the Holiday

Inn where Kuo and I used to push hands. I remember standing here years ago arguing with my friend Hank, a Chinese-American, who in a fit of frustration said to me, "The trouble is you're east and I'm west." Although he was referring to the cultures of the east and west coasts of the United States, I heard the reversal that, in Gestalt terms, rearranged the field. I had found the point where east and west meet, and henceforth my life would never be the same.

In San Francisco there are neighborhoods for everyone— African-Americans, Hispanics, Gays, Lesbians, WASPs, Japanese-Americans, Italian-Americans, every possible other; but it's the Chinese who set the tone and in some strange way make the city their own. In every neighborhood the smells and sounds of Guangzhou permeate all the others, leaving their mark and reminding us of China, the five-thousand-year-old civilization that taught the Japanese to write 1500 years ago. Deep into the twenty-first century its government will continue to hector other nations from its perceived position at the center of the world. China is now shorthand for a quarter of the world's population, and, on this shrinking globe we share, we are all increasingly involved with it and with them.

On the eastern cusp of the Pacific Rim the sun comes through the fog and bounces around the city like a golden ball as I come to my center and begin my morning practice. It's time to begin again.

AFTERWORD

Riding on the train recently in Japan, I notice three men seated across from me. All would be identified by themselves and others as Japanese, and yet their physical appearance varies so greatly that people in the U.S. would designate them members of distinct ethnic groups. One is a pale, bald man in a business suit who could be Phil Gramm's twin brother. Another is dark-skinned with a mustache, dressed in causal clothes—a bit shabby for Tokyo, where most people's clothes look like they were bought yesterday (or maybe even this morning), yet well within the normal range of wear for the United States. The third is a tall, handsome man with a square jaw and heavy black eyebrows arching neatly over finely tapered eyes.

What impresses me about the variety of faces and forms in Japan is the way Japanese have made these distinctions irrelevant. It's not that they don't have groups—they do: Koreans are singled out for prejudice and limitations, and so are the burakumin, descendants of the old untouchable class of tanners and others who traditionally handled dead things. It's just that in Japan this prejudice is not accorded on the basis of appearance. Almost by fiat, if you have a Japanese surname you are Japanese. Everyone is included by an act of will. I look forward to the day when sufficient numbers of citizens of the United States become psychically whole and no longer require an "other" for psychic survival, and we can and do include everyone in the United States.

When I turn from my traveling companions to the newspaper, I am only slightly surprised to discover the following paragraphs in USA Today:

> *The official Xinhua News Agency...recently criticized the market reforms for causing a moral crisis and widening China's economic imbalance.*
> *As an ideological alternative, Xinhua proposed Confucianism, which measures success in terms of community, rather than individuals, and stresses submission to higher authority—*
> *ideals uncannily similar to the Maoist ideals embraces by the Laosanjie [the generation that went to the countryside during the Cultural Revolution].*

If there is such a thing as a philosophical equivalent to vampirism, it has to be the blood-sucking Confucianism, which those who wish to maintain submission to authority in China invite to rise from its ragged coffin again and again as they struggle with the human impulse toward freedom. One of my greatest regrets about leaving China when I did was that I did not have a chance to teach my students to sing "We shall Overcome," for I knew they would need it again and again before their revolution is complete and they are free to speak, to read, to travel, and to assemble.

The harshness of Chinese culture on Taiwan revealed itself in the self-hatred among the young people in the group I led there. My shock on meeting their misery recalled my feelings in Shanghai. Before I went to Shanghai I had read dozens of books about China and knew the words: Life in China is hard. Nothing I knew about China could ever have prepared me, though, for the reality of experiencing China. I was stunned by people's everyday aggression. Clerks in shops literally threw the change at the customer. I remarked once to a friend, "They're passive-aggressive;" when he asked, "Who?" I said, "Everyone." And in public it truly seemed so.

The contrast between people in public and in private is perhaps the greatest anomaly of China, for the soul and spirit that is present in friendship and personal contact seems to vanish within a dark shell of public behavior. Often it seemed that the only people who weren't passive-aggressive in public were the ones who were actively aggressive. I have never seen so many street collisions in the entire rest of my life as I saw in ten months in Shanghai: a van hitting a man and probably killing him (although I didn't crowd close enough to know for sure); several cars hitting cars; a car hitting a bike; a motorcycle hitting a bike; another one hitting a car; several bikes hitting pedestrians, and a man bloodying another man's face with his fist.

As there were apparently no right-of-way laws in Shanghai, large trucks roared from side streets onto main thoroughfares without stopping—truly terrifying events for bicyclists, who would surely die in China if they did not remain alert to this possibility. Riding my bike through Shanghai's chaotic streets, I often felt my entire skin contract as I involuntarily tried to make myself safe by becoming small. For those who take public transportation, there are literal battles to get on and off buses and trains as crowds of people collide head-on in doors and aisles in truly violent encounters that leave bodies bruised and hearts racing.

A friend told of seeing soldiers on a train in Szechuan escorting condemned prisoners, who sat shackled on the floor under the table while their guards ate. And there are still public executions—now embellished by rumors of organs being quickly removed and rushed to hospitals for transplant. So far as I know severed heads are no longer displayed as they were in Imperial times.

I am writing all this because I don't want to deny it, and also because I imagine that most Americans, if they think of China at all, cannot imagine what life is like there. I made good friends among the people of China and am continually touched by their unremitting struggle for peace and livelihood. I know from experience that life in China is abrasive and that I am soft, for when I lived there I would at times feel abraded, as though someone had been sandpapering my skin.

From my experience in the Taiwan group I see that while life may be easier in Taiwan, there is still a hard, harsh edge to existence, made publicly visible in the filthy air and wild behavior of people in wheeled vehicles (although I didn't see any collisions in Taipei).

I want to emphasize that much of this harshness comes from a rotten history during which plain people—the peasants who grew the food and created the wealth—were despised and abased by a bureaucratic class that never doubted its right to impoverish and degrade them. I do not believe that his kind of cruelty and disrespect for other human beings is natural, and I agree with Sun Yat-sen that "Nature originally did not make men equal; but when autocracy developed, the despotic kings and princes pushed human difference to an extreme, and the result was an inequality far worse than Nature's inequality."

The evils of inequality are taught and learned, and Chinese history is one long lesson. People who degrade others degrade themselves, regardless of how thoroughly they disguise and hide their dishonor. The face that people hide is the shamed face, and even the elders of the Chinese gerontocracy—the Long Marchers who, given the intense suffering of their own past, are some of the most deservedly shameless people in the world—tried to close out the foreign press before Tienanmen. What I hide and what I show is the deepest expression of my moral code.

Traditional Chinese culture created a harsh and stringent split within people: a brutal division enhanced by life under the crushing Mongol, Manchu, and (most recently) the Euro-American and Japanese conquerors. If I am abused over time, I will most likely come to believe that I deserve it; and, in order to maintain a semblance of wholeness, I will internalize the aggressor, making him or her part of myself. Then, as soon as I have a chance to abuse someone else, I will, even if I have to wait until I have children.

The Irish people in California were the most enthusiastic Chinese-bashers, even thought they were not even a generation away from the same mistreatment themselves. The Bible says this devastation goes on unto the fourth generation, but in some parts of the world like China, the four hundredth generation would be more accurate. The Chinese have had a hell of a time, and they are still coming out of it. The people of Africa, too, are scarred by an awful history: two hundred years of the mass kidnappings labeled "slave trade" and two hundred years of European colonialism, some of which was as bad as or worse than slavery.

This kind of past torment becomes embedded in people and does not go away when the conquerors leave. Just as World War II did not end in 1945 for the people of Hiroshima or the Jews released from the death camps, the millennia of imperial power in China did not end in 1911 or the centuries of foreign conquest in 1949. The years of conquest and war have lodged themselves in people's psyches, where they burst forth in incredibly self-destructive episodes like the Cultural Revolution in China and the civil war in Rwanda. Such events come naturally from centuries of domination, and they will not end quickly.

The present outbursts of anger and violence in the United States are a similar phenomenon. As he was acting to end the Cold War Mikhail Gorbachev warned the Americans that he was doing them a disservice by taking away their enemy. Events have proven him an astute psychologist, for the role of the enemy in maintaining equilibrium within many peoples' psyches has come to the foreground as those for whom communism served that role now discover the needed enemy next door or downtown. It's important both to acknowledge people's fear and to confront their irrationality as they identify people who have never hurt them as enemies.

Human beings are capable of ending even the most ancient and irrational violence. We can see it happening in Europe: after hundreds of years of violent outbursts like the Thirty Years' War in Germany, the Napoleonic wars, innumerable wars between France and England, and the two world wars, the historical antipathies of Europe have mellowed until now national groups who once despised one another and killed each other with malicious glee are now discussing a common currency and allowing each other into their countries without checking passports.

Among the peasants of imperial China, eternal vigilance was the price, not of liberty, but of life, and often even the prudence and caution of peasant life was not enough to guarantee survival. Living in China and working in Taiwan, I have become aware that the peace and plenty I have lived with all my life are not given to all people, and I am grateful for the incredible good fortune which has come to me through no effort of my own. If ever the words "fate" or "destiny" have meaning, it is in their reference to being the person born in a particular place at a specific time. Time, place, and parentage are the givens of our existence over which we have no more control than a butterfly has over a Mack truck. It is within the boundaries of our fate that we have choice and freedom to create from what is given the existence that we desire. Liberty surrounds destiny, and the human journey encompasses both. Whether fortunate or unfortunate in our origin, each one of us is still responsible for our life.

Nelson Mandela was born a black African in South Africa under apartheid. Few would consider this a lucky break, and yet look what he did with his life. He walked out of prison after 24 years with a smile on his face and forgiveness in his heart. Seizing the freedom that existence brings, he formed himself into the person we see today. The human spirit can never be conquered; it can only submit.

Existentialism, with its emphasis on choice and responsibility in the here and now, is the perfect philosophy for a time when the uncertainly of life, which is nothing new, becomes increasingly frightening by being juxtaposed with the potential for long and healthy lives for everyone. This combination, which makes arbitrary and unnatural death a greater loss than ever before, comes just as technology and urbanization make it increasing simple for a few confused and desperate people to kill a great many others without reason and without warning. As our human vulnerability within urban systems becomes increasingly explicit, we must recognize that this is not an accident: as a species, we have chosen to perfect and publicize the technology of death far beyond our willingness to study and communicate the enhancement of life.

Although not so well supported financially and emotionally, there are technologies of life, and I believe that Gestalt therapy is among these. This book has been an attempt to illuminate some of the ways people may creatively enhance their lives without harming each other or depleting our precious planet, as well as have some fun in the process; for fun is the operational word for joy and pleasure which are our natural birthright and genetic inheritance.

We are both the materials of our birth and the artists of our existence. Individually and collectively, we are the dancer and the dance. I wish you joy as you shape your being, both in solitude with nature and among other people, into ever-changing forms of movement and response. Don't forget to remember, with the Beatles, that "in the end the love you take is equal to the love you make."

Together and separately, we choose.

BIBLIOGRAPHIC REMARKS

Fritz Perls's *Gestalt Therapy Verbatim*, a good one-volume introduction to Gestalt, has recently been reissued by the press of *The Gestalt Journal*, Highland, New York. *Living at the Boundary*, Laura Perls's melodic presentation of her Gestalt song, is also available from the same press. To taste both the teacher and the teaching, I like *In and Out of the Garbage Pail*, Fritz's irreverent autobiography which is unfortunately out of print. There is a substantial Gestalt literature for anyone who wishes to explore it further. *The Body in Psychotherapy* by Edward Smith is an excellent overview of holistic explorations of the human organism.

I greatly value the work of the Swiss psychoanalyst Alice Miller, who has brilliantly and comprehensively unclothed the connections between childhood suffering and what many call mental illness, which is a configuration, a gestalt if you will, of creative adaptations to impossible existential dilemmas experienced by the immature human being. Her *Thou Shalt Not Be Aware* is a brilliant exposition of how adults, often in the name of love, victimize children, and I recommend it to anyone who finds it easier to entertain the possibility that we might be mistaken in how we treat our young than to believe that people are born evil.

The finest single one-volume explication of Japanese history and culture is *The Japanese Today: Change and Continuity*, by Edwin O. Reischauer. For Hong Kong I relied extensively on Jan Morris's *Hong Kong: Epilogue to an Empire*, and for the Opium War, Maurice Collis's *Foreign Mud*.

From the literature on China, which is nearly as vast as the land itself, I value Owen Lattimore's *Inner Asia: Frontiers of China*, for its integration of cultural, political, and geographic details. With his firsthand experience of the peoples, lands, and languages of inner Asia, Lattimore is a unique commentator on the importance of this area to our conception of China. For a more focused picture of the events in twentieth-century China,

Barbara Tuchmann's *Stilwell and the American Experience in China* places the story of Chiang Kai-shek's army and the Kuomintang's struggle for China within a world perspective. Regarding Sun Yat-sen's activities I have quoted Lucien Bianco, *Origins of the Chinese Revolution, 1915-1949*, and Harold Z. Schiffrin, *Sun Yat-sen and the Origins of the Chinese Revolution*. I have also quoted from Sun's own writings. For details of the early Chinese American experience as well as Sun Yat-sen's time in the United States, I used *Chinatown San Jose, USA* by Connie Young Yu, whose reports of the daily lives of early Chinese immigrants in the United States makes it a rare portrayal among histories.

I have read widely in the literature of the various Chinese revolutions, and most of the ideas not otherwise attributed are my own. Reports of recent events in China are extremely vulnerable to distortion by the prejudices of the one who tells the story. I am no different in this respect, and fully understand, with Benedetto Croce, that all history is history of the present—modified, I would add, by the experiences of this person writing in this place. This conception in no way diminishes both the fascination and the significance of history, for it only makes more explicit how irrevocably we are embedded in what has gone before. In order to make sense of the present, each one creates their own story of the past, and the more the big story called history is our story, the more nearly accurate it will be. Just as with the blind men and the elephant, we need to hear from everyone.

The section on the pleasure center is quoted from Lewis Thomas's essay "The Life in the Mind," which appears in *The Fragile Species*. Thomas, who was a medical doctor, writes in the great tradition of the humanistic English essay, and I recommend his books to all who love to read.